CERTIFICATE OF
NOMINATION
FOR AWARD

Be it Known That

Brenda Blethyn

was Nominated for an

ACADEMY AWARD
OF MERIT

for Outstanding Performance
in 1998

ACTRESS IN A SUPPORTING ROLE
"Little Voice"

President

ACADEMY OF

MOTION PICTURE

ARTS AND

SCIENCES

Olivier

THE
LAURENCE
OLIVIER
AWARDS
1 · 9 · 8 · 4

PRESENTED BY
THE SOCIETY OF WEST END THEATRE

...MINATION

...Blethyn

...or

Actress of the year in a...

PRESIDENT

BOB SWASH
PRESIDENT OF
THE SOCIETY OF WEST END THEATRE

English
Tourist Bo...

AND BY SPECIAL ARR...
THE OBS...

D0275602

PRIX D'INTERPRÉTATION FÉMININE
DU
49e FESTIVAL INTERNATIONAL
DU
FILM
CANNES 1996

DÉCERNÉ A

Brenda Blethyn
DANS
"Secrets and Lies"
RÉALISÉ PAR
Mike Leigh

CANNES

BRENDA BLETHYN
RICHARD JOHNSON   PETER BLY...

★★★★
Brenda Blethyn is a stunning 'Mrs War...
in Peter Hall's excellent revival

'Blethyn is PURE COMIC PLEASURE...
Evening Standard

MRS WARREN
PROFESSIO...

'BERNARD SHAW...
play has lost none of its power, wit r...

'PETER HALL'S
production is one of his be...
REBECCA HALL IS EXTRAORDIN...

★★★★
Mail on Sunday

'FINE PERFORMANCES, a spot o...
Daily Telegraph

Mixed Fancies

Mixed Fancies
A Memoir

BRENDA BLETHYN

SIMON &
SCHUSTER

London · New York · Sydney · Toronto

A CBS COMPANY

First published in Great Britain by Simon & Schuster UK Ltd, 2006
A CBS COMPANY

1 3 5 7 9 10 8 6 4 2

Simon & Schuster UK Ltd
Africa House
64–78 Kingsway
London WC2B 6AH

www.simonsays.co.uk

Simon & Schuster Australia
Sydney

A CIP catalogue record for this book
is available from the British Library.

Hardback ISBN-13: 978-0-7432-4859-4
ISBN-10: 0-7432-4859-7

Trade paperback ISBN-13: 978-1-4165-2786-2
ISBN-10: 1-4165-2786-9

Typeset in Goudy by M Rules
Printed and bound in Great Britain by
CPI Bath

Picture credits
The publishers have made every effort to contact those holding rights in material
reproduced in this work. Where this has not been possible the publishers will be
happy to hear from anyone who recognises their material.

Rex: p. 206, plate 10 (bottom), plate 13 (bottom), plate 14 (bottom);
Kobal: p. 230, plate 10 (top); Corbis: p. 240, plate 12 (top)

In memory of Mum and Dad
with much love and gratitude

CONTENTS

CONTENTS

Contents

ACKNOWLEDGEMENTS

I give heartfelt thanks to my niece Valerie Winstone for all her help. I couldn't possibly have written *Mixed Fancies* without her encouragement and guidance. Thanks too to my brothers and sister for reading proofs and also to my extended family and friends for listening to my ramblings and for jogging my memory. Thanks also to my agent Paul Stevens, and to my editor, Angela Herlihy, for giving me directions when I got lost and, more importantly, for not letting me give up even when it seemed to me the most sensible thing to do. Especial thanks to those who turned their lofts inside out to find photographs to include herein, and to my partner Michael for hearing about *Mixed Fancies* day in and day out for the best part of two years and not complaining. Finally, many thanks to all the aforementioned for not ridiculing my effort.

FOREWORD

As I sat on the balcony of the luxurious Belage Hotel, basking in the glorious Los Angeles sun, it was tempting to reflect that I had truly 'arrived'. It was 1996 and Marianne Jean-Baptiste and I had been on an international tour to promote Mike Leigh's *Secrets & Lies*, visiting many countries including such far-flung places as South Korea and Brazil, and had finally ended up in Hollywood prior to the push for Golden Globe and Oscar consideration.

We had a three-week break from our schedule but, instead of returning home, my agent suggested that I remain in Los Angeles to meet some producers and discuss various projects which were presenting themselves. However, this meant staying on at my own expense. If I was to pay my own way in Tinseltown, it would be necessary, to use a favourite expression of my mother's, to 'pull in my horns'. I couldn't afford room service and consequently went to a local store and bought cereal and milk, quite forgetting that there were no dishes or cutlery in the room. So what? Improvising was no problem for me – indeed, I had been trained to do it from a very early age. With our large family it wasn't unusual to have to wait for a vacant spoon before we could start our breakfast.

And as I ate my cereal from a vase, using a shoe-horn for a spoon, I realised I had travelled a very long distance in more ways than one!

Making an entrance

1

LIFE ON THE PLAINS

'Pulling in our horns' was, more or less, a permanent aspect of family life. Our horns must surely have been the most vigorously exercised part of us, pulled in as they constantly were. Life on the Plains of Waterloo, in Ramsgate, could sometimes seem to be an uphill struggle, apparently combining many elements of the battle for which it was named. Occasional discomforts, frequent skirmishes and the constant possibility of ambush from my loving, but somewhat volatile mother were tempered by the loyalty, affection and protection of my father and of my brothers- and occasional sisters-in-arms.

Mum and Dad met c. 1922 while working for the same household in Broadstairs. Mum had worked for the family since leaving school aged fourteen and had worked her way up to become parlour maid. She told us that her first job before leaving school was collecting basketsful of acorns for a local pig breeder who fed them to the pigs, which she really enjoyed because she loved to be outdoors. Dad's first job, before leaving school, was as a shepherd. Ten years her senior, he had spent six years in India with the Royal Field Artillery immediately prior to meeting Mum, and had returned home to Broadstairs to become the family's chauffeur, the proud driver of a gleaming Delage. According to Dad, when he met Mum it was love at first sight and it wasn't long before he popped the question. Mum, however, although she felt the same way, said she needed a little more persuading. Quite a lot more persuading as it turned out! Even after the birth of their eighth child in 1943.

Mum was born in 1904. She was a small, bright, pretty lady, with beautiful creamy skin and soft dark hair, which was occasionally permed into a style that she'd had since the 1930s, when she was herself in her thirties and probably a time when she thought she looked her prettiest. She was the oldest girl of fourteen siblings and had spent almost her entire life caring for children. It was second nature. In her younger days she was a beauty with the finest teeth Dad said he had ever seen, although by the time I was old enough to notice them they had long been gone. That's just one of the penalties of having nine children. But also this was a time before the National Health Service, before subsidised medical and dental treatment. Mum said it was quite common for people to lose their teeth to decay and that a popular twenty-first birthday present was a new set of false teeth! A Taurean, home loving, stubborn, loyal, resilient and brave, she was a hardy woman and would never give in to sickness if she could at all help it.

Dad, born in 1894, was of medium build, clever, handsome and with a ready laugh. He had plenty of time for us children. He was a storyteller and a natural teacher. Dad was an avid reader and was, in fact, offered the opportunity of training to be a teacher on his return from India but he declined. He was easygoing and unhampered by ambition. A typical Piscean, he was compassionate, loving, artistic, intuitive, indecisive. It was Mum who wore the trousers in our house, but he was happy with that. He adored her. He was mildly spoken and I never heard him swear unless he was talking about politics, and even then not excessively. They were both staunch Conservatives, surprisingly. Unlike Mum, though, he was on occasion prone to hypochondria.

Together they were passionate. Either laughing fit to burst, or arguing fit to kill. A lot of their arguments followed the same pattern. One or other of them would shout 'Sit down!'

And the other would say, 'No, YOU sit down.'

'Siiiiiiit down.'

'YOUUUUUUUU sit down.' And on it went, ad infinitum. And all the while they were both already sitting down.

Before the war, Dad was working away at the Vauxhall car factory in Luton. (His claim to fame is that his suggestion of the use of a crescent-shaped washer to hold one part or other of the engine together was adopted and went into mass production. Mum said, 'If you believe that, you'll believe anything!') He could only occasionally get home to see her and the children, but he regularly sent money. The problem was that when he sent money home he couldn't afford the fare to come home himself. So Mum became extra thrifty and scrimped and scraped sufficiently to save enough money for Dad's fare. But he soon saw the necessity of coming home to find work locally and applied for a job as a driver for the local council, which we called the corporation. The wages were not generous and Mum was obliged to take several part-time jobs to compensate, while at the same time running a home.

In 1944 after an engagement of twenty years, and eight children into the bargain, Louisa Kathleen Supple finally agreed to marry William Charles Bottle. I suppose wartime puts a lot of things into perspective, and makes you understand more fully the value of things. Gran lost three sons in the war, Mum's three younger brothers. Uncle Sid died when the *Firedrake* was torpedoed; Uncle Bert was shot in Greece, and Uncle Fred tragically fell down the stairs while home on leave. And if that wasn't enough, Gran died in 1944. Mum was heartbroken. It was enough to drive anyone to drink. And did.

At the start of the war and the threat of bombardment, three of their children – Ted, Bernard and Jeannie – had been evacuated for three years to Stafford. Aged eleven, nine and six respectively they were each housed with a different family. Dad said it was not a very satisfactory arrangement, but the phrase 'there's a war on' justified any kind of hardship. At Gran's funeral, it was decided that Jeannie should temporarily go to live with an aunt in London. Mercifully, she survived the Blitz.

In 1945 the war was over and just when things were looking up my 42-year-old mother found she was pregnant again. The last straw!

I was born Brenda Anne Bottle in 1946, nine months after the end of the war, and I like to believe I was conceived in celebration – a product of rejoicing. Even though it meant Mum and Dad had another mouth to feed along with my six brothers and two sisters. In later years when Mum got really cross about something or other she would invariably say that I was the cause of all the trouble, but sometimes she would say it with affection. No wonder I'm confused with a guilt complex!

We were not well off, but just after the war it seemed that everyone was in the same boat. By the time I came along the three eldest, Pam, Ted and Bernard, had flown the nest. Pam, my eldest sister, was shortly to marry and my two eldest brothers, Ted and Bernard, had both become seamen. This seemed a natural progression as they both loved to watch the ships come and go

6

from the harbour, as indeed we all did. That left just the seven of us, Jeannie, Brian, Bill, Terry, Martin, me and Dad, for Mum to care for. 'Dear oh dear!'

When baby Brenda came into the world, relatives galore turned up to see the new arrival, and apparently it was my cousin, Noreen, who was playing 'This little piggy went to market' with my one-day-old fingers who discovered that I had eleven of them. Had I been born a couple of centuries earlier I would probably have been drowned as a witch. Mum promptly took me to the doctor's surgery and the extra finger on my left hand was removed. Dr Crawford, for reasons best known to himself, told my mum that I was going to be a film star. Had he known I was first going to be a typist presumably he would have left the extra finger on.

We lived in a rented house, which was in a very poor state of repair, but despite many pleas to the landlord we found that we had to like it or lump it. Whenever the landlord turned up at the house to demand his rent, invariably my mother would ask him cryptically if he was afraid of getting lockjaw. What did she mean? None of us knew. Had I known then that I would be capable of DIY in adulthood I might have started my apprenticeship a little earlier and repaired the scullery ceiling when it caved in, narrowly missing Dad.

Many of the houses surrounding ours had been bombed out of existence during the war, including the one immediately behind ours on the opposite side of the alley in La Belle Alliance Square. A lot of our playtime was spent on these bombed sites. In 1943 my brother Bill narrowly escaped death when this particular house fell, as he had toddled out into the alley and was playing only yards from it. Fortunately my pregnant mother noticed his absence whilst shepherding the rest of her flock to the safety of the air-raid shelter, and sent the most reliable person, my sister

Pam, to retrieve him. Apparently with only seconds to spare she snatched him up and managed to get back indoors and under the stairs, covering Bill with her own body just before the bomb fell. Pam was thrown into such a state of shock that it took a considerable time to release Bill from her arms.

We had a scullery and a basement sitting room, but there were only two bedrooms to accommodate the lot of us, so the parlour also had to be used as a bedroom. The boys all slept in a line at the top of the house. Whenever Mum sent me up there to give an instruction to one or other of them, if they were asleep I couldn't tell them apart. And nor could Mum sometimes. If one of them was due a clout, they'd all get one just to be on the safe side. Whack whack whack whack. One each. It created a sort of collective responsibility between them! But my mum was never cross with us for very long. And Dad never got cross with us at all. Irritated frequently, but never cross. Mum had the job of getting cross for both of them.

The rooms were small, and the parlour was made even smaller by the addition of a huge dining table in the middle that would have suited King Arthur. There was a sort of narrow path around the edge of the room, blocked by my little bed and an out-of-tune upright piano. Dad was the only one of us who could actually play, although he couldn't read music, but he'd only play it if Mum was out, otherwise she'd holler 'Cut that racket out!' or 'If ever a woman suffered.' He taught me to play one or two tunes, one of which I still churn out at parties, 'When You Are in Love', but I sound like Les Dawson. The lavatory was in the back yard, and although we didn't expect luxury, a door would have been nice! But there is always a plus to any situation, isn't there? The lack of a door meant there was light, making it much easier to locate and avoid the resident spiders. At night, we'd take a lighted candle, which lasted all of two seconds before it blew out.

There was no electricity in the scullery or upper part of the house, and the only supply was in the basement and parlour, but even for that you had to clamber across the rooms in darkness to locate a plug and socket. Fortunately there was a lamppost located just outside the front of our house, and at night we'd sometimes leave the curtains open and the room would be dimly lit from outside. Nowadays we pay a fortune to get that subtle atmospheric lighting, casting interesting shadows around the room. We'd take a candle up to bed with us, if we had one, otherwise we'd just have to go up in the dark, in which case Mum would direct us to 'Get in the same way as you got out!' I was sometimes scared of the dark because Mum used to hang her white overall on the back of the cupboard door, and if someone walked past the house with a torch casting shadows into the room, the overall would appear to be moving. But Dad would come upstairs and sit in the dark with me and tell me stories of swimming in the harbour and of catching fish with a stick. Or he'd find a torch and leave it by my bed until I'd fallen asleep.

How I missed my dad recently, while filming *Clubland* in Australia. A beautiful, huge apartment had been rented for me by the production company overlooking Rushcutters Bay, Sydney. It was fabulous. The first night I was there I was suddenly awoken at 3 a.m. by something falling on my face. I screamed and leapt out of bed in a panic and switched on the light. There on the pillow was a cockroach the size of a kangaroo. I couldn't get around to the other side of the bed to get my sandals or my specs because I could see several others scuttling about on the floor. When I got my breath back, I told myself not to be a wimp and ran down the hall to get a dustpan and brush, but before I could get there the entire flat was plunged into darkness. 'If ever a woman suffered.' I was to spend the entire night curled up in a vibrating chair, which was mercifully still as the electricity had blown, waiting for the sun to come up. Needless to say when the property agent arrived the next day, there were no cockroaches to be seen, except an insy spinsy tiny one lurking along the skirting board which I was almost reluctant to point out. But I'm glad I did because she said it was too small to have flown in and that there must be a nest in there somewhere. I moved to Quay West at The Rocks, overlooking Sydney Harbour, a far cry from the Plains of Waterloo.

The lighting in the scullery was supplied by gas through a very flimsy mantle, which we children were drawn to like moths to a flame, constantly testing its fragility. One gentle touch with the finger made the mantle disintegrate before our eyes, and presented the distinct possibility of the lot of us being gassed. What fun! But woe betide any of us if Mum caught us doing it. To add to the excitement, many were the times when the scullery was plunged into darkness because the gas had run out, and I would either have to run to a neighbour or up to my sister Pam's house to borrow a shilling for the meter. Even more frustrating was when Mum *could* afford more gas but didn't have the appropriate coin to feed into the meter. In desperation I once saw Mum sliding a knife into the coin slot to try and lever one of those coins out again! My brothers, too, once. But Mum's teaching of 'Do as I say, NOT do as I do' never seemed to sink in until they each got a clout round the ear, where the phrase resonated for a very long time. Of course, she didn't even know they'd tampered with the meter until the meter-man came one day to empty it and to tally the money with the register.

'Only doing my job, missus, you'd better cough up what's missing.'

'I'll give you cough up,' said Mum, 'you loppity eyed article! You afraid of getting lockjaw?'

The boys were in such trouble for that, from Dad as well as from Mum. They didn't do it again.

There was only one tap in the house, which supplied cold water, and when I think of all the modern conveniences we have nowadays to make our lives easier, the more I realise how heroic my mother and father were in bringing up nine children with no labour-saving devices at all. Luckily for me and all the other baby boomers, soon after we were born so was the Labour government's National Health Service, providing free health care for all. The Labour government also introduced other benefits including dental care, free milk at schools and other benefits. But obviously it didn't provide new kitchen appliances and on wash day, Mum had to boil gallons of water on the gas stove, in what resembled a witch's cauldron, in order to do the washing. In winter her hands would be red raw.

One of my jobs was to help her to take the washing out into the back yard and put it through the mangle, a magnificent contraption, which stood about five feet high, with a huge ornate iron frame and two wooden rollers each measuring about 9 inches in diameter. So old was the mangle that the centre of each of the rollers was worn thinner than the outer edges. Washing would be fed through the rollers with one hand while the other hand turned the huge wheel at the side. It had a giant adjustable iron screw at the top which allowed the rollers to accommodate different thicknesses of washing. I was warned not to operate the mangle alone for fear of crushing my fingers, but my brothers spent many a happy hour trying to crush each other's fingers, or preferably heads, in its mighty rollers. There was a line strung from one end of the yard to the other to peg the washing to, but there wasn't much room for it to blow in the breeze because the yard was so small. Mind you, that was a blessing because if it did, the washing would hit the wall and get dirty again. It took for ever to drip dry. Sometimes the washing froze, but that was a bonus because Mum could crack off the ice and bring the washing inside to dry in front of the fire.

When it came to ironing, Mum would spread a blanket on the scullery table and cover it with a sheet. We didn't have an ironing board. Two flat irons would be used alternately, one warming on the gas flame while the other was in use. 'Stand back,' said Mum, as she tested the heat of the iron by spitting on its underside. Only a sizzle said the iron was ready for use. I loved the wonderful, slightly singey smell of the fresh ironing. And I love the smell of laundry that has dried outside on a washing line. I can definitely tell the difference. When not in use these heavy flat irons were used as doorstops, or alternatively as handy weapons. I remember being totally awestruck when my friend Patsy said her mum had got an electric iron. It seemed the *height* of luxury. I think Patsy's family was also the first family I knew to get a television. Its tiny eight-inch screen was housed in a dark brown cabinet about three feet high and the screen was covered with a huge magnifying glass.

A wonderful sense of expectation came on smelling the sweet lavender furniture polish when we came home from school. This meant that Mum was home, it meant she hadn't been up the Alma, she was in a good mood and probably expecting company. Whenever we had visitors we'd usually end up with threepence in our pocket, sometimes sixpence. It didn't always mean that though. Sometimes Mum would wake up with a sense of regret and tried to put all her wrongs to right by cleaning the house from top to bottom on her hands and knees. She'd clean the windows by sitting perilously on the outside windowsill until they were gleaming. She'd spray the carpets with water to minimise the dust rising when the stiff broom did its stuff, and I'd watch in a daze as the motes floated out of the window into the sunshine.

Sometimes the smell of Brobat bleach would hit you halfway up the Plains, which told you that Mum had washed down the area steps. I always expected it to be one of the neighbours washing their steps, but it never was. It was lovely. Or she would swill down the back yard drain after scrubbing the scullery floor.

Having no bathroom, washing arrangements were in the scullery, and it was quite normal for us to use cold water and carbolic soap. It's surprising how often people comment with envy on the clearness and youthfulness of our skin, and we think this is probably attributable to these archaic arrangements. Or it could be due to the less sophisticated version of washing when Mum would just spit on the corner of her apron and wipe it around our faces. In winter it was really cold in the scullery so stripping off for a wash was avoided at all costs if we thought we could get away with it. But Mum had eyes like a hawk, and she'd announce 'Look at the dirt on that child's neck!' Or 'You could grow potatoes on that child's feet!' Or 'Come here, Shuckyucks, let me put a rake through that hair.' So once a week, whether I needed to or not, I would have to use the West Cliff Public Baths, situated next door to the dance hall. It was lovely and warm in there because there was a gas fire in the corner keeping the attendant warm. She would use a ruler to measure out the permitted six inches of water, and included in the price of the bath was a square inch of soap, but Mum always supplied me with a sachet of Beecham's shampoo, which came in powder form. A poster advertised WASH AND BRUSH UP 3d, BATH WITHOUT TOWEL 6d, BATH WITH TOWEL 9d. The water was far too hot to sit down in and I would go home on the bus with telltale red rims round my legs, wearing an itchy clean woollen vest and skin-tight liberty bodice, and a most stylish home-made pixie-hood to cover my wet hair. And before leaving the baths I always liked to peek through the doors to the dance hall and see the variety acts on stage, including the

Singing Coon (I'm not kidding!), or watch couples taking a turn around the floor.

But sometimes, bath night would be organised at home, when every saucepan in the house would be used to heat the water. A large grey tin bath, which hung on a nail in the back yard, was hauled inside and placed in front of the fire. One by one we would get into the same water, girls first, and top it up with another saucepan of hot water when it cooled. Sometimes the boys splashed one another and Mum would holler, 'This ain't a public swimming pool!' She'd always suspect Terry of being the instigator of the hilarity so she'd add, 'I'll dance on you in a minute, you little box o'tricks!' Of course, the bath had to be emptied just as methodically, because it was too heavy to lift when full. A chain gang would be formed from the front room to the backyard drain, and the bath would eventually be emptied and hung back on its nail in the yard. What a palaver! No wonder Mum preferred the expense of sending us up the West Cliff, although fortunately for us, we were privileged customers for a couple of seasons because the attendant at the baths was none other than my sister Pam. The glow of knowing someone in such a position of authority would keep us warm on the cold bus journey home.

But I was never as clean as I was after an unfortunate incident while out playing on Abbotts Hill with my best friend, Patsy. A middle-aged man approached us and asked if we knew where he could go to wee wee. We were about nine or ten. We said that the nearest public toilets were down at the harbour or perhaps Charlotte Court in the town, but he spotted an alley almost opposite Patsy's house and he said he would go up there to relieve himself and that I should go with him in order to keep watch. We had never heard of child molesters or paedophiles or rapists or anything like that. Although we had been taught not to go with strangers, we had also been taught to obey our elders. I was taken firmly by the shoulder and escorted up the alley while Patsy ran indoors. As instructed I diligently kept watch while he urinated, except he wasn't urinating was he, and he then took my hand and told me to give it a good old shake dry. Oh dear, oh dear, I thought, why won't it get dry? Surprisingly, having grown up with brothers, I had never seen a boy's private parts. Obviously I wasn't aware of what he was really doing, and although I intensely disliked what was happening, I wasn't traumatised by it because I didn't understand, but I was greatly relieved when Patsy came running down the alley with her father, and the man fled. Devout Catholics, they took me into their house and scrubbed my hands cleaner than they had ever been and my mother was summoned, who was absolutely livid and over-affectionate all at the same time. I had to describe time and time again what had happened, and then she took me home where my underwear was examined and every inch of me was gone over with a fine toothcomb and the bath was taken from its nail in the yard. Oh what a stupid little girl I had been to go with him. Why hadn't I shouted out or screamed? The realisation of the narrow escape I'd had made me sickened and scared. Once satisfied that her daughter was still intact and spotlessly clean, Mum stopped quizzing me, but I was very aware and ashamed of the drama I had caused for a very long time. Except I hadn't caused it, had I, HE had. Mum possibly thought that she was scaring me more than the man had, so let me climb into bed with her and she cuddled me to sleep, running her fingers through my hair and I could smell her powder and beautiful scent. I thought it heavenly. Even though it was inexpensive, no designer perfume I've come across since smelt as good. Whether the man was reported to the police or not, I don't know.

In fact I was wanted by the police at a very early age, when I was reported as trying to hang my niece Valerie on the school railings with a length of rubber hosepipe. Honestly, we were only playing cowboys and Indians and *of course* I was the sheriff and Val was wanted dead or alive. Anyway, some nosy parker had witnessed the lynching and dutifully rushed and told my sister, who summoned me to her presence. Pam convinced me that the police had been informed and were now scouring Ramsgate for a little girl matching my description wearing a red coat who was wanted for attempted murder. I protested that I was only playing and wouldn't have *actually* lifted Val off her feet (although I'm not absolutely sure about that) and, anyway, it was her turn to be sheriff next. My protests fell on deaf ears. I was petrified. I walked home in absolute terror, walking sideways with my back to the wall just in case I was being followed (I'd seen too many films). My head was turning from side to side on constant lookout. How unfair of my sister to frighten me so. After all, I had only tried to hang her daughter. When I got home, Mum asked me why I looked so shifty. I explained what had happened and she said she'd felt like hanging the lot of us on more than one occasion!

Of course, Pam wasn't the only celebrity in our family. My dad was the operator of the Waterfall on Madeira Walk and the Fountain on the East Cliff. He'd cross the stepping-stones at the bottom of the falls and disappear into a cave behind the cascading water to switch it off on our way home from the cinema. I could never understand why he never got wet. But more important than that, Dad was the driver of the Aqua Lovelies in the carnival every year. Not only the Ramsgate carnival at that. The float displayed the Aqua Lovelies (bathing beauties) posing on water skis behind a speed boat being driven by my dad. Of course, he was also driving the float itself. Mum was a bit jealous, and wasn't shy of showing it. 'I lay he does think he's something,' she'd goad and then say he looked like 'a whelk' or 'a barnacle' on the boat. But that wouldn't stop her from cheering as the float passed by. 'What do you think you look like!' 'Look out, here's Gregory!' (She often accused him of thinking he looked like Gregory Peck.) Or 'Hey-up, here's Humpty!' 'Ever to be associated with such an article!'

Ne'er cast a clout till May is out

2

KEEPING THE HOME FIRES BURNING

UNLIKE TODAY WHERE FAMILY MEMBERS COME AND GO OR watch television while eating, our mealtimes were extremely rigid. I think it is such a pity that the convention of families having their meals together is going out of fashion. It's so valuable, to simply face someone across the table, and give the meal the attention it's due. The meal didn't arrive there by magic. Someone planned it, bought it, carried it home, cooked it and served it. And in Mum's case, also made it stretch. We'd all sit down together around the *huge* table, depending upon when Dad would be home from work, leaving time for him to wash and change out of his overalls. Dad always sat sideways at the table, never with his knees under it. (The only time I saw him with his knees under the table was at Val's wedding. Her veil was getting in her way and she asked Dad if he had a pin. He said, 'Why, are we having winkles?') Anyway, either myself as the youngest, or whoever happened to be in the most trouble at the time, would sit on my mother's left side. She was left-handed, so if there was any misbehaving, the unfortunate in the hot seat was conveniently positioned for a clout. She could-n't bear sapping, noisy eating or greediness. If we were greedy, she'd say, 'There's another day!' Or if we said we wanted another cake, she'd say, 'More still when there's none!' Which, of course, meant we'd be craving even more for a cake if we'd had none today. Such pearls of wisdom. Catch 22 though was when there was a little pudding left over and we were all fighting for it. By way of resolving the situation she would say, 'Those who ask, don't get. Those who don't ask, don't want!' and promptly put the pudding away in the cupboard.

The table was covered in newspapers, except on the rare occasions we were expecting 'company', in which case a nice clean cloth would materialise and be spread. Having visitors meant Mum's special tea – tinned salmon and cucumber sand-wiches and two shillings' worth of mixed fancies. These were a selection of little iced cakes of different colours, shapes and sizes, jam tarts, cheese tarts with twisted coconut shreds on the top (I didn't care for that one), cream slice, Eccles cake, angel cake and cream horn. Two shillings bought a dozen. Oh, oh, what a huge treat this was, although admittedly it was usually marred by an unseemly scuffle for the cream horn. Oh, the cream horn! It's making my mouth water just thinking about it. But Mum simply would *not* tolerate bad behaviour at the table, and would only allow herself to throw a punch if absolutely necessary.

I loved hearing the back gate opening and knowing that Dad was home. He would invariably have a present for us. Comics or some toy or other that someone had thrown out. And we would rush to the back door to greet him, our little hands diving into his pockets to see what treasures were there. I would hold on to his hands and walk up his legs while Martin and Terry climbed up on to his back. And Dad would protest, 'Aw gawd crickey ay, give me a chance to gid in the door!'

We'd have to make our own breakfast because Mum would already be at work. She had a regular cleaning job at Albion House, the offices of Thanet Council, and had to be there by six o'clock. Come rain, snow, hail or shine, off she went. We'd make either porridge or have cornflakes with the milk mixed with water. I didn't know then that I'd come to prefer this humble breakfast to the breakfasts served in LA that come on a plate the size of a manhole cover. 'Dinner' was at one o'clock. My brothers and I went through phases of having school meals, but sometimes Mum couldn't afford it, and we would have to come home – it was only a ten-minute walk. Some children got free school dinners and my brothers remember that we did too, so why can I remember being made to stand in the corner of the classroom for not having my dinner money?

On entering our house we could see along the passageway straight into the scullery, and we'd know instantly whether there was any dinner or not, for sometimes Mum, bless her heart, would get sidetracked at the Alma, get a bit squiffy, and there'd be nothing on the table to eat at all. On good days though there might be corned beef and potatoes. 'What's for afters, Mum?' was a familiar cry. 'Think yourself lucky you've got befores' invariably bounced back. But sometimes, though, on entering the house we could smell baked rice or the spicy aroma of bread pudding. It was such a welcome smell, because not only did it mean we had a tasty treat for afters, but that if there was a pudding at all, it meant that Mum was home, sober, and in a good mood. It felt like a cuddle. We would negotiate about who was going to scrape out the rice-dish in lieu of a portion, because of all the lovely crispy bits round the edge, even though the first one of us to enter the house would shout 'BAGSY THE DISH' and felt there was no need for further discussion on the matter. Mum thought differently, however, and unreasonably made us take it in turns.

21

I have yet to taste bread pudding as good as my mother's. It was an event just watching her make it. We'd all gather round in the scullery marvelling as all the different ingredients went in. Soaked stale bread, suet, sugar, spice, sultanas and raisins – sometimes even the odd bit of fag-ash if Mum happened to be smoking. She had the uncanny knack of balancing about two inches of ash on the end of her cigarette before it fell. 'How long will it take to cook, Mum?' 'About as long as a piece of string' came the reply. Whoops, there goes the ash! Mum's Yorkshire pudding was also in a class of its own – so light and fluffy that when she ran the knife round the tin, the pudding would spring into the air and flip over. It tasted so good that we never noticed how little meat there was to go with it. Whenever Mum did cook beef she would always make 'dripping' by pouring the excess fat and juices into a pudding basin to cool, for spreading on to our bread for tea. The brown jelly, which had settled at the bottom of the basin, was particularly tasty. In winter the dish usually lasted all week because it would stay cool on the outside windowsill.

One of our neighbours made an improvised fridge by digging a hole in a shady part of the back yard, filling it with a big metal box and putting in all their perishable food. The box was then covered over with a big rock. What a performance! We didn't own a fridge until I was about fifteen, which my brother Bernard bought for us, amongst other things, when he returned home after working as a chef for several years for the New Zealand shipping company. All the time he was away, he religiously sent money to Mum to buy shoes for us children or winter coats or school uniforms. To Mum he was a godsend. On one of his trips home he introduced us to a very peculiar dish called spaghetti bolognaise. I can remember being terrified of it. It took a lot of persuading to get us to taste those worms but when we did, oh! It was delicious.

Being a Catholic household, every Friday was fish day, or to be more precise, fish and chips day. Inexplicably, almost every Friday after fish and chips I got a toothache, I've no idea why, and the thought of having to visit the dentist filled me with terror. Mind you, I never even owned a toothbrush until I was thirteen when I went on a Girl Guides camping trip and Pam bought one for me, but this was more for appearances' sake than for cleaning my teeth. Considering our lack of oral hygiene, it's surprising that we all have such good teeth.

Having a tooth pulled out at the dentist was a most traumatic affair and I can remember sitting in a huge leather chair surrounded by torturous contraptions and the white-coated dentist coming at me with a mask to fit over my face. The gas knocked me out while the tooth was pulled, and it was disconcerting on waking up to find my mother tussling with the dentist, who was covered with my blood and holding my tooth with a pair of pliers. My mum, who'd been waiting in the next room, had heard me screaming blue murder while the tooth was being pulled. She apparently came charging into the surgery and accused him of not knocking me out properly and told him to keep his hands off me! She nearly knocked *him* out.

Tea was around five o'clock, and sometimes Dad being the breadwinner would have bacon and egg. My brothers and I would sit and watch him eat it, pretending to be starving slaves and begging him to let us dip our bread into his egg yolk – he rarely got it all to himself. He might have done had he been a faster eater. But Dad religiously chewed every mouthful thirty-two times. He maintained it was good for the digestion. Mum, however, maintained it was good for sending her to an early grave! The whole procedure was like a well-rehearsed comedy routine. Our tea was more likely to be bread and jam and a cup of tea, or an old favourite – *wait for it* – condensed milk sandwiches. Ugh, it sounds awful now, but when that tin of condensed milk was placed on the table, it was a real treat.

In the 1940s and 50s the American Air Force was stationed at Manston on the outskirts of Ramsgate, and on one occasion we came into the possession of a *huge* tin of jam, that had apparently started life at this base. The tin was so big that I had to stand on tiptoes just to reach into the top of it – we didn't possess a dainty jam dish. On the contrary, it was quite a hazardous exercise just getting a spoonful of the stuff, for the serrated edge of the tin was quite capable of cutting your arm off. This tin of jam couldn't possibly have fallen off the back of a lorry, because theft in our house was absolutely forbidden, and any offenders were severely punished. Oh no, absolutely, it couldn't possibly have been nicked. Curious to recall then, that if there was an unexpected rat-a-tat at the door the cry went up immediately, 'Quick – hide the jam!' This would be followed by a mad scurry to lift the massive tin from the centre of the table and conceal it in the cupboard, lest the unexpected visitor would come in (there were no locks on the doors in those days) and spot the offending article.

It was also around this time that I first experienced the taste of a new beverage called coffee. It might have been well known to everybody else but it certainly hadn't been in our house before. It wasn't the freshly ground beans ready to filter, or the instant freeze-dried kind, it was in a bottle, made of chicory and its name was Camp. How appropriate. It smelled so sweet and I remember the smell of it made my nose itch with excitement. The black sticky liquid was measured into the cup with a teaspoon, just like medicine. The fact that it was only for adults made it even more exciting. I have often asked myself where it came from because we certainly couldn't have afforded such an exotic extravagance, so it must have come from the same place as the jam, i.e. the American Air Force Base.

24

When Mum and Dad were out one day my brothers decided it was time for us to check out this mysterious potion. They boiled a kettle of water on the gas stove and poured out some of the Camp coffee, filling the bottle up with the exact amount of water to hide the theft. Perhaps we used the wrong measurements or something because the vile taste of the stuff made us screw up our noses in disgust. Eeeeeergh! Why would anybody drink this muck called 'coffee' for pleasure. In our young wisdom we decided that it would never catch on! A few days later, our theft was discovered when Mum was making a cup of coffee for Dad and not a single one of us was whining to have a taste. She twigged at once. It wasn't a proper clout, it was one of those terrifying ones she did quite often. She would raise her hand until you could visualise the *almighty* clout coming, and with a cry of GEEEEERCHA down came the thump with force but mercifully stopping just short of impact.

Sometimes on a winter's night, Mum would pose the question 'Do you know what I fancy?'

'What?'

'A nice four penn'orth of pease pudding. So who's going to nip down Woods the butchers to get it?'

'Me! Me! Me!' we chorused

After Mum had broken up the ensuing fight, she would announce that we *all* had to go, for there was safety in numbers. In retrospect I think she only sent us all together so she could have a little precious time on her own in front of the fire with Dad. It was freezing cold upstairs in the bedroom! You could only buy pease pudding on Tuesday and Thursday nights from 7 until 9 p.m. It was delicious, especially accompanied by faggots or a saveloy. My brothers and I would eat our share with our index fingers on Abbotts Hill until our fingers went all crinkly because we were too impatient to wait until we got home.

Also available were pigs' trotters. I couldn't understand how anyone could eat them, but they were a favourite with Mum and Dad. Neither could I stand the look or smell of tripe cooking. At least I think it was tripe, Mum called it chitlings. It made me feel physically ill. And Dad. But that didn't deter her from tucking into a handsome helping. It was probably the only dish she could have all to herself with not a starving slave in sight. If she was annoyed with Dad over something or other you can bet your bottom dollar she'd cook chitlings for tea just to irritate him.

Because there was no heating in the house, in winter we had a coal fire in the parlour and the basement, but never both at the same time. If money was short, there'd only be a small fire in the hearth, and we'd all crowd around elbowing our way in, and Mum would be heard to say, 'It's like heaven in here – you can't get near the fire' or 'Let's *see* it even if we can't feel it!' She would supplement the fuel by throwing the vegetable peelings on to the fire, and they'd hiss and sizzle on the coals. Or we would be dispatched around to the various greengrocers to see if they had any empty wooden fruit boxes going begging, whereupon we would take them home to the back yard and chop them up. In fact, we'd chop up anything wooden if it was no good and burn it. Anything to keep warm. We had one giant log in the yard that you had to place the piece of wood on before bringing the chopper down. I got quite expert at it.

To supplement the bedding, winter coats were laid on top of the blankets. On my bed there was a thick khaki army coat to keep me warm. But one summer, the prettiest rose-covered satin eiderdown suddenly materialised on my bed. Goodness only knows where it came from! Probably Daniel Bing's, the second-hand shop, and along with it came a pretty little nightgown. There was a name-tag in the collar. Brenda Chips. Wherever you are Brenda, thank you very much. And Martin also got a very smart dressing gown. He looked remarkably like Noel Coward in a smoking jacket!

One night when Mum and Dad had to go out, my brother Martin was left in charge of me, and he thought it would be a good idea to bank up the fire so that it would be nice and warm when they came home. It was a wretchedly cold night. He made a beauty, and we had to sit on the other side of the room so we wouldn't get scorched. Oh it was lovely. Well, Dad nearly went ballistic when he saw it – fearing the blaze was halfway up the chimney! His face was redder than the fire. Now I never saw my dad raise his hand to any of us, but on this occasion we thought a clout was definitely on the cards and it seemed more than appropriate to get out of his reach and retreat to the passageway. We watched the action through the crack of the door.

With the speed of an athlete he'd gone to the back yard and returned with a shovel and a couple of metal buckets and started to lift out the hot coals, and then shoved loads of sodden wet sacks into the fireplace and up the chimney to stop the house burning down. (I suppose it was a precautionary measure to send steam up the flue.) He took the buckets of hot coals and rushed them downstairs to the grate in the basement. No point in wasting them. When he was certain he had made the chimney safe he sat for a while on his heels in front of the diminished fire and slowly calmed down. He glanced at the four wide eyes staring at him through the crack in the door and with his finger crooked he beckoned us in. Look out, we thought, here it comes! Get ready to dodge! Blow me down if he didn't thank Martin for being so thoughtful. It was just a bit too thoughtful. So the expected clout turned into a pat on the back. Honestly, grown ups! Who could understand them? I have this strange recollection of Mum finding this all hilarious – but surely that can't be right! Especially as I remember her calling Dad a prat!

Mum, c. 1924

3

ESOTERIC COGITATIONS

Bυτ THIS WASN'T THE ONLY TIME MARTIN GOT ME INTO DEEP water. He is closest to me in age, being three years older. He and Terry were always together as children, as there is only one year between them, and naturally they didn't always want their sissy little sister hanging around all the time. While Terry excelled in business acumen even as a boy, Martin was more studious, reading anything he could lay his hands on, and has a remarkable memory. Martin was in the school choir, sang as an altar boy in church, and excelled in the school production of *HMS Pinafore*. I was so proud to see my brother on stage singing 'Polish Up the Knocker on the Big Front Door'. He is also a very sharp snooker player, taught by my dad who in his younger days ran a snooker hall, and Martin has played and won demonstration frames against two world champions. But as a boy, Martin was only allowed in the snooker hall accompanied by an adult. However, he didn't let this small detail stop him from sneaking in.

On one occasion he was forbidden to go to watch a snooker

tournament at Swan's snooker hall (always referred to as Swanies) because he'd been told to stay indoors to look after little me. It was simply too much for him to bear. He *had* to go, and came up with a brilliant idea. What if he had a little *brother* instead of a little sister? As girls were not allowed in the snooker hall at all, he told me to dress up in Terry's shirt, tie, rolled up trousers, braces, big boots, jacket, cloth cap and muffler, and took me with him to the snooker hall.

Wearing one of Dad's trilby hats, he said 'act nonchalant' as we swaggered in the door past the doorman, who was fortunately chatting to someone, and clonked up the stairs, where we could hear the snooker balls enticingly smacking together on the green baize.

'Where d'ye think you're going?' called the doorman up the stairs after us, just when we thought we'd got away with it.

'Just 'aving a couple of frames, guvnor,' I growled, effecting as deep a voice as I could muster, and gave a big gobby cough.

'Not in here you're not,' he said, 'not with a cough like that. You little scamps. Sling your hook!'

But Martin was already through the door and watching the match. So I ran through the door after him. The players weren't best pleased to see and hear a four-foot bloke, with boots several sizes too big, clumping into the hall.

And just as one player was about to take a shot, in came the doorman.

'OUT,' he hollered, 'THE PAIR OF YOU.'

The player mis-cued and was more annoyed with the door-man than with Martin and me. But our cover was blown and poor Martin had to take me home again.

To cheer us up, Martin announced that because Dad had given him some pocket money for looking after me, we had enough to buy some pease pudding on the way home.

Meanwhile, my mother, who had returned home unexpectedly early, worked out what had happened and launched herself like an Exocet missile towards Swanies, but her fury fizzled out when she passed Woods the butchers, finding us outside tucking into our pease pudding. My outfit was a giveaway though, and she told Martin she would 'Dance on him when she got him home' and dived into Woods and bought an extra large portion of chitlings.

Despite the incident of nearly burning the house down, and at the risk of singeing all the hairs off our arms, we were still allowed to toast our bread on the fire using the iron toasting fork. You'd think we'd be scarred for life. In fact, I probably am scarred for life because apparently when I was a toddler I ventured too close to the unguarded fire, stumbled and sat on a red-hot poker. Not being a contortionist I don't know if I'm scarred or not, and not wanting to draw attention to my rear, I have never sought confirmation from anybody else! We'd also toast chestnuts by lining them up along the top rail of the grate. We knew they were done when they flew off into the fender, or occasionally one would ricochet around the room, and the first person to find it could eat it, invariably burning a layer of skin from the tongue! Sometimes Mum would cook on the range in the basement, especially in winter because it was warmer than the scullery and it saved on gas.

Mum didn't have a social life. I don't remember her ever going out with a friend for pleasure, although there were plenty of 'friends' who would turn up on the doorstep to borrow this or that. But she was well liked. She'd sometimes stand at the back gate and chat for a while to a neighbour but that was the extent of her socialising. In fact, my earliest memory is of standing with my mother at the back gate while she chatted to a neighbour. I was fascinated by my leggings, which had flaps over my shoes, straps underneath and were buttoned all the way up the sides. I was trying to count them. I must have been two or three.

Dad didn't socialise much either, except for his annual reunion dinner with the Royal Field Artillery. It was such a special occasion, long and eagerly awaited, that he'd stand tall for ages in front of the mirror over the mantelpiece, combing his thick dark brilliantine-soaked hair, admiring his good looks and adjusting his stiff white collar and tie. This would always put Mum's nose out of joint and she would encouragingly remark that he 'looked like a donkey looking over a whitewashed wall'! She was never invited to accompany him on this very special occasion, but maybe it was men only. 'I lay he does think he's something,' goaded Mum to the rest of us. 'What does he think he looks like?' They would, however, occasionally go out together, for a bracing walk 'around four corners' which didn't cost a farthing, or go to the pub or to the cinema, if they weren't pulling in their horns.

Mum and Dad were both great storytellers. My brothers and I would love to sit at their feet, in front of the range in the basement, and listen to tales of Dad's time in India. Of how he nearly died of smallpox, not having been vaccinated, and how fortunate it was for him that he had previously been very fit, which he thought was probably the reason for his survival. And how important it was for all of us to keep fit and to eat our vegetables in case we should ever find ourselves in the same situation! And of how, when he was once pulling a gun carriage across India en route to Mesopotamia (now Iraq), he met a battalion of British soldiers travelling in the opposite direction, and was amazed to learn that one of the soldiers was his young brother Tom. Dad didn't even know Tom was in India. He'd tell us graphic tales of falling sick again on the banks of the Tigris, and of how he wrestled with a black mamba snake that had crawled into his kitbag. He'd jump up for emphasis and act out the whole scenario for us using the entire room as his stage. He'd show us the scar on the side of his hand where the snake had sunk its fangs into his flesh! And of how he only had moments to get an antidote and tourniquet, and how he was GASPING for breath. And of another time when he'd dragged himself, barely alive, across the desert in search of water. And of how he again narrowly escaped death when a scorpion had crawled inside the netting around his bed. He told us of how he had to break ranks in order to vomit at the side of the dusty road, in the soaring heat, and of how delirium had set in. Mum said he still had it! It was riveting. We'd ask to hear the stories time and time again. Who needed a television, we had live entertainment. Or as Mum would say, 'live fantasy'!

And we'd love to hear them both reminiscing, midst gales of laughter, about hop picking each summer. Mum told us that for four or five weeks every year they would pack up home along with hundreds of Londoners and go off to the hop farms in the Kent countryside, and camp out in small huts on the farm. Sharing the hut would be Mum, Gran, Auntie Fran, Uncle Sid, my sister Pam, my brother Ted, Uncle Bert and cousin Beryl. They apparently slept on wooden pallets, rather like large upturned orange boxes, filled with spare clothing for comfort. They all welcomed Mum getting a visit from my dad because that meant there would be straw to lie on. He was treated like a prince. At which point in the story Dad would start heckling, saying he wasn't treated like a prince at all! It was him who had to go and get the straw! And they'd nudge and laugh and croon. It sounded such a happy romantic time. She said their clothes would be damp in the mornings from the dew, and would need to be hung out to air in the midday sun, making them fresh and dry again for wearing. She told us that the job entailed taking small camp chairs along the long line of hops, and of pulling the hop vine over your lap and plucking the hops away to fill as many wicker baskets as possible. As a child I thought the whole operation had to be done on one leg! She said care had to be taken to avoid pulling off the leaves as these did not count at the weigh-in at the end of the day, although most people threw a few in at the bottom of the basket where they would pass undetected. At weekends most of the hoppers would get doled up in their finest and walk along the country lane to the village pub and have crisps and lemonade in the garden. At that time none of my mum's party drank alcohol. Occasionally there would be a dance organised either by the farmer or the villagers. A local baker would open his ovens on Sunday when many of the hop-pickers, for a few pence a time, would bring along tins of all shapes and sizes, containing various roasts and vegetables and pies, and pop them into his oven. Many friendships were made and remade each year. Auntie Fran, aged twelve, had her first taste of butterflies when she fell in unrequited love with the farmer, an apparently gorgeous man who resembled the Duke of Windsor!

In fact, Auntie Fran and Uncle Norman often talk about how beautiful Mum was and how totally in love she was with my father, and he with her. According to Auntie Fran they were happy times. She fondly remembers that when she was a little girl and Mum was about nineteen, Gran had taken her to see the carnival with a surprise in store. Delirious with excitement and sucking on an ice cream she was overjoyed to hear the cheering and to see the carnival approaching. Proudly leading the parade was Micky Mottler, the chief of police, and striding alongside him was a huge shire horse bedecked with ribbons and frills and to Auntie Fran's astonishment sitting astride it was my mother wearing a silk jockey outfit and wielding a rider's crop. Auntie Fran said it was a magnificent sight and that Mum looked absolutely beautiful.

After supper, if we weren't listening to stories, or if Mum had a headache, we would sit around the big table and play board games or draw or do jigsaws. Dad enjoyed any kind of puzzle or brainteaser and we'd all help to solve them. The Chaotic anagram in the daily *Evening News* was a favourite. He'd often give us a word to study to see who could make up the most words from it, and most of us are passionate crossword puzzlers today. I was once writing a story and asked Dad for some new words to incorporate. He did give me some but told me it was far better to write simply. He then proceeded to teach me, parrot fashion, a paragraph he had found in the *Reader's Digest*,

> In promulgating esoteric cogitations, or articulating superficial sentimentalities and philosophical or psychological observations, beware of platitudinous ponderosity. Allow your conversation to possess a clarified conciseness, coalescent consistency and a concentrated cogency. Eschew all conglomerations of flatulent garrulity, jejune babblement, and asinine affectation. Shun double entendre and spurious jocosity whether obscure or apparent.

Which in other words meant don't be pompous, don't use long pretentious words just for the sake of it. Say what you want to say in simple everyday language, and be sincere. I'm trying to do that with this book, Dad.

We'd make up songs together but this was a risky business if Mum was in a bad mood because there was the danger of 'tears before bedtime' when the most raucous of us would get a clout.

Just before I was born Dad and Jeannie entered a radio 'write a song for £1,000' competition run by Lou Preager and the winning song was 'Cruising Down the River'. I wonder if there's a copy of Dad and Jeannie's entry on file somewhere? I'd love to hear it. Listening to the wireless was a popular pastime. In the early days, of course, we didn't know anyone with a television, none of the 20 million who had access to TV sets to watch the Coronation of Queen Elizabeth II in 1953 lived in our street. Radio was all we had, that is if the Rediffusion hadn't been cut off for not paying the bill. There were only two stations, the Light and Home Service, but there seemed to be a wealth of good programmes to listen to: *Meet the Huggetts*, *Worker's Playtime*, *The Navy Lark*, *In Town Tonight*, *Hancock's Half Hour*, *Journey into Space*, *Life with the Lyons*, *Two-way Family Favourites*, *Friday Night Is Music Night*.

During the war a Spitfire had crashed into Wellington Crescent on the east cliff. My brother Ted and his friends, of course, were fascinated by this and after the authorities had finished examining it, they crawled all over it and retrieved a set of headphones. Ted gave them to Dad, who thought they might come in useful one day. Much to Mum's annoyance, Dad was one of those people who kept everything: little pieces of string, the odd chair leg, hooks, old screws, old nails, paper bags, bicycle wheels, ball bearings, tins of oil, brackets, hinges, handles, *anything* salvageable, and kept it all in a huge cupboard in the yard, grandly called the Lodge. He kept us children out by fixing a big padlock on the door. It was a treasure trove. I loved peeking inside whenever it was unlocked. So naturally he was right about the headphones. On one of our many evenings around the table he gave them to Terry, who was ten years old, to enable him to make a crystal set. Bill had learnt how to do it at school and was passing the knowledge on to his younger brother. All I remember is that bits of wire, a crystal and a cat's whisker were mentioned. Suffice it to say that the assembly process culminated in Terry dicing with death by climbing out of the third floor bedroom window in order to fix the end of the wire into the roof guttering to act as an aerial. He then attached the headphones and fiddled and fiddled and fiddled until miraculously he tuned into the BBC and heard the strains of Wilfred Pickles' theme tune, 'Have a Go Joe, Come and Have a Go'. 'And now Mabel, what have we on the table?' We took it in turns to listen on the headphones. Mum said she thought he was a clever 'little box of tricks'. I thought my brothers were wizards. Still do actually.

Bill for his part, by way of amusing himself, once completely dismantled a radiogram simply to study the workings inside. Dad was furious at first but then became as interested as Bill. Mum said she'd be interested 'to see the inside of his skull when she got hold of him'. We are all inquisitive. Mum taught us all how to knit, explaining that it was originally a fisherman's craft. She also taught us how to cook. Boys as well. In fact, in those days cookery, along with needlework and woodwork, was taught as a matter of course in secondary school to boys and girls. Terry excelled at baking, taking after Bernard who later became a master baker and who made all of our beautiful wedding cakes. Martin read anything in sight and has a remarkable memory for all kinds of data. Sister Jeannie also has a fantastic memory and is probably the most well read amongst us, neck and neck with my niece Valerie. But as far as memory goes we all pale into insignificance compared to my sister Pam. I discovered recently via a distant relative, John Bottle, who is keen on genealogy, that a celebrated Victorian Music Hall artiste called Datas is thought to be an ancestor of ours. He had an extraordinary memory for data. So intrigued was the medical profession at his astonishing memory, he is reputed to have sold his brain for £2000 for medical research after his demise. Fortunately for him though the surgeons he sold it to died before he did.

Dad would bring home second-hand books and magazines from work, which he got from the dustmen. He was an avid reader of the *Reader's Digest*. He rarely failed to bring us something home. Mum complained that as fast as she threw rubbish out he brought it back again. He once brought home a timer he reasoned had also been salvaged from a wrecked plane, and he made himself an alarm clock from it. My brother Bill still has it. However, you do need a couple of hours' spare time and a degree in mathematics to work out the actual time, by doing something like adding five hours and subtracting nine minutes per hour, and then taking away the first number you thought of! But it certainly worked for Dad. I can remember the bell ringing at least an hour before it was time to get up in the morning. It drove Mum mad. 'If ever a woman suffered!' I'm a bit like Dad in this respect. I often set my alarm to wake me up when I don't have to get up at all, simply for the pleasure of disobeying it. Mum, however, had a built-in alarm clock. She never overslept.

Ramsgate was a bustling seaside resort and in the summer the beach was absolutely crowded with visitors. You'd be hard pushed to find a square foot to yourself, and once having left your square foot to go into the sea, you'd spend the next couple of hours looking for your belongings again. There were amusement arcades galore, teashops, novelty stalls, deckchair hire, and ice-cream and fruit salesmen parading the beach, my Uncle Norman being one of them. His daughter Noreen was his assistant and if sales were a little on the slow side she would shout at the top of her voice right across the crowded beach, 'DAD, THE PINEAPPLE BOAT HAS JUST DOCKED!' And on cue Uncle Norman would go to his lock-up and slice up his delicious juicy shop-bought pineapples and sell the slices for a tidy profit. Donkeys paraded up and down the beach to give the younger visitors a ride, and each of the donkeys had the name of a popular film star painted on to its bridle.

When I was about four, I cried and cried for a ride on a

donkey until Mum's patience ran out and she took me to the donkey line. The man lifted me on to the saddle and the prickly hairs of Myrna Loy made my legs itch. It was a lovely long ride from the centre of the beach to the harbour wall and back, with the bells on the bridle jingling merrily. When the donkey man lifted me down again, my mother was nowhere to be seen. I howled. There were thousands of faces laughing and smiling at me, but there were none I recognised. As young as I was, I knew with certainty that I would never ever see my mum again. She was lost to me for ever. I screamed even louder. But a responsible visitor took this screaming child to the bathing station at the top of the beach, whereupon a nurse made an announcement, which blasted from a huge megaphone right across the entire beach, 'We have a little girl at the bathing station wearing NAVY BLUE KNICKERS and answering to the name of BRENDA. Will her parent or guardian please come and fetch her.' My mum, who hadn't actually moved from the spot where I was put on to the donkey, came stumbling and panting up the beach to the bathing station in a fury, saying that the donkey man had set me down at the wrong place and that he should be horsewhipped. She had already made a 'song and dance' with the donkey man when she saw him making a return trip without me.

All the amusement arcades opened for the summer season around April time. Mum's favourite gamble was on the Film Stars stall. For sixpence you could purchase a ticket showing the names of six stars. About two dozen photographs of film stars were illuminated alternately and then the light came to rest on one of them, and if the name of that star appeared on your card you tore off the little tab at the end. The original hanging chad! The first person to get all six stars was the winner. This was such a glamorous game – Hedy Lamarr, Lana Turner, Grace Kelly, Jane Russell, Bette Davis, Myrna Loy, Greta Garbo, Marlene Dietrich,

Betty Grable, Marilyn Monroe, Doris Day, Barbara Stanwyck, Anna Neagle. We once had four goes which cost two shillings and we won a cruet. We could have bought one for 1s 3d.

If I played my cards right I'd probably be allowed to have a go on something. The bowl slide maybe. Aye! Aye! On the Bowl Slide! Threepence a slide. Aye! Aye! After paying the fee, you'd take a coconut mat and clamber up inside the tower until reaching the door at the top, then sit on the mat and push off. It was wonderful sliding down the long, polished wooden chute into the deep bowl at the bottom. I remember the first time I was allowed to go up on my own. It was absolutely exhilarating. Previously I'd had to ride between Dad's or one of my brothers' knees for safety. There were lots of variations on how to slide down. You could just do the conventional sit. Or you could lie flat, on your stomach or back. Whizz down on your side, either side. Or head first. But this method was only recommended in the summer months when the bowl was at the bottom. In the winter, the bowl was removed until the next season. My cousin Wendy and I and some friends would feel intrepid and, ignoring the signs warning us to keep out, would climb up the chute on our knees using our plimsoles as leverage against the sides. On reaching the top we'd about turn, hoping not to die from tumbling over the top, and come hurtling back down, shuddering to a halt at the bottom or else go straight into a head over heels on the tarmac. Once was never enough and we'd spend hours going up and down and eventually arriving home covered from head to foot in cuts and bruises. But considering we used to climb the cliffs for amusement the bowl slide was the lesser of two evils.

Val and me, c. 1954

4

LIFE AT PAM'S

My SISTER PAM WAS TWENTY-ONE YEARS MY SENIOR. THERE was a special bond between my mum and Pam as there had been between Mum and Gran, perhaps because they were the eldest daughters. According to Auntie Fran, my mother and my gran were inseparable and you'd very seldom see one without the other. Pam is the only one of Mum's children who didn't move away from Ramsgate, so Mum saw more of her than anyone else.

I had to go to live with my sister Pam on a number of occasions, because coping with us lot at home was sometimes a bit too much for Mum. She was drinking a little more and the domestics of the house were sometimes left wanting. Pam was decency itself. All her life she stifled her own personality to deliver whatever was expected of her. A hard worker, and *spotlessly clean*!! Her assessment of anybody she became acquainted with was usually somewhere between *spotlessly clean* and *putrid*! Any other attributes paled into insignificance. When she was a young girl she was expected to help Mum with all the other siblings and she probably nurtured some kind of resentment, but she never *ever* neglected her duties. Her friend was Mum's youngest sister, Auntie Fran (who was only five years her senior), and they would go to dances together, get crushes on visiting soldiers, and run giggling home in the wartime blackout. But Mum was as strict with her as she was with the rest of us, probably more so, because there were no older brothers to keep an eye on her. Pam was a nervous lady, indignant, and strove to be strong. She was a very bright pupil at school but because of the war and the need to help Mum, she was never encouraged to take further education.

She longed for her own home to take care of, and not be at Mum's beck and call all the time. So when I was a year old, she married John and went to live in a small rented flat. But still she would come to our house to make sure we were all looked after, and sometimes took one or other of us home with her if the need arose.

Living at Pam's I had three meals a day, clean clothes daily and was looked after very well indeed, but I couldn't help feeling like a displaced person and that I was a burden and would rather be at home with my mum. My sister once told me that beggars couldn't be choosers. Secretly I didn't agree with her, I thought everyone had choices, but her words still resonate.

The first time I went to live with Pam was in 1953. I was seven years old. I remember it clearly because Mum had taken me there to celebrate the Coronation of Queen Elizabeth II, when street parties were held all over the country. Kitchen tables, trestle tables, dining-room tables, tables of every description were placed end to end along the centre of the street and laden with sandwiches, trifles, cakes, crown-shaped money boxes, Coronation spoons and Coronation mugs. And when it started to drizzle, waterproof tablecloths were held aloft to keep all the children dry underneath.

After the tea party, Val and I played games and won prizes. There were races for everyone, parents too, and someone's mum fell over during the egg and spoon race, which caused a little consternation. They soon helped her off the road though and made way for the sack race, during which I fell over. Someone told me my feet were too small to keep me upright, which only worried me for a few years. However, the day was wonderful and when it was over, I was told I could stay for a week's holiday with Val. Hoorah! But the following weekend I was told my stay was extended indefinitely because Mum had had an accident.

One of Mum's many jobs was cleaning the Alma pub at the top of the alley, and whenever there was a coach outing, known as a beano, she would be invited along for free. Unfortunately, on one of these outings, some railings on which she was leaning gave way and Mum fell, banging her head quite badly. While she was fit enough to travel home with the rest of the party, the injury needed further investigation. She was taken to hospital for tests and as a result was transferred to Brook Hospital in London for yet further investigation, and this is where she remained for several months. She was suffering from a suspected skull fracture or, at the very least, severe concussion. Thereafter Mum was constantly complaining of severe headaches.

While Mum was away, life at the Plains was tranquil. Jeannie took care of everyone at home, and at Pam's, within five minutes of arrival, I was rendered squeaky clean. But I missed my mother and was constantly asking: 'When is Mummy coming home?' My brother Terry would wait to see me in the school playground and give me any news of her. Dad had been to visit her as often as possible, but it was very difficult as he didn't have transport and the train fare was not affordable. Val and I sent a message to Dad telling him not to worry because the Queen lived in London and would probably visit Mum since we had been to her street party.

Sometimes Uncle Norman, my mother's brother, would give Dad a lift, or failing that, Uncle Lal, another of Mum's brothers, would go to visit her as the hospital wasn't very far from his home in Peckham, south London. Uncle Lal would then telephone Dawson's Café, opposite our house on the Plains, to leave a message about Mum's condition. When she did finally return home everyone said she looked ten years younger. I was so happy. She brought a huge cardboard box, almost big enough to sit in, filled with the sweets and chocolates she had been given while in hospital and which she had saved for us children. But better than all of the sweets, she said I could come home again. I was delighted. While it was very nice staying with Val, I always seemed to be getting into trouble. Having me there meant twice the amount of work for Pam. She'd line Val and me up for a wash. One face, two face. One arm, two arm, three arm, four arm. One leg, two leg, three leg, four leg. When we were playing tents with the sheets, and one of them got torn, it was me who got the clout, even though Val owned up to it a fortnight later. If I was particularly irritating, and I'm sure I was most of the time, Pam's threat of putting me in the cupboard under the stairs with the 'eeriwigs' made me behave myself immediately. None of these threats was ever carried out I hasten to add. Not even the threat of being put in a home. She said I was enough to try the patience of a saint, and took me with a packed suitcase to wait at the bus stop for the bus to take me to a home. I was howling. For the life of me I can't remember what I had done that was so bad, other than drop Val on her head at Sunshine Corner, while teaching her to do a cartwheel. I was so glad to be going home, where I could play nurses and look after Mum.

It's a curious thing, as a child, time and time again I would imagine heavy objects falling from the ceiling or the sky. And in my imagination I would always throw myself across my mother to protect her from injury, letting my own back take the impact. And my dad, too. He would laugh often, long and hard, in fact so long that his face would turn puce. I'd sit in readiness to slap him on the back in case he should choke. I was terrified of losing either of them. My concern was magnified by the fact that they were the same age as most of my friends' grandparents. I needn't have worried. They were both blessed with longevity.

Pam and John were thrifty and saved religiously until they were able to buy their own house in St George's Road. They then supplemented their income by taking in holidaymakers on a bed, breakfast and evening meal basis. One evening just before the meal was to be served, Pam instructed me very carefully to go quietly upstairs to the guests' room, to knock on their door very gently and to say in a clear polite voice (posh voice if possible) that the guests' meal would be ready whenever *they* were ready. Remember, slowly and quietly. Oh dear, I don't know if I was more hungry than everyone else or if I was just being belligerent, but I went to the foot of the stairs and hollered, 'YER DINNER'S READY.' As far as Pam was concerned it was as if I had thrown a hand grenade up the stairs. To use a modern phrase – I was grounded.

Back at the Plains, on my eleventh birthday, miracle of miracles, Mum promised me a party, to which I had invited six friends. I was beside myself with excitement. But when the day arrived, my cake and jelly and mixed fancies didn't, and neither did Mum because unfortunately she'd been waylaid at the Alma, was in the blackest of moods, and had to sleep it off. Pam turned up with a gift for me, saw the situation and instantly went into action. The floor was swept, rubbish cleared, the newspaper taken from the table and disposed of and a clean tablecloth spread. She rushed to Vyes the grocers and bought bread, butter, ham, *peanut butter*, biscuits and cake. She made dainty sandwiches fit for silver service and placed them on paper doilies. Presentation meant a lot to Pam. Meanwhile she called on my sister Jeannie to leave work early and come to her assistance. Jeannie set about making a parcel out of newspapers for 'pass the parcel' which was full of packets of sweets and pencils and trinkets. By four o'clock the scene was set and I had a party royal.

We played musical chairs but as we had no music of any kind, or radio because the Rediffusion bill hadn't been paid, Jeannie sang with her back to us and stopped when she thought fit, whereupon we all dived for a chair. The hilarity woke Mum up and she came downstairs feeling a little the worse for wear. Oh blimey, look out! Mum's grumpy face could put the fear of God into you because she was so unpredictable. But when she smiled it was like the sun coming out. After a tense moment or two she happily joined in the fun. She sang, suspiciously happily, for pass the parcel, making her headache worse, and I'm sure she was peeping because she made sure every single guest received a gift. When all of my friends had gone, we waited with baited breath in case Mum's happy smile got put away with the leftovers. But it didn't. Instead, she went to the cupboard and produced a lovely, brand new, hand-knitted cardigan for me that must have taken her several days to make in secret.

As a child I looked forward to my Christmases with my niece Valerie at Pam's house. They were lovely. I remember getting a gift of a doll's cradle that I was deliriously happy to receive, even though I came to realise it was last year's present disguised with a new coat of paint on it, and Pam had made new covers for the cradle and a new outfit for the doll. I must have been so easy to please. But I remember getting a clout for teaching Val slang words, such as grub (for food) and arse! We still sniggered about it though when Pam wasn't in earshot. We were allowed to stay up late sometimes to listen to the wireless, our favourite programme being *Journey into Space*. One of Val's friends who lived nearby had a television and we really felt privileged when we were allowed to go to watch *Popeye the Sailor Man*.

It was at Pam's once that Val and I were playing travel agents. She had amassed a collection of picture postcards that various people had sent from all over the world, including my merchant navy seamen brothers Bernard and Ted and the wealthy people who Pam had been working for as housekeeper. As everything is of Val's, they were immaculately kept. She was the travel agent and I was the customer.

'Good morning, madam, may I help you?'

'Yes, please, I would like to go on a very relaxing holiday please.'

After flicking her fingers through the file of cards, *à la* a librarian, flickedy flickedy flick, she eventually produced a postcard and suggested, 'Africa, madam?'

The photograph on the card presented was of a ferocious lion, for all the world looking as if he was about to eat the unfortunate photographer, and probably did, and of course the *very last* thing one would want to encounter on a relaxing holiday! It was at that moment that Val and I found we had a shared sense of humour and we laughed uncontrollably for days, in fact we are still laughing at it. Whenever either one of us feels down, we only have to say the magic words 'Africa, madam?' and all will be well. There were gales of laughter when I told her that the offices of Simon and Schuster, the publishers of this book, were at Africa House!

But prior to the travel agents, I was sometimes jealous of Val, who was only four years younger than me, because she was very clever and wholesome, and everyone was nice to her and insisted that I should be as well – I couldn't understand why, I was only a little girl, too. She had nice things and took care of them, and when my brother Brian came home from Germany on leave from the army, bringing me a lovely musical box with a dancing ballerina inside, I hid myself away and sobbed and sobbed because I thought it was so lovely and far too nice for me to own, I didn't deserve it and it should be given to Val.

I still feel remnants of that today. I dislike getting presents. For some reason it makes me feel uncomfortable. I think it has something to do with being in debt, which I avoid like the plague. If I can't afford something I go without, or I save up until I can afford it. It could be that I think getting a present puts me in someone's debt and I don't like it. An assistant of mine, against all my entreaties, persisted in buying me gifts. Time and time again it would happen. I found it so irritating and seriously thought about finding a more stingy assistant, but I made myself get over it. Of course, there are exceptions to this rule, but very few. I also know it's ungracious of me especially since I enjoy *giving* gifts.

I can remember the wonderful sense of pride I had when I saved up and bought Mum a lovely new leather handbag from Whitehead's in King Street, the best leather goods shop in town. Well, actually, it was the *only* leather goods shop as far as I knew. But it was really posh. My cousin Noreen was a sales assistant there at that time. The wonderful smell of leather in the shop made me dizzy. It was expensive and long lasting. I'd sometimes loiter in the shop doorway just to get a whiff of the leather as the other customers went in or out. The bag had been displayed in the window for two weeks at two shillings, equivalent today to 10p but in those days to a little girl of ten years old a fortune. But it wasn't available for purchase until the sale started. I stopped and looked at it in the window every day leading up to Mum's birthday. On the first day of the sale I was up with the lark and got to the shop as early as I could only to find that someone else had bought my precious bag. How could that have happened? I did all the right things. It was an outrage! But Noreen produced another *almost* as good bag and I bought that instead. I ran home as fast as I could and in my excitement slammed the door. 'YOU'LL HAVE THAT DOOR OFF IT'S HINGES,' hollered Mum.

'But Mummy, look what I've got for you. Happy Birthday.' Mum was taken aback, and my spirits were only dampened for a few moments when she asked me where I'd got the money from. I explained that I'd saved the money I'd got from running errands, which was true, and she believed me. She was thrilled and so was I, especially as she gave me sixpence to spend.

But gifts didn't have to mean material things. When we were children, if we couldn't afford to buy a gift for a friend or neighbour for instance, we'd offer to clean their windows for them, if they couldn't manage it themselves, as a present. Or shovel the snow from the path and steps. Collect coal from the merchant in an old pram. Run a few errands. But I baulk if someone wants to return the favour. Come to think of it, I'm not comfortable with direct compliments either. Although I like my work to be appreciated, I'd much rather *overhear* something complimentary or read it, in privacy. But then I don't suppose I'm alone on that score.

Sporting new plimsoles, 1955

5

GOING TO SCHOOL

AT FOUR AND A HALF, EVEN THOUGH I HADN'T BEEN CHRIS-
tened a Catholic, I was sent to St Augustine's, the Catholic
school, because that's where my brothers went. The only reason
I wasn't christened was probably because my parents got bored
with christenings, me being the last in a line of nine, or maybe
they simply forgot. Pam was christened Church of England
but the other seven were all christened Catholics. Most of our
teachers were nuns. The headmistress, Sister Patricia, on first
acquaintance seemed to be rather fierce but her bark was much
worse than her bite, unlike some of the other nuns at the infant
school, especially one of them. Her punishment was to squash
your little finger in half. Of course, it looked as though she was
gently holding your hand but, in fact, you were being subjected to
torture. I was given the little finger treatment when I was accused
of pulling down the ivy on the rockery at the edge of the playground. I hadn't been anywhere near the rockery and protested
my innocence, and in any case I knew for definite it was Tony

Grey. On the other hand, Sister Lou-Lilly was an angel and sneaked us pieces of home-made butterscotch when no one was looking. In infant school there were always two 'volunteers' forced to do washing-up duty after dinner and I was usually one of them. But it was lovely when all the drying-up had been done because along came Sister Lou-Lilly with the big iron key to the cupboard in the hall and out came the jar of home-made butterscotch. Mmmmm. The best butterscotch ever!

I remember screaming in agony on one occasion in infant school because I'd stuck a pencil in my ear, but the pain inflicted by the pencil was nothing compared to the pain inflicted by the angel of mercy when she clouted me for being so stupid.

'You could have peeeeeeeerforated your eardrum,' she screamed and punctuated it with another thump.

She made me stand in the corner as an example of stupidity and laid a chair-leg (her weapon of choice) on the desk in front of her. She would pick it up and wave it about lest we should forget. She wouldn't hesitate to whack someone with it, and did quite often. It's a miracle I didn't get the chair-leg wrapped around my ear.

Sister Agnes who taught us needlework in secondary school was a different kettle of fish altogether. A lovely lady, she was very pretty indeed and sometimes she would blush terribly and be reduced to tears if teased by some of the boys in my class. I made her cry with laughter once when I tried on a dress I'd been making. I eventually made out what she was saying amidst gasping and gagging and it was that she thought my dress looked like a suit of mail! She had such a lilting soft Irish accent that when showing me where I had gone wrong with a line of stitching she actually lulled me to sleep while I was standing at her desk, and I fell with a clatter to the floor! Unfortunately that happened again when I was seventeen, while being interviewed for a job at

Marshall and Snelgrove in Oxford Street. The personnel manager had a similar accent and was 'tilling me ahll aboat the different depertments in the stohrr and how ahl the gerhls gut alang verry well' and whoops, here I go, I slumped off the chair! I didn't get the job.

I loved every Thursday afternoon in infant school because it was dressing-up day, when a huge trunk would be brought out into the hall. I would go into a deep panic if I didn't get there first and bagsy the clown's outfit, climbing into it as fast as lightning, and then prance around thinking I was terribly funny. That should have told me something. Actually, sometimes I think I was funny. My mum thought I was anyhow. Her dentures would fall out because she was laughing so hard and she'd lose control of her jaw. Try as she might she couldn't keep her teeth in. They just sort of lay on her chin until she could get her breath back. That happened once in the Odeon cinema while watching Norman Wisdom, so she took them out for safety. It was only when we'd got home and were about to tuck into some fish and chips that she discovered she'd lost them. I was dispatched forthwith back to the cinema to see if they'd been found, whereupon the manager brought out a box of lost property from under his desk and asked if I'd recognise them. I thought he was joking until he opened the box and I saw about a dozen sets of false teeth grinning at me. That was definitely one for Mum to sort out! Norman Wisdom has a lot to answer for.

I told Norman about this when I worked with him on the TV series, *Between the Sheets*. It was such a thrill to work with one of my childhood heroes. A lovely man and a nonstop entertainer. I was delighted when he said he thought I was really funny too. I told him that in our family my brother Terry is the real comedian. He frequently has the whole lot of us in absolute hysterics for hours. He and his wife Penny are wonderful company and she is the perfect foil to his comedy, and really cuts him down to size in such a charming way. I asked Penny once, if she won the lottery, what would be her dream? She told me there was nothing she wanted that she didn't already have. She was already living her dream with Terry. Well, how enviable is that? Terry is a wonderful raconteur and I sometimes think that if he did after-dinner speeches, he'd make a fortune, especially if Penny was a guest at the table!

Although my brothers were very mindful of taking care of me as a child they could sometimes be little gits. They would dress up as ghosts by covering themselves with sheets and holding a torch under a mop for a face and frighten me. When Mum came home and I told her, they would get a clout, but I would also get one for snitching. Another source of terror for me was hearing the alley cats howling outside, especially if I had sneaked into Mum and Dad's room. Their bedroom window was always wide open because the sashes had broken, and if I could hear the alley cats outside I would be terrified that Korky the Cat (from the *Dandy*) would climb in and get me. A bit Freudian don't you think? Those sashes were broken from my earliest memory and were never mended. Come hail, snow, wind or sunshine, that window was wide open.

I remember one Christmas spent at home when Terry and Martin were looking after me. We could hear bells jingling in the distance and they said it was Father Christmas getting closer and closer, perhaps just past the Brown Jug at Dumpton Gap, and now approaching Bellevue Road, which was very close indeed, and I should go to sleep immediately if I wanted some presents. I totally believed them. They could only have been seven or eight themselves. Oh the joy of that Christmas morning as I ripped open parcel after parcel looking for the tap shoes that I just knew would be there. Oh, yes, they were! Oh just look! They were from Pam and they were red, and they were to drive the entire family mad before the day was out. Tap tap tap up and down the stairs, tap tap tap up and down the passageway, tap tap tap up and down the alley. My mum said she would tap tap tap me around the ears if I didn't give them a little rest! And even though I asked a dozen times she told me I would NOT be wearing them to school! That year I also got a stencil set, and a book called *Charlotte's Web* about the friendship between a spider and a pig. Mind you, I don't think I read it for about five years. Although everyone else in our house read a lot, I didn't. At least not until I was about ten, when my friend Morag's sister, Margaret Morrison, introduced me to reading. She was a pupil at Clarendon House grammar school and was horrified to overhear me say that I didn't do much reading. She produced a book from the shelf and she literally had to *persuade* me to read it. It was one of Enid Blyton's Famous Five books. I read it hungrily. And I was hooked. For a while she was my very own personal library. What a lovely gift to give to somebody – a passion for reading. Thanks Margaret.

Christmas parties at school were always enormous fun and eagerly awaited. Each pupil would contribute to the party by taking, say, a jelly or blancmange, a tin of fruit or bag of sugar or flour to school each week, starting from as early as October. On the big day we were allowed to wear party frocks, if we had one. One year I didn't have one and had to wear my uniform. My dad told me it didn't matter because I'd be the prettiest one there. We'd take our hair out of plaits making it hang in violent crinkly waves. My hair had usually been plastered with Amami wave set before plaiting so it would stick out at right angles before curling madly as if I'd been given some sort of electric shock.

The party usually took place in the afternoon at about 4.30 and was followed by party games in the assembly hall. O'Grady says, musical chairs, statues and many others. Mr Jones our geography teacher would be O'Grady, shouting out his commands. He was a very popular man whose hobby was playing bowls. My best friend Patsy and I once volunteered to clean out the school loft, and when we came across an old bowling ball we decided that it would be a wonderful idea to clean it up and give it to Mr Jones. He was thrilled and delighted and told the whole assembly so, concluding that it would go very nicely with one he had up in the loft. Oops. The winner of each game could choose a prize from a selection of board games, jigsaws, books, dolls or Dinky toys. My brother Bill was called a sissy once when at age eight he won a game of statues and instead of collecting a boy's prize for himself he chose a rag doll for me. I was two years old. Fortunately the teachers knew the reason for his choice of gift and made sure that he won another prize for himself.

As Christmas approached each year we tuned up our voices for carol singing. The boys were allowed to go door to door singing and, cry as I might, I wasn't allowed to go with them. 'Why can't I get some money for Christmas presents as well?' I howled, and pointed out that they were allowed to go when they were *much* younger than me. Mum relented and gave me permission. The trouble was my brothers didn't want a sissy girl along with them. Especially since they had the band all worked out and I would go and spoil it all. Usually, Martin who had the best voice would sing, Terry was on mouth organ, it didn't matter that he couldn't play it, and their friend Ricky was on the tin whistle, similarly accomplished. They'd practise along the promenade all the way to Winterstoke, with me trailing about a hundred yards behind. They had to keep checking that I was still there, because even though they didn't want me with them, they didn't want to lose me either. But as it got dark I was dutifully ordered to stay close. I felt like part of the gang. It was wonderful. And I wanted to play an instrument. But if I wanted to stay with them I had to observe the first rule. And that was to keep schtum, especially while they were practising. While Martin sang 'The Holly and the Ivy', Terry huffed and puffed into the mouth organ playing a different tune altogether, if indeed you could call it a tune. I whiningly complained that I could play the tin whistle better than their friend Ricky, who sounded like a guard at Ramsgate Station. To shut me up Terry said he would think of something for me to play tomorrow evening if I behaved myself. And he kept his word.

The next evening we met up for practice on the promenade and he presented me with a comb wrapped in a piece of shiny toilet paper, and he told me to blow through it, paper and all. How melodic! 'O Little Town of Bethlehem' had never sounded better. But not as good as 'Away in a Manger' or 'Ding Dong Merrily on High'. It got better and better. I played my heart out and by the end of the evening my lips were completely numb and felt four times the size. (Beauty Tip: Girls should play the comb and paper nowadays instead of having all those collagen or Botox injections or whatever they are!) When told to join in the singing instead, I found I couldn't move my mouth and did a sort of nasal hum. But we were very successful and collected quite a bit. At the end of the evening, when we counted our pennies we discovered that one of the pennies given to us was, in fact, a florin (two shillings). As this bunch of coins had come from my pocket we were able to deduce who had given it to us. Obviously it was a mistake, and although it was nice to have a florin we decided we had better take it back. We thought it had come from an old lady who had asked us to sing 'Adeste Fidelis', which is the Latin version of 'O Come All Ye Faithful'. To her utter astonishment we knew it. She might not have recognised it though from our rendition, although she did wave thank you through the window before shutting the curtains. Actually, I think it was that one that did my lips in. After ascertaining which door we thought was hers, we knocked and she appeared and said, 'Oh no, not you again.'

All speaking at once we told her that we thought she'd given us too much money.

'Well sing another song then,' she barked.

'Oh, all right,' we enthused. 'What would you like to hear?'

She asked if we knew 'The Bell Bottom Blues'.

'The Bell Bottom Blues'?

Yes, of course, we knew 'The Bell Bottom Blues' because our sister Jeannie used to sing it. For a while I actually thought Jeannie *was* Alma Cogan! Although 'The Bell Bottom Blues' was not at all festive, we sang it with gusto.

The old lady didn't come to the door again although we waited and waited. We even started to sing an encore but her next-door neighbour opened the window and told us to 'Ef off!!' It was a good job my mother hadn't heard her. Although Mum's language could sometimes turn the air blue, she would have been incensed because absolutely NO ONE was allowed to swear at her children. Except herself! So, not at all disappointed, we went home with 1s 11d more than we should have.

At a Christmas fancy dress party at the church hall I also got something I shouldn't have. A clout. I was about nine. Val went as Little Red Riding Hood and I went as a gypsy. Jeannie made my costume for me, which was made up of a white ruffled blouse and a flared skirt she'd trimmed with brightly coloured zig-zag binding. She tied my hair in a turban and clipped big hooped earrings on to my ears. Bright red lipstick completed the picture. How was I supposed to know she was only joking when she told me to swing my hips in an exaggerated fashion and to give a saucy wink at the audience of churchgoing parents? I was positioned in the line between a canary and a stick of rock. The canary got a lovely round of applause along with 'ahs' and 'ohs' and was obviously in line for a prize, and then I sashayed on to the floor. I could see a look of apprehension cross Mum's face, but I thought she was just nervous for me, hoping I'd win. So I gave an extra large saucy wink, nudge nudge, to reassure her and an intake of breath and embarrassed murmur spread through the hall. Mum nearly erupted. I thought it was an eruption of approval so I did it again. It was more than she could bear. She hoiked me off the floor and out the door saying 'Wait till I get you home, you little mare' and, 'I've never been so shown up in all my life.'

'But Mum, what if I've won a prize?'

'The only prize you've won is an early night in bed. *I could swing for you!*'

But if she was so cross, why did I hear her downstairs with Jeannie telling Dad, and doubled up with laughter!

Martin and me look after Val at Aunt Lil's Christmas party, c. 1955

6

POCKET MONEY

My BROTHERS AND I WERE QUITE GOOD AT MAKING A BIT OF pocket money as none of us were afraid of hard work. Indeed, our parents instilled in us that if we wanted anything at all in life we had to work for it. During the summer months Ramsgate was swarming with holiday-makers. It was a bustling seaside resort. Street after street, and row upon row of terraced houses, advertised BED AND BREAKFAST or VACANCIES in their front-room windows. NO VACANCIES was displayed at the height of the season when the hotels were full. Ramsgate was one of the favourite holiday destinations for Londoners and there'd be a constant stream of them pouring from the railway and bus stations lugging along their suitcases and bags and other tackle. Not many people had cars waiting for them and few people took taxis, they simply walked to their destination. Terry along with lots of local boys had a great idea. They would each make a wheelbarrow big enough to carry several pieces of luggage. Terry enlisted my brother Brian's help (who was always good at woodwork even at an early age) and together they found two sets of old pram wheels, some old wooden floorboards and a sturdy wooden orange box, and fashioned a cart big enough to carry four or five suitcases. Terry then launched his new enterprise by waiting outside the station for the London train to arrive. 'Carry your luggage, sir/madam?' 'Carry your luggage?' He probably made a bob (5p) a time, sometimes half a crown (12½p). Of course, there was the added advantage of Terry's excellent knowledge of the town and knowing exactly where the guesthouses and hotels were situated. He and the other local boys did a roaring trade. I sometimes cried until he let me go with him. He didn't really want me around because I was more of a hindrance than a help, but he usually relented just to keep me quiet. And if Terry had a lucrative day he would give me some spending money.

On one particularly good day, I rushed home very happy indeed with my pockets bulging with coppers, only to have the joy drained out of me completely by finding my mother in the scullery drowning several kittens in a bucket of water. I tried to intervene and as I tried to pluck them out of the water, I got a clout. In any case, they were already dead. I was mortified and cried for hours. Mum said the kittens wouldn't have lived long anyway because they couldn't afford to feed them. It was a common occurrence. I had often heard about someone, somewhere, drowning kittens, but I had never seen it before. That night she let me squash into her chair with her and she cuddled me and ran her fingers through my hair. The cat searched for days for her litter and so I cuddled the cat.

For my part, moneymaking consisted of running errands for several people who lived nearby for tuppence or threepence a time or for nothing at all if they were worse off than us. Or help with washing-up at one or other of the many guesthouses. This is how I later saved enough money to buy my books and equipment to go to commercial college, although Mum and Dad helped as much as they could.

Cobbling also brought in a few pennies. This was something I picked up from watching Mr Tippler through the window of his cobbler's shop on the hill. Dad happened to have an old iron cobbler's last, which he was using as a doorstop, so I commandeered it for my new venture. I saved up and bought a supply of rubber heels, little tacks, steel tips and studs and a selection of rubber stick-on soles and glue. I did quite well for a time, mending shoes for family, friends and some neighbours, but this enterprise was brought to a sudden end, almost along with my life. Dad interrupted me once by fancying a cup of tea, and walked bare-footed into the scullery, which doubled as my workshop. He trod on a rubber heel I had just pulled from a boot and which was ringed with tacks and nails lying upward on the floor. You could have heard the yell in Margate. *What* he didn't call me! The cobbler's iron last, hammer and pliers were all confiscated even before he went off for his tetanus jab. So after that, all I was allowed to do was polish the shoes. And I made them gleam. I'd learnt how to do it from my brothers who were in the army cadets. Spit and polish. Tiny circular movements with the cloth wrapped over the index finger. Our shoes might have been falling off of our feet but they shone magnificently. You could almost see your face in them. I read somewhere that you can tell a lot about a person just by looking at their shoes. Goodness knows what anybody made of ours.

Which reminds me of when I was promoting *Secrets & Lies* in 1996. We had a special screening in San Francisco, which went very well indeed. The audience loved it and were very moved by it. We were required to wait by the exit to have little chats as the audience departed and perhaps answer any questions. One very smart lady approached me, with tears in her eyes, having difficulty in speaking. I smugly thought, 'Oh boy, she really thought I was good in the film.' Finally, she said to me, 'You—' and words failed her. She tried again. 'You are—' 'I'm so sorry,' she said, 'I'm feeling a little emotional— You are—' She couldn't continue. I told her to take her time, she was obviously very moved by my performance and I asked if I should find her somewhere to sit down? She tried again. 'No, you don't understand,' she said. 'You are— You are wearing the BEST pair of shoes I have ever seen!' There's no answer to that is there. Actually, they were rather nice, Escada, two tone, light grey and green. About the same shade as my ego on that occasion.

Our friend's mother was on a nice little earner. She would boil up a load of sugar water in a metal chamber pot (a new one I hasten to add) and make toffee apples. She'd then sell them from her front-room window for a handsome profit. We would have liked to follow her example but Mum wouldn't let us. We tried it once and she said we made such a mess with the toffee that her shoes got stuck to the scullery floor. Which was a pity, because my brother Brian who was working at the greengrocer's at the top of the hill at the time had bought us a load of leftover apples cheaply for our venture. Mum made us eat apple pie till it was coming out of our ears.

My brother Brian has a heart of gold. He was the last of my brothers to be conscripted into the army, aged eighteen, and had to report to the barracks at Canterbury. My father gave him a lift to Ramsgate railway station on the snow-plough he drove for the council, with his belongings in a brown paper carrier bag and seven shillings in his pocket. Dad waved goodbye and predicted he wouldn't last in the army for more than two weeks. But Brian had the last laugh because Dad couldn't have been more wrong as the army was the making of Brian where he discovered, like Dad, that he had a talent for music. Although he was on active duty in the Middle East, he was in the Corps of Drums and pro-gressed up through the ranks to become Divisional Drum Major, Queen's Division. He married a lovely woman, Pat, who has the gentlest nature and who is a wonderful homemaker, excelling in all things domestic, cooking, dressmaking etc., and their daughter Karen is the same. Back at home in those early days we would go to watch him leading the Junior Band and Drums of the Home Counties Brigade as they paraded through the streets at carnival time. Brian was majestically smart and ramrod straight as he tossed and caught the spinning mace. It was a wonderful spectacle. At the time of one parade Terry was working temporarily as a bus driver during the summer holidays and I happened to be a passenger on his bus. Traffic had been stopped to allow a parade through Canterbury, and, what a lovely surprise, along came Brian, the mace glinting as it spun in the sunshine. The band wasn't playing a military tune, but a popular tune from the hit parade, believe it or not, and Terry thought it would be acceptable to join in on his bus hooter in time with the music, to amuse me more than anything else! Brian heard this, and with an imperceptible flick of his eye saw it was Terry in the driver's seat. With a spin of the mace he gave the command to momentarily halt the march. His boots crashed into the tarmac. 'Oh look out, Terry,' I thought, 'you're going to get a striping for sounding your hooter.' But I was wrong, Brian was simply treating us to an extra special stationary display. Terry took advantage of the situation, and in a BOOMING voice hollered, 'OI BRIAN, MUM'S JUST DOWN THE ROAD!' But Brian would not be distracted from the task in hand and, with a ONE, TWO, QUIIIIIIICK MARCH, carried on with the parade, a figure of perfection. But he did stop again down the road especially for Mum's benefit, much to the delight of the crowd in general.

Brian is a perfectionist in *everything* he does. His tool-shed, unlike Dad's Lodge, is totally shipshape and in Bristol fashion, even down to the many screws in their little boxes, all facing the same way. Whenever he tackles jobs around the house, they're done with a master's touch. He's a brilliant carpenter. He not only builds practical things like kitchens and cabinets, but also toys, rocking horses, cradles, birdhouses, and all impeccably made. His two sons, Terry and Martin, are just as meticulous. His garden is textbook perfect, each blade of grass standing to attention even when their dog, a border collie called Fudge, frolicked on it. For Fudge's entire life, he absolutely refused to go for a walk.

Dog walking was another pocket money winner. Especially Peter, the huge German shepherd dog from the Alma pub. My sister Pam didn't like dogs very much, especially that particular one because it looked as though it could swallow me whole. I suppose it was quite ferocious, it was a guard dog after all. But against all warnings I secretly continued to take Peter for a walk and once, inadvisedly, I took my niece Valerie with me and swore her to secrecy. Peter was as tall as Val and probably twice as heavy but just to secure her allegiance I let her have a turn at holding Peter's lead. But Peter had other ideas and took off like a greyhound out of the trap, taking Val with him. Her feet left the ground. Fortunately there was a lamppost conveniently placed in her path, which stopped her flight. She hit it side on and her ear swelled up to prize cauliflower proportions and shone like a beacon. I made her promise to stop crying and to act normally when we got back to my sister's house and to her credit she did try. But her ear made an entrance ten minutes before we did and I was given the third degree.

That was the last time I took Peter for a walk. Even though the landlady asked me several times, I said no. However, that didn't stop her from buying me an Italian perm for my twelfth birthday. My God, what was she *thinking*. I looked forty-five years old when I walked out of the salon. It was probably her revenge. Mum made me wear a hat for six months.

I thought of this when I was making Nicole Holfcener's *Lovely and Amazing*. In this film I played the mother of three daughters, played by Catherine Keener, Emily Mortimer and 8-year-old Raven Goodwin. In the story the youngest daughter decided without anyone's permission to go to a friend's house to get her frizzy hair straightened. My character was in hospital having cosmetic surgery at the time and was horrified when the three daughters came to visit. She was so cross with her 8-year-old for doing this to her hair that I was reminded of my mum and the Italian perm. So when visiting time was over and the daughters were all leaving I found myself ad-libbing 'and buy her a hat'.

Collecting empty 'Bing' bottles was quite lucrative. Bing was a fizzy drink sold in thick glass bottles with a strong lever top. A deposit of threepence was paid on the bottle but, luckily for us, some people couldn't be bothered to return them to collect the refund and just threw them away. So armed with a cardboard box we'd scour the beach and seafront, collecting as many as we could carry and taking them back to the off-licence. The most I collected in one go was six. Threepence a bottle × 6 = 1s 6d, equivalent today to 7½p. It doesn't sound very much now but then it would have bought two cinema tickets, and posh seats at that. Theoretically the bottles should have been returned to the same shop they came from, but we were nearly always lucky enough to get the threepence refund wherever we went. One newspaper vendor paid Terry a penny for every unsoiled magazine he could find and return to him, whereupon the vendor resold them for the full price. Mum wasn't so keen on this venture, not because it was dishonest but more probably because she thought Terry deserved to earn more than a penny.

In fact, so strict was Mum about us being law-abiding she

once confiscated my stash of chocolate bars. I had been playing in the amusement arcade along the seafront when I came across a faulty machine. Usually one would have to insert a penny to obtain a ball to flick around the face of the machine, hoping for it to land in one of the two winning slots. But this machine already had a ball nestling in the start position. I flicked it and alas it went into the losing slot. But, wait a minute, out came a chocolate bar AND the ball reappeared. I flicked again and again and again, and win or lose out came a chocolate bar and the ball returned. After about half an hour I had completely emptied the machine of chocolate bars. There were so many that I had to make a bag out of the front of my skirt in order to get them home. To avoid detection from my mother I crept in the back door and went straight to my bedroom and hid them under the pillow. Not being practised in this sort of deception I didn't consider the possibility of Mum changing the sheets the next morning, since it didn't happen that often. Oh dear! She was livid. I was playing on the bandstand on the east cliff when I got the message, which always put terror into all our hearts, 'Mum's looking for you.' Oh no. In trepidation I went home, again creeping in the back door. But Mum, who should have worked in the War Office for such was her uncanny intuition about such things, was lying in ambush inside the door armed with a pillowslip filled with the chocolate bars. After a clout I was frogmarched back to the sea front arcade and made to wait until the manager arrived. On the way there Mum drummed into me in her own very colourful language ('I'll give you go choring, you thieving little whelp!') why it was wrong of me to have done what I'd done and why it was necessary to return the contraband, to apologise to the man, and to understand why I must never do it again. Full of shame, I dutifully obeyed, and although I thought my punishment harsh, I have never done anything like that again, and probably never will. A lesson had well and truly been taught and learnt. At teatime that day, after our bread and jam, surprisingly we each had a chocolate bar. The next day too. Mum wasn't daft, and was never one to look a gift horse in the mouth.

But believe it or not, one of the best ways to earn a little extra pocket money was to walk along streets lined with guesthouses at about 11.30 in the morning and look for NO VACANCIES signs. Then listen for a baby crying. If the hardworking mother of the house was trying to prepare lunch for a house full of holiday-makers there would be little time for the baby. So for sixpence an hour, my friends and I would take the baby for a walk in the pram along the promenade, thus enabling the lady of the house to pre-pare lunch. We did this lots of times. We were told not to take the baby out of the pram, but, of course, we did, especially if it was crying, and gave it lots of cuddles. Can you imagine doing that nowadays. 'Excuse me, missus, may we take your baby for a walk? Oh, by the way, my name is Brenda.' We'd be locked up.

Every year, about a month before 5 November my brothers and I would make an effigy of Guy Fawkes. The better the guy we made the more money we would make for fireworks, sweets and chips on the big night. We'd stuff an old pair of men's trousers and a shirt with newspapers, old rags and a little straw and tie them up in the middle. A small sack would be used to make the head, also stuffed with straw and then pinned to the torso. A scarf would be tied around the neck to cover the join. The legs would be stuffed into old boots. If we couldn't afford to buy a mask, we'd make a face using bits of coloured paper cut from magazines and then stitched on to the head. An old overcoat and one of Dad's trilby hats would complete the effigy, usually nearly six feet tall. It would then be lifted and tied on to a chair, which the boys would have fixed on to a wheelbarrow ready to carry to our position on King Street. We got to be quite expert and made pretty good guys. As there was a guy on nearly every street corner in the town, the pressure was on to make a better guy than the ones along the road, because shoppers tended to reward the best one. 'Penny for the guy, please? Penny for the guy?' Sometimes we'd get a penny, sometimes threepence, sometimes sixpence, but mostly a halfpenny.

Nineteen fifty-four was a bumper year, because we decided to make the guy a little more intellectual by adding a pair of glasses. An open copy of the *Reader's Digest* was then put into his hands. The *pièce de résistance* was when Terry attached a length of fishing line to the guy's arm, and every time somebody gave us a penny he pulled the wire and the guy saluted. Some people paid another penny in order to see it again! Come rain or shine we'd be out with the guy. We were in terrible trouble one year when we came home soaked through to our skins. The guy was perfectly dry as he'd been seated under Mum's old gamp. She was furious and forbade us to go any more. She didn't like it anyway because she said it was begging (which didn't stop her trying to cadge a shilling if she was skint). The next evening was dry but Mum still refused to let us go. We grizzled and moaned and whined but she wouldn't change her mind. We tried every trick in the book to get around her but she was resolute. As luck would have it, she asked Terry to nip to the corner shop for a new gas mantle, and then went to the scullery for some money. While she was out of the room Terry told me and Martin to go downstairs to the cellar and to await further instructions. We thought it a very odd request. Neither of us liked the dark or spiders and we were a little reluctant, but such was the glint in Terry's eye that we did as we were bid. Feeling rather foolish and bewildered standing in the blackness of the cellar we were surprised to hear the coal-hole cover lifting, and along with the light flooding in came Terry's face.

'Quick, get the guy.'

'What?'

'Quick, get the guy.'

Knowing that we were really going to be in trouble, Martin and I nevertheless lifted the guy from the corner shelf and dragged it into the cellar and between us managed to lift it up to Terry, who reached in through the coal-hole in the pavement at the front of our house. After a lot of heaving, pushing and pulling, Terry pulled it through and replaced the coal-hole cover. Passers-by would have wondered what on earth was happening, seeing a body being pulled up through the ground. The guy was too big for Terry to manage on his own without wheels, so he left it sitting on the front steps like a weary traveller while he ran around the block to the back yard to get the barrow. And off he went to the appointed spot on King Street.

'WHAT ARE YOU TWO UP TO DOWN THERE?' Mum hollered. 'Come upstairs for your tea.'

We said we weren't up to anything and went upstairs like little angels, not realising until we got into the light that we were covered from head to foot in coal dust. In a flash Mum worked out what had happened. It was never any use lying to Mum and we reluctantly had to confirm her suspicions. Oh we were in such trouble, and in fury she spat on the corner of her apron and dived at the coal on our faces. 'Woe betide Terry when he gets home,' she predicted. 'That is definitely the last time you have a guy!'

Dad came home before Terry, however, and I'll swear they were laughing when I heard Mum tell him what had happened. While they frowned on disobedience, they applauded ingenuity and enterprise, and when Terry eventually returned home he was greeted with a clout, but it was not for going out with the guy, it was for forgetting the gas mantle.

But one year we really overstepped the mark. Each evening when we returned home we sat Mister Guy on a dismal little corner shelf at the bottom of the stairs in the basement. The only lighting on this alcove spilt from the open door of the sitting room, which was itself dismal. We decided it would be such fun if Terry dressed up in the guy's clothes and sat on the corner shelf. Not an easy task since the guy was twice the size of Terry. But we managed it by only removing some of the stuffing, and adding two stumps of wood for him to stand on before attaching the boots. Straw was added to cuffs and collar. He sat there for over an hour before we heard our first victim coming down the stairs. It was Mum. She was carrying several skeins of wool for winding. So used was she to seeing the guy sitting there in the shadows, she didn't give it another thought.

Imagine her paralysed shock then as she reached the bottom stair and the guy said, 'Hallooo, missus' and jumped off the shelf to give her a kiss.

It's a wonder Mum didn't die on the spot. Or more specifically it's a wonder that we didn't all die on the spot, because when she was eventually able to breathe she let out a cry that turned the air blue and came at us twirling those skeins of wool and whipped us around the ears.

'*I'll swing for you, you little whelps!*' she hollered. We really had scared her half to death but the fact that she came to laugh at it by the end of the evening was a tribute to her powers of recovery. 'If ever a woman suffered!'

Terry in his lovely made-to-measure Italian suit

7

'HEY JOE, SAY, WHERE D'YOU GET THEM FANCY CLOTHES?'

GOING TO THE PICTURES WAS A REAL TREAT AND IT CAME TO be a weekly event. We had the luxury of four cinemas to choose from: the Odeon and the Palace being the poshest, then the Kings, and finally the Picture House, which was considered to be a bit of a fleapit. The programmes included an A film and a B film and usually a cartoon was shown as well. Also trailers of future films would be shown along with Pearl & Dean advertisements. The Pathe newsreel was included and, if I remember rightly, updated once a week. In those days the programmes were shown continuously and we didn't bother to find out what time the film started, we simply bought our tickets and went in regardless, even if it was right in the middle of the film. Continuous screening meant we just stayed there until it came right round again to the point where we came in, and then everyone had to get up to let us out. If a certificate A film was showing we would have to be accompanied by an adult and if we weren't with Mum or Dad, we would loiter outside and ask someone in the queue to take us in, 'Will you take us in, mister?' or 'Please take us in, missus.' And usually they did. Can you imagine doing that nowadays?

When I was about nine, I went to the Picture House with some friends to see *Calamity Jane*. Doris Day was and still is a favourite of mine. We went into the cinema at about one o'clock and while my friends left after the screening, I was still there at 9.30 in the evening having watched the programme three times. I was brought back to reality when a torch shone in my face and at the other end of the beam was my mother and a policeman who had been scouring the town for me.

'I'll give you Calamity Jane when I get you home,' she sang, with 'Never mind homeward bound safe and sound' as an encore.

I ducked as I reached the end of the row, fearing there was a 'whipcrackaway' coming. But surprisingly there wasn't. Mum was so glad to have found me. She even took me to see it again with Dad the following week. Oh I loved it! It was wonderful. 'Hey Joe, say where d'ye get them fancy clothes – I know, from some feller's laundry line.' Great lyrics.

I loved going to the cinema and we all especially liked musicals. The first time I actually remember crying at a film was at *The Student Prince*, with Edmund Purdom singing 'Drink, Drink, Drink', da da da dah (lip-syncing to Mario Lanza, I've since discovered). At the end of the film the barmaid, played by Ann Blyth, realised that the Prince couldn't love her because he was a Prince, and she doubled up in grief over the counter. Oooh! I sobbed.

And the joy of watching *Snow White and the Seven Dwarfs*, *The Wizard of Oz*, Tommy Steele in *Tommy the Toreador*, *Oklahoma* with Gordon MacRae and Shirley Jones. *Seven Brides*

'Hey Joe, say, where d'you get them fancy clothes?'

for Seven Brothers with Howard Keel I found desperately romantic and the dancing sublime. Mum and I went to a live concert
given by Howard Keel at the Folkestone Leas Cliff Pavilion
shortly before she died and she was absolutely enchanted when
he threw her a rose followed by a kiss.

If Mum and Dad went out by themselves on Saturday night,
then they'd take us to the pictures on Sunday, or vice versa. The
Odeon was our favourite cinema and we'd always sit in the same
seats downstairs and about six rows from the front on the right-
hand side. Seats upstairs in the circle were more expensive. One
advantage of being a little closer to the screen was that you didn't
have to squint through such a dense cloud of cigarette smoke.
Smoking was so popular, there was an ashtray affixed to the back
of every seat. Another advantage of being close to the front was
that there was an exit near to our seats and sometimes, to the
loud accompaniment of tutting from other cinemagoers, Martin
would nip out the side exit door and return with a portion of the
aforementioned pease pudding from the butcher's shop opposite.
Terry would stand guard at the door to let him back in, and also
a couple of their mates if they were in the vicinity.

Whenever we went out anywhere, Mum would always issue a
warning 'Ask for anything' (with the emphasis on the 'ask'),
which, of course, meant, 'Don't you dare ask for anything' while
we're out, especially if we're in company. It didn't take us long to
work out that if you did ask for sweets or a lolly in company, Mum
would be too embarrassed to refuse. But there'd be a merry dance
when you got home! If Dad and I were at the pictures on our own
though, he'd buy me a tub of ice cream, or occasionally a packet
of Butterkist popcorn, but it was too expensive if there were a lot
of us.

One of the very best things as far as Mum was concerned
about sitting in these favourite seats, was that they were right

next to a huge fat radiator that would keep us toasty warm, and dry our cold wet feet in winter. And it was in these particular seats one night that she had a brainwave. A brilliant brainwave. I told you she was clever. Because it was winter, drying the laundry was a problem, especially the woolly cardigans and socks. So why not load all the wet laundry into a big handbag and take it with her to the pictures? Making sure we filled the seats next to the radiator, she draped the wet items along the top to dry while we watched Audie Murphy, Barbara Stanwyck or Rory Calhoun being heroic and romantic. But the steam on screen couldn't possibly match the steam rising in the auditorium, where we all sat ostensibly oblivious. It worked a treat. I don't know which the other people preferred, the smell of spicy pease pudding or the fog made by the laundry. Either way, nobody complained, and who knows, some may have followed her lead. And meanwhile, we returned home with bone dry laundry, albeit smelling of Woodbines.

I was reminded of this more recently while staying at the Four Seasons Hotel in Los Angeles. Whenever I am required to travel to LA it is usually either to make a film, or to do the endless tour of interviews to promote a film I've already made. Normally, on these occasions, all expenses are paid by the distributors of the film. There is no denying that the laundry service in the hotel is first class, but even so, I simply cannot shake off my working-class roots and bring myself to pay $6 per T-shirt to be laundered, no matter who is footing the bill. Instead I go to the launderette. Easy. The one I found on this occasion was at the Pavilion shopping centre on Santa Monica Boulevard and North Robertson, but a little too far to walk with a bag of laundry. So I took advantage of the car allocated to me, which just happened to be a mile-long stretch limousine. Chico, the driver, was a rather suave Puerto Rican, and looked totally nonplussed when I told him our destination. He took pains to explain to me that there was a perfectly good laundry service at the hotel. I told him I was fully aware of the fact but that I preferred to go to the launderette. He gazed at me quizzically for some time with his mouth slightly open, wondering if he'd picked up the wrong passenger, and then made a call on his cell phone, occasionally glancing over his shoulder to look at me. Whomever he was speaking to obviously also thought my destination a little bizarre because he was told to ask me to confirm that I was indeed Miss Blethyn. Fortunately, at that moment some guests emerged from the hotel and cried, 'Oh Miss Blethyn, may we have an autograph?' Persuaded now that he had the right cargo he became a little more polite. It only took about ten minutes to drive there but it took an eternity to park the stretch limousine outside the launderette. It caused such consternation amongst the staff and other shoppers that they thought it was some kind of advertising stunt, and wanted to pose for photos with me and my laundry. Usually I would do the laundry myself but I decided it would be more prudent to push the boat out and have a service wash instead. Wash, Fluff and Fold. Ten dollars all in. And while my laundry was being dealt with I took the opportunity of going to the nearby cinema. And as I sat watching the film I laughed to myself thinking of Mum in the cinema also waiting for her laundry to dry. Like mother, like daughter. A smiling Chico was waiting for me outside the cinema in the limousine and proudly presented me with my neatly packaged bundle of clean laundry.

We seldom got new clothes. They were either bought from the second-hand shops or were hand-me-downs from relatives. Because there was an age gap of twelve years between myself and Jeannie, her old clothes were not an option, and neither, of course, were Terry's, Martin's or Bill's. Thank God. They had already been handed down a dozen times. I loved to visit my mum's sister Aunt Lil at the Northwood Social Club, not only because she was a lovely lady, but because she would generally go through her beautiful daughter's wardrobe and give me whatever Janice had grown out of. She was only a year or two older than me. On one occasion, when I was about twelve, I was given five skirts and five pairs of shoes. It didn't matter that they were a little big. I dressed up in my new skirt and shoes and promenaded along the east cliff as proud as Punch, then went home and changed into a new set and did the same again. Five times in all.

When I was eleven, I espied a turquoise and white spotted dress in the tiny haberdashery shop opposite our house. It had a matching turquoise and white striped cardigan. It was impossible for me to pass the shop without stopping to gaze inside. I didn't tell Mum about it, knowing full well I wasn't able to have it. No fuss was ever made because we all knew from experience it would be fruitless. Mum couldn't afford it and that was that. It was Easter time, it was warm and the visitors were flocking to Ramsgate for the start of the holiday season. Easter eggs were lining up on the sideboard, given to us by neighbours, relatives and friends. The first thing we'd do is to give them a shake to see if there were chocolates inside but we weren't allowed to open them until Easter Sunday. This was the day we would get dressed up and go out as a family and stroll along the seafront. Imagine my delight then when it was my turn to go the scullery for a wash, to find my new underwear (underwear was always new), new white socks, blancoed plimsoles, and the turquoise and white dress and cardigan. I was delirious with joy, even though the sight of stripes and spots on the same hanger made everyone feel giddy. Mum must have seen me constantly looking in the shop window. I flung my arms around Mum's neck and kissed her and she told me to stop being such a cranky cow and to get washed. It turned out that Terry and Martin had new outfits too. I learnt later that my brother Bernard had sent money home from New Zealand, where he was working as a chef on board a ship. Mum always referred to this as a windfall. Bernard often sent money home to Mum, but sometimes it arrived when Mum was feeling down, and instead of cheering her up, she would go to the Alma and drown her sorrows. But luckily for us, this was not one of those occasions.

Bill's pretty girlfriend gave me a party dress she had grown out of. It was beautiful and made of turquoise green taffeta. Of course, it was far too big for me and had to be altered. Mum took it to be altered in the dry cleaner's in King Street opposite the Duke of Kent pub. We were told to collect it in two weeks' time. But when we went to retrieve it the cost of the alterations was so exorbitant that we had to leave it there. The proprietress protested that we couldn't have got it done cheaper anywhere else, which was probably true. I don't expect it was that much money but to us it was a fortune. I was heartbroken.

But not quite so upset as in New York a couple of years ago when I took my lovely white silk trouser suit to be cleaned and delivered back to the hotel the same day. I needed it for a television interview I was going to do. Evening came but my suit didn't. The following morning I went to the cleaner's myself to retrieve it and they said that they had absolutely no record of it. Arguing was a waste of time. They simply didn't have the suit. Returning back to the hotel to my surprise we passed a small oriental lady hurrying in the opposite direction, wearing what I thought to be MY suit. We gave chase and guess where we ended up? At the dry cleaner's. But the lady and the suit had disappeared into the back of the shop. We demanded an explanation. They were quite adamant that I had been mistaken, but on further inspection in the back of the shop they returned with good news! They had found the suit but it wouldn't be ready until the afternoon. They absolutely denied all accusations of it having been worn by one of their staff and the suit was returned to the hotel that afternoon as promised. Maybe I had been seeing things after all. It wasn't the only white suit in the world. Perhaps I was being paranoid. I didn't have occasion to wear the suit for some months after, but when I did, imagine my surprise when I put on the trousers to find they had been temporarily shortened by 4 inches!

Ready for secretarial college

8

MOVING TO NIXON

IN 1960 I WAS FOURTEEN. *THE* BIG EVENT OF THE YEAR, actually of my life so far, was that we were lucky enough to be allocated a council house in Nixon Avenue on the Whitehall Estate. Mum and Dad weren't overenthusiastic about the move because although many benefits came with the new house, it was a bus ride out of town or at least a long walk, and we all missed the proximity of the cliff with its promenade, the seafront, and the bustle and convenience of the town. But apart from that, I was ecstatic because it meant, at long last, my own bedroom and even better than that, an inside toilet. The most beautiful music I had ever heard was the sound of the cistern filling in the toilet below my bedroom. We also had a bathroom. It didn't matter that we only had hot water in the winter when the fire was lit in the sitting room downstairs, we had a bathroom, and I'd sometimes force myself to have a cold bath, because it was such a pleasure to have one at all. Also we had a garden front and back but none of us knew how to enjoy it or tend it. All it was ever used for was drying the washing. I don't think any of us ever sat in it because it would have felt so odd. We'd never experienced the convention of being private in public. Come to think of it I can't remember any of the neighbours enjoying their gardens either. Nowadays we don't think twice about stretching out in the garden.

On one of the occasions I visited Mum and Dad, I was surprised to see four strangers digging the front garden and mowing the grass. (It had needed doing for some time.) I found Brian in the front room and learnt the four men were his friends in the army and they'd volunteered to do the garden. Mum insisted on giving the men a cup of tea and slice of cake for their labours. Brian agreed but said that although it was very generous of them to do the garden he had to maintain discipline. Out he went. 'ATTEEEEEEEENSHUN!!' And then, 'AT EASE!!' My mum came out with the tray. 'You don't listen to him, do you?' she said to the men, much to their amusement. 'He's not too old for a slapped arse you know!' 'Oi, don't tell them that,' said Brian, 'let's get the garden finished first!' But everyone was laughing, it was obvious that the four men liked Brian enormously and were very happy to be off barracks and to be enjoying a little barracking instead. We all ended up having tea and cake on our perfectly manicured grass; alas the one and only time.

When we moved, my sister Jean had been married for two years and had gone to live in America with her USAF husband Herbie. Brian had long been in the army, promoted to Corporal and then Drum Major. Bill at this time was at university in London. Terry and Martin were both working but still living at home with Mum, Dad and me.

Terry was working temporarily as a driver for the K Laundry service in Ramsgate that summer. He hated to be idle. He could turn his hand to anything and make a success of it, so he was never out of work. He had a regular pay packet. I'll never forget how generous he was to Martin and me and to Mum and Dad too. He couldn't have earned an enormous amount yet he still gave me and Martin pocket money. In return I did little jobs for him. I made sure his shoes were nicely polished, that his laundry was attended to and that his suit was pressed. But on one momentous occasion, after a special bonus at work, he treated himself to a brand new made-to-measure Italian mohair suit. It was gorgeous and the height of fashion. To make sure he absolutely looked his best when he went out with his girlfriend, I decided to give it a nice little press. I had the trousers laid out carefully on the table covered with a damp cloth, when a knock came at the front door. I carefully set the iron on its little stand and went to answer it. It was the coal man with a bag of coal balanced on his shoulders and a sack of logs hanging from his wrist. I guided him through the house to the coal-hole on the other side of the kitchen, paid him with the money Mum had left, and showed him out again. When I returned to the pressing I found to my horror that Terry's lovely mohair made-to-measure suit trousers had fallen against the iron which had burnt a hole the size of half a crown right through the middle of the waistband! Oh my God!! Oh no! What on earth was I to do? Oh, his lovely new, EXPENSIVE, made-to-measure mohair suit. And as I quaked, Terry walked in the front door whistling.

'Hiya Bren!'

It took him a few minutes to realise that I had somehow been paralysed, and when he enquired if I was OK the floodgates opened!

'Oooooh Terry. Ooooooh I couldn't help it, Oooh I'm so sorry, it was an accident,' I cried, tears streaming down my face.

He looked at me and very calmly and clearly said, 'I don't care what you've done Bren, as long as you haven't done anything to my suit'.

I howled.

When his eyes fell upon the table and he saw the burn, he put his hands on his hips, closed his eyes, lowered his head and whispered, 'I don't believe this' and was then deafeningly silent.

I waited.

Eventually, he looked at me and said, 'Right.'

Another silence.

'I'll see if I can cover the burn up. Go upstairs and see if you can find one of Dad's belts.'

I went up the stairs two at a time, and returned with the only belt I could find which would have been capable of securing a large trunk on a long tempestuous journey. But Terry, being Terry, managed to trim the belt to fit. It wasn't ideal but in the circumstances it was better than nothing.

He didn't speak to me any more until he was washed, dressed and all ready to go out on his date. I felt so wretched. He was halfway out of the front door when he paused, turned, smiled and said, 'Bren, it was so very nice of you to press my suit. Very thoughtful of you. Thank you,' and went out the door.

I burst into tears again, but this time with tears of relief.

That same year, I was allowed to join the local youth club in St Luke's Avenue. Lots of activities were organised for teenagers, including outdoor sports matches, indoor sports matches, dances, outings, canoe camping, etc. It's a pity such youth clubs aren't as popular today. I once went on a terrific canoe camping holiday with three friends. We borrowed a couple of canoes from the youth club and my friend's dad loaded them on top of his van and drove us all out to Plucks Gutter on the River Stour. It had been raining but that didn't bother us at all, because we were going to get wet on the river anyway. Neither did we have sophisticated tents. Before pitching the tent a groundsheet would have to be laid down and pegged as soon as we'd found a few square yards free of cow dung. We had two two-man tents. My friend Patricia and I shared one, and our friends Jim and Mick, shared the other. The first morning I woke up, I found that I'd slid out of the tent. Only my head was left inside. So the next night I tried sleeping around the other way and when I woke up there was a cow staring at me and only my feet were left inside the tent. So I tried sideways, and rolled completely out of the tent. Of course, tents nowadays are far more sophisticated with built-in groundsheets, so the occupants are kept safe inside all night long. But how lovely it was to wake up, slide the canoe into the river and paddle up and down as the sun came up and we'd see the mist over the river slowly evaporate. And our voices and laughter on the early morning river seemed so clear, intermingled with the bird song and the busy scurrying of river creatures in the reeds along the bank. The boys were far more competent canoers than Pat and myself, but it didn't really matter. We had a great time just messing about on the river, and playing in barns, bird watching, and cooking on our little Bunsen burner. There was one minor hiccup. Our tin of beans exploded when we tried heating the beans without opening the tin. It was like a World War Two bomb going off, but twice as messy. Ah well, live and learn.

And here was another lesson. I once foolishly hazarded the sea in a canoe. It was such a silly thing for a novice to do, although I was with someone more experienced. We paddled from Ramsgate harbour around the coast to Broadstairs. The outward journey was so enjoyable and remarkably quick, about forty minutes. But while we were having fun out on the sea, the tide had turned making it very difficult for us to paddle home. This was a different kettle of fish altogether. It took over two hours. The pier was lined with people watching us struggling towards the harbour, and both of my thumbs were worn away with the effort. Being a novice I was required to sit in the front of the canoe, with the more experienced canoer at the rear, and seeing the swell of the sea crashing over the bows was really scary. My young instructor told me afterwards, with a good deal of bravado, that we hadn't been in any danger at all, even though we'd just learnt that the lifeboat was on the point of being launched.

Our house on the Plains of Waterloo was demolished along with the other ten or so houses in our terrace, including Vyes the grocers on the corner. I loved Vyes the grocers. I have many memories of the manager or other members of staff cheering me up with a bag of broken biscuits. Or sometimes, if I couldn't find my mum when I came home from school earlier than expected, they would take me into the office, dry my tears, and equip me with pencils and drawing paper until she came to retrieve me. From the office there was a hatch into the shop itself and I was small enough to sit inside it and watch the shoppers choosing their cheeses or bacon. I loved to watch them cut the cheese on the huge marble slab, slicing neatly through with the cheesewire. When I grew up I was definitely going to be a cheese cutter. When Terry was about eight years old, Mum sent him to Vyes to buy a packet of tea. The assistant manager George, who was a very handsome man with thick black hair, told Terry that Mum had won the Christmas raffle and the prize was a massive box of groceries. He instructed Terry to tell Mum to come to collect it. Mum was naturally puzzled when Terry gave her the message because she said she hadn't bought any raffle tickets, she couldn't *afford* to buy raffle tickets, and that there must be some mistake. 'What was the silly bugger talking about?' But when she made enquiries it transpired that the 'silly bugger' and the staff at Vyes the grocers had made up the story just so that Mum would accept their gift of the groceries. It was so generous of them. The hamper was full of delights. Besides the usual provisions of tea, sugar, butter, cheese, bacon, bread and pickles, there was a sticky fruitcake, biscuits, bags of raisins and a jar of juicy cherries. And a big bag of sweets.

When we were allocated the council house, a number of our neighbours were also relocated to the Whitehall Estate, so we weren't suddenly living alongside total strangers. I often dream of our house on the Plains, and in my dream it has been beautifully renovated with all mod cons, and Mum and Dad don't have any money worries and everybody who passes says 'What a lovely house.' It was a lovely house, or at least it would have been, if it hadn't been shaken to its foundations by the Luftwaffe.

At around this time, I really started to miss my sister Jeannie, even though she hadn't lived at home very often. She'd have spells of living with Pam or other relatives and I didn't know her as well as I knew my brothers. But I thought she was beautiful and exciting. She was glamorous then and now. And when she was at the Plains she was very kind to me, and would always bring me chocolate home or some small trinket or other, if she'd been out on a date. And we played a lot of games. I really looked up to her. She and I became good friends when I became an adult, and we still do play a lot of games whenever I visit her and her husband in Florida. We're both crossword puzzle fanatics. Scrabble enthusiasts. Cryptogram decipherers. Puzzle solvers. And laugh ourselves silly.

But when I was just fifteen or so, and my friends started going out with boys, and I was being made aware of the importance of fashion and style, I needed guidance, and wished that Jeannie lived nearby. Obviously we didn't have a telephone. I had my mum, but the only advice she would dispense was 'Keep away from boys OR ELSE.' Or 'I WANNA BE BEHIND YOU', meaning woe betide you if I catch you with boys. It used to put the fear of God into me. Pam would dispense the same advice because she was also a figure of authority and perhaps even stricter than

Mum, and her daughter Val didn't count because she was only eleven years old. Of course, I had my friends at school to consult and confide in but they all seemed much more liberated than me. My mum was stricter than their parents were, or so I unreasonably thought. If I was allowed out in the evening at all, I had to be home before dark. Just as well really, because we got up to all sorts of mischief in daylight! Knock down ginger being the least of it. Or if I'd been invited to a party or was going to a dance I could only go if one or other of my brothers accompanied me. Or my cousin Wendy, but that was great because we were best friends anyway.

Whether it was the constant warnings of 'keep away from boys OR ELSE' and not to get myself into trouble or whether I was just painfully shy as far as boys were concerned I don't know, but all my friends seemed to have boyfriends and I didn't. At least, not until I was seventeen. Who would have predicted that a couple of decades later, in the line of duty, my job would sometimes entail kissing and climbing into bed with chaps I'd only met the day before!

I had very little experience of acting at school, save for a couple of productions, scenes from Jane Austen's *Pride and Prejudice* and a full production of Sheridan's *The School for Scandal*. We were encouraged and championed by one of our teachers, Mr John McAllister. He was a wonderful teacher, making every class he taught exciting. There was very little misbehaving in his classes because pupils paid attention. I always sought the approval of Mr McAllister in everything. We made our own costumes in needlework class under the watchful eye of Sister Agnes and also made our own wigs out of cotton wool. During a performance of *School for Scandal*, somebody emerged from a cupboard instead of the door by mistake, and the entire place was in uproar. The audience was howling with laughter. I was playing Lady Teazel, opposite my best friend Patsy who was playing Sir Peter Teazel, and my favourite speech was coming up. It was when Lady Teazel has a secret assignation with Charles, a cad. Unfortunately for her, Sir Peter also turns up to see him. In desperation she hides behind a screen and overhears her husband pouring his heart out, saying how much he cares for her. But when he discovers her behind the screen he is hurt and outraged. I launched into my speech as seriously as I could to regain the audience's attention. The exposed cad Charles feigns surprise and says 'She's mad!' To which Lady Teazel replies,

No, sir, she has recovered her senses and your own arts have furnished her with the means. Sir Peter, I do not expect you to credit me but the tenderness you expressed for me when I am sure you could not think I was witness to it has penetrated my heart, that had I left the place, without the shame of this discovery, my future life would have shown the sincerity of my gratitude. As for that smooth tongued hypocrite, who would have seduced the wife of his too credulous friend, whilst he effected honourable advances to his ward, I behold him now in a light so truly despicable that I shall never again respect myself for having listened to him.

We got a round of applause.

When I came off stage, Mr McAllister was in the wings and he said 'Brilliant, Brenda. Well done!' It's amazing what a few encouraging words can do for a teenager. I was especially delighted because my mum and dad were in the audience, although I learnt later that when they arrived at the hall they were told all the tickets were taken, so Dad pretended he was a reporter writing for the local paper and flashed the inside of his lapel.

While I had thoroughly enjoyed the whole experience, I had no idea that acting was a talent that could be nurtured or pursued as a career – I was just pleased to have done something well. Ever since I was a toddler my mum would announce that I was going to be an actress. But that prophecy had little to do with my working in theatre, nothing could have been further from her thoughts, it was simply a comment on the way I would stamp my foot and make a dramatic exit from the room whenever I was reprimanded. 'She's the cause of all the trouble!'

You shall go to the ball!

9

MAKING MY WAY

I was in the top group of six pupils in my class and, when at fifteen most people left school and took a job, for some reason best known to the headmaster, one other pupil, Catherine Grist, and myself were chosen to go on to further education at nearby superior schools. Catherine to concentrate on English, she was a talented writer and artist, and myself to study mathematics. I was rather good at maths although I only ever scratched the surface of the subject. It would probably be more accurate to say I was rather good at 'sums'. (I'd love to know what became of Catherine.) My sister Pam, however, persuaded Mum and Dad that it would be much better for me to follow my friend Maureen's example and go to Thanet Technical College to learn secretarial duties. So the decision was made for me. I applied to the Thanet Technical College and was accepted. I realise now that it must have been a big sacrifice for my parents to let me continue learning because they could certainly have done with another income, but nevertheless they agreed to let me go. It meant that I would have to work full time through the summer to raise enough money for books etc. because I certainly wouldn't be getting a grant. Mum got a pound a week family allowance while I was at college. I was offered a job washing-up in a guesthouse on Wellington Crescent and gratefully took it. In those days the guesthouses were all full in the summer months and some of them in the winter too. I worked really hard doing one of two shifts, either the breakfast and dinner shift, or the dinner and tea shift.

The college issued a list of books to buy in preparation for my first term, and, since each student was expected to dress as befitted a respectable secretary, I had to save enough money for a couple of skirts and blouses and a pair of stout shoes as well as my books. Because I grew up at the seaside, my legs were always lovely and brown and smooth, therefore I didn't need to wear stockings, which was just as well really because we couldn't afford to buy them. The college rules stated that girls were expected to wear stockings but nobody could ever tell that my legs were bare. However, one day after tennis practice, we were all in the changing rooms getting ready for a shorthand lesson when one of the lady teachers came in, and was horrified to observe that I didn't put on a suspender belt and stockings. 'ANY RESPECTABLE GIRL WEARS STOCKINGS,' she bellowed. It was so embarrassing and somewhat hurtful because she was suggesting I wasn't respectable. So from that day on Mum and Dad and myself had to stretch our already stretched budget even further to buy stockings every week. The cheapest were 1s 11d a pair (equivalent to just under 10p today but with the purchasing power of buying two cinema tickets). The 2s 11d ones were more durable. Tights had only just been invented and weren't yet available, and in any case they would have been beyond our means. My stockings would get washed each night ready for the next day.

Actually, while at college in 1961, I had a Saturday job at Littlewoods, and I was usually positioned on the stockings counter. This was in the happy days when each section had an assistant allocated to it. But once during the pre-Christmas rush I was transferred to the furniture counter. They had a surplus of poufs to sell and I came up with the idea that if I put a dirty great SOLD sign on each of them, they might become a little more popular. I was right. People kept asking if there were any left. 'I'll just check with the stockroom, madam.' Or, 'Oh yes, you're in luck, sir, we just have a couple left, what colour would you like?' I shifted the lot in a day. No doubt Littlewoods wouldn't have been best pleased with my methods, but there again, maybe they would. Nobody said anything.

It was the fashion at the time to have a beehive hairdo and dark eyeliner. Some girls had their hair coiffed, backcombed and stiffened with lacquer on a Saturday, and that's how it stayed all week. And I'm talking *really* backcombed, about six inches high. How they ever slept at nights I don't know. I wasn't allowed to have a great big hairdo, because Mum said I'd get nits if I didn't comb it every day. She was probably right. However I did have a go at the black eyeliner, until Pam came into the shop one day.

'What do you think you look like?' she said. 'It looks like you've put that on with a matchstick! AND it looks like you've been up all night.'

I was crushed.

'Go and wipe it off,' she said. 'Now!'

I had to ask the supervisor if I could be excused for a few minutes to nip to the toilet. I wiped all my lovely eye liner off and returned to my counter. 'That's better,' said Pam, who had waited to check me out. 'Now then, have you got any of them poufs left?'

I had a good mind to say 'no' but I didn't. I just waited until she had left with her purchases and nipped back to the ladies' and put my lovely eyeliner back on again.

Previously I'd had a Saturday job in Woolworths on the pick and mix counter, which I loved. It was so satisfying to weigh up the sweets and whoosh them into little paper bags, taking two corners and flipping them over. I'd seen them do that in Vyes the grocers. And then one day, joy of joys, I was put on the cold meat and cheese counter.

'A pound of Cheddar, please.'

'Certainly, madam, won't keep you a moment.'

I'd place the cheese on to the marble slab, lift the cutting wire over the cheese and pull. Ooh it was lovely! In my mind I was in Vyes the grocers. At first it was, 'It's just a little over, madam' or 'It's just a little under, madam. Is that all right for you, madam?' But I soon got pretty accurate. The cold meats were cut in a little room upstairs. I suppose this was a safety measure because the machine had a rotating blade. A small pretty lady called Lily operated the machine and I had to measure out 4 oz sections separated by sheets of greaseproof paper, pile it all on to a tray and take it to the shop floor. But all in all I suppose I preferred to be in Littlewoods smelling of leather poufs than of smelling like a side of bacon.

Mum was feeling particularly depressed during that first year I was at college, she was probably menopausal, and it was less than harmonious at home. As a result I didn't do as well as I should have. After the first year, we were asked to raise our hands if we were staying on for a second year, and I was crushed when my raised hand was greeted by the remark 'Oh, I'd rather hoped you were leaving' from the teacher. My brother Bill persuaded me to stay on nevertheless, and because of conditions at home, I went to live with my sister Pam for the rest of the course. As a result my work improved, because I was having three good meals a day and going to bed early, and also because her husband John got me an old heavy Remington typewriter to practise on in the evenings. The deafening clatter must have driven them mad as I pounded the keys, but they never complained. It wasn't unusual at that time to meet retired secretaries with gnarled arthritic fingers, the result of pounding those old typewriters for so many years.

Every year since 2001, I have held special screenings of one or other of my films at the Granville Theatre Ramsgate or Windsor Cinema Broadstairs to raise funds for the restoration of St George's Church lamp tower. At a recent screening it was lovely to see my shorthand and typing teacher Mrs Wallace and I was delighted that she remembered me. It was also gratifying to find some of my old school friends and play mates turning up, including one of my youth club pals.

I continued going to the youth club even when I started college. There were weekly dances and it was here, when I was seventeen, I got such a crush on Stanley, a local boy who was a reserve footballer with Crystal Palace Football Club in London. Or to be more precise, I got a crush on the back of his neck. He always looked so smart and his hair was fair, slightly curly and neatly cut. It was just that little gap between hair and collar that looked so vulnerable. However, lots of girls liked Stanley, so I thought he was hardly likely to take any notice of me. I had stepped out with one or two boyfriends before, Mick *one* the caterer and Mick *two* the soon-to-be graphic designer, and the curly haired trainee manager of Littlewoods, but none gave me the butterflies as Stanley did. Actually they weren't very keen on me either as it turned out, because Mum's 'OR ELSE' threat was ringing in my ears so loudly that *they* could probably hear it. For them I wasn't an easy target. Plus my brothers were always on the look out for me. From the age of sixteen, provided I was with Wendy or my brothers I was allowed to go to the dances at Dreamland in Margate on Sundays, St Lo in Broadstairs on

Saturdays, or the Pleasurama Ballroom at Ramsgate which was open most nights in the summer. Live music played at these venues and lots of well-known bands visited, including Joe Brown and the Bruvvers, the Springfields, Screaming Lord Sutch (with a toilet seat around his neck), Freddie and the Dreamers, Gerry and the Pacemakers, the Karl Denver Trio, Manfred Mann, Jim Dale and many more.

But, blow me down with a feather, Stanley did like me and we started 'stepping out' as my mother called it. We courted for about a year and before the end of my course at college we got engaged to be married. Nowadays that seems very young, but not then. A lot of my friends were already married. On graduation I was successful in getting a job as a shorthand typist at the Royal Bank of Scotland in the Haymarket, London, and, of course, as a bonus, I'd be able to see more of my fiancé.

My parents must have been inordinately sad as they helped their youngest child to pack, but they felt confident my wellbeing would be taken care of since the accommodation chosen for me was right next door to where my brother Bill and his wife Fran lived. It had been organised for me to stay at the Cecil Residential Club, a young ladies' hostel in Gower Street, and I was horrified when the matron, seeing my completed arrival form, announced that I could not stay as I was only seventeen and the minimum age was eighteen. However, to my relief, she relented, and I unpacked by bags in a room to be shared by three other girls.

I loved working at the bank. I was at a desk with two other typists and since the design of the place was open plan we could see all the comings and goings. I earned the grand sum of £6 per week, and with my rent at the hostel being £3 15s which included food, I was able to save a little. I felt rich.

But I had only been in London a couple of months when Stanley announced that he had been offered a transfer to

Johannesburg, South Africa. He said he would only go if I went with him, but the stipulation was that we would have to be married. I was not yet eighteen. Just think, I could have been a footballer's wife! Representatives of the football club, whom we called 'the millionaires', came to London and we met them at the Strand Palace Hotel, where they bought us lunch and told us of all the benefits of moving to South Africa. Obviously I couldn't go without my parents' permission, so they agreed to go to Ramsgate to talk it over with them, and to reassure them that their daughter would be well taken care of.

The following Sunday the millionaires turned up at my parents' house in a Rolls Royce. My dad didn't believe for a second that they would come down to Ramsgate so he went upstairs for his customary forty winks. Mum hadn't yet cleared away the dinner table. In came the millionaires and their imposing presence almost overwhelmed her. I went upstairs and woke Dad up. Down he came with his tousled hair. Dad always wore his trousers about four inches above his waist, and, as well as braces, wore a belt about his waist that had no purpose at all, like someone out of a D.H. Lawrence novel. He entered the room and said, 'Good shot, sir!' to one, and 'Good shot, sir' to the other, which was his euphemism for 'welcome'. Mum was livid because Dad hadn't combed his hair and was doing an elaborate mime behind the millionaires' backs. In an effort to overcome her embarrassment Mum asked them to 'excuse her prat of a husband and would they care for a naice cup of tea?' and 'Did they mind tinned milk?' the 'fresh milk being on the turn'. They sat and chatted for about an hour.

Dad never had any intention of letting me get married and go off to South Africa, but he hadn't given it much thinking time because he thought the whole idea was pie in the sky. He didn't realise that things would get so far as having millionaires sitting in his front room and asking for his permission. Eventually he said that he didn't want his daughter going to South Africa in the current political climate. They argued their case but Dad was adamant. Not to be deterred, and because they really wanted Stanley, they then turned to Mum, expecting a little more support from her, but she said, 'With the greatest respect, I totally agree with my prat of an 'usband!' But to soften the blow she said, 'There's a bit of meat left over from dinner, would you like a sandwich?' They didn't. So that was that.

I was in floods of tears because I thought that since they'd come all the way from London, the least Mum and Dad could do was let their 17-year-old daughter get married and move 6000 miles away! When they left the house there was a circle of neighbours around the Rolls Royce, and by way of compensation, one was giving the bonnet a little polish with the sleeve of his jacket.

About eight months later, Stanley was transferred to Dover in Kent and he wanted me to return home also. I was just a young girl and besotted by him, so I reluctantly gave up my lovely job at the bank and returned home, which really put Mum and Dad's noses out of joint. They were thrilled to have me home, of course, but felt I had done the wrong thing. But what did they know? Quite a lot, as it happened, because I wasn't home long before it all went pear shaped. I'd found work in Ramsgate as a receptionist at Nelbarden Swimwear Factory. As well as my typing work, I was responsible for playing the records for the seamstresses in the factory. The girls would send music requests to me at reception.

But then, a couple of months after my return, Stan told me that he'd had a little bit of a fling with a former girlfriend, and that I was chucked. I was devastated and because of our intimacy I felt like a fallen woman of Victorian times, and was beside myself with guilt. I was *physically* ill. I felt sullied. I couldn't do my work properly. Complaints came from the shop floor that I wasn't playing the records, and that the ones I did play were crap!

My brother Bill came to the rescue and suggested I went back to London. He advised that I should contact the bank to see if I could have my job back and also approach the hostel to see if a room was available. I followed his advice, especially as I was spurred on to do so by Mum and Dad. Fortunately the bank did have a job for me to go back to, and not only did the hostel have a bed for me, it was in the same room as previously. Poor Stanley was so repentant and didn't want me to go, but the damage was done. For me there was no going back. I've since learnt, of course, that everyone makes mistakes, myself included, and maybe I should have forgiven him. But I was so hurt. It was a double-edged sword for Mum and Dad to be saying goodbye again. They loved me living at home and working, but they knew that much better opportunities existed for me in London.

The same weekend that I arrived in London, I was Bill's guest at the London University Ball attended by the Queen Mother. He even bought me a gorgeous ball gown for the occasion. It was long and sparkling pink with long white silky gloves to go with it. He was so supportive and tried to open my eyes to the fact that I was not the Jezebel I believed myself to be. By the time I had settled into my old routine, my centre forward friend had again asked for a reconciliation. But to use a football analogy, the whistle had gone and the match was over, whereupon Stanley went to play football in South Africa.

I was very surprised, nearly forty years later, while clearing out an old trunk, to come across Stanley's scrapbook recording many of his football triumphs. I didn't have the heart to throw it away, because I felt sure it would have been precious to him. I remembered receiving a letter from him some ten or fifteen years earlier, and after searching high and low and after turning every cupboard and drawer inside out, I found it. Stan was living in Sydney and I posted the book to him. He was delighted. I made a film in Australia in 1996 called *In the Winter Dark*, set in the Megalong Valley, and while there I went to visit Stan in Coogee, near Bondi Beach. It was strange seeing someone I once might have married, after all those years. He told me about his life and I was pleased to hear that he'd had a very successful career as a footballer, first in South Africa, then Australia and Hong Kong, but had long since hung up his boots. More recently I returned to Australia to make a film called *Clubland* and paid him another visit. I was shocked to find that he'd had his leg amputated, the result of advanced diabetes. He'd had a new prosthetic leg fitted and was trying to get used to it with the same determination he had as a successful sportsman. Stan said he was very pleased to see me and despite these tragic circumstances, I was very pleased to see him, and I remembered with clarity what a very nice young man he had been, and it made me feel terribly, terribly sad. But Stan was remarkably philosophical about it, and as upbeat as he could be. 'No point in being miserable about it, is there, Brenda,' he said.

No Stan, there isn't.

And I remembered my dad giving me those same words of wisdom as I sadly packed my bags again to return to London.

A few weeks after I arrived back at the hostel, a girl from a neighbouring room invited me out to a party to meet a friend of a friend of hers on a blind date. She could see I was miserable and was just trying to cheer me up. Oh boy, did it work!

Alan wearing a jumper I had knitted him.
Perhaps that was my first mistake.

10

ALAN

THE PARTY WAS AT BUSHEY HEATH NEAR HARROW, AND THE chap I was to meet was named Alan, who later became my husband. Talk about on the rebound! When he walked into the room I was gobsmacked. He was so handsome, with such a pleasant manner and ready smile. I was instantly drawn to him and Mr Centre Forward from that moment was history. He drove me home to Euston in his little car with the sticky-out trafficators and asked me for a date! He had also just split up from a long relationship. And that was it.

We were married on 6 January 1966 at Harrow Registry Office, six weeks short of my twentieth birthday. We chose Thursday for the ceremony for the simple reason it was half-day closing in the town and it would be easy to park! I wore an ivory-coloured two-piece suit with silver and gold embroidery, and a turban style hat. It was a modest wedding, and the only guests were family and a couple of friends, Dave and Sliz. The reception was held at Alan's parents' flat in Harrow, and, of course, Bernard made the cake. Mum and Dad gave me £5 to buy an electric kettle for our wedding present and it made me so happy. Because Alan worked for British Rail we travelled free on the train to Poole in Dorset for our honeymoon, to a guesthouse I'd found in a copy of *The Lady*. But it wasn't all that it was cracked up to be. It was deathly quiet in the house and we were the only guests. And it was bitterly cold. We spent practically our entire honeymoon with our winter coats on. Not long after our wedding there were a couple of spies apprehended in that area and I fantasised it was the same people whose house we'd stayed in. We didn't have en-suite facilities and every time we left our room, they were either lurking outside our door or they opened the door of their own room about an inch and peeped out. Fortunately, Alan and I had taken a basket of leftover food from the reception with us, so we mostly stayed in our room and ate from it. We only ventured outside once to go to the cinema to see *The Guns of Navarone*. We couldn't wait to go home. We should have read the signs!

For a long time we got on very well indeed. Alan was extremely witty, talented, warm, easy-going, and generally a good egg. He was the only bloke I knew who could wear a pale blue velvet suit and get away with it. It was the sixties after all. I ribbed him mercilessly about it and said he looked like a detergent salesman, but really I thought he had great panache.

His mother had been a beauty in her day and was blessed with a remarkable talent to whistle! She could have made a living whistling, and given Ronnie Ronalde a run for his money! But I didn't get on so well with his father. He made me feel I wasn't good enough for his son. Well, as it turned out, he was right. Although I seemed outgoing, I was very naive sexually, and remained so after our marriage. I suppose my frigidity was caused by a combination of a Catholic education, the OR ELSE threat issued by my mother and the badge of Jezebel.

Alan

Presented with the opportunity of studying graphic design at Watford College of Technology, Alan gave up his job at British Rail and embarked on the three-year graphic design course. He was popular and made lots of friends, most of whom were very talented, and I couldn't help feeling like a bit of a parasite. I wished I had a more creative job. However, I started to work at Euston as a secretary to support us both and lo and behold, British Rail's amateur dramatic group asked me if I would take part in a one-act play, which they were entering in an annual competition. The play was *His Other Love* (his other love being mountaineering). I hadn't done anything like that before save for the couple of productions at school, but they said they were 'desperate'. Oh, I see! Thanks very much! But since it was only one line, I agreed to help them out. 'It's a real dirty old night. Evans the post said the mist is right down to the pass. Quite thick he said it was!' I thought to myself, 'Yes Brenda. Go on. You can manage that!' Needless to say we didn't win the competition although I found I really enjoyed the experience, despite the fact that, in rehearsal, the lady director threw her eyes to the ceiling and pressed the back of her hand to her forehead every time I said my line. Anyway, they must have thought I was eventually OK because they asked me to become a regular member of the group. I loved it. I felt good, although I had no idea that acting was anything other than a hobby. I too made friends. I was asked by the camera club, who took photographs of our drama productions, to pose for some portrait photographs, which I did a couple of times. Considering my ambivalent attitude to sex, i.e. my frigidity, it's surprising that one photographer persuaded me to pose for some topless photographs in the interests of 'art'. But I soon saw the 'artlessness' of it when asked to remove my knickers. Of course I refused and got dressed as quick as lightning, realising my naivety had led me into an error of judgement.

At this time, it so happened that the daughter of one of the senior members of staff worked at the Young Vic Theatre's press office. He told me that the theatre always needed voluntary help to type envelopes, etc. and asked if I would offer my services. I did so quite readily. It was the perfect solution to help me regain some sense of worth. I enjoyed going to the Young Vic, even though I was confined to the press office with thousands of envelopes to type, because I could occasionally sneak out and watch from the back of the balcony Jim Dale, Jane Lapotaire, Nicky Henson and Denise Coffey being wonderful in *The Taming of The Shrew*. Who could possibly have foreseen that only six years later I would be performing there myself as Cassandra in a National Theatre production of *Troilus and Cressida*? Coincidentally, it was the same press officer, Lynn Kirwin, who took care of me and the publicity for Sir Peter Hall's production of *Mrs Warren's Profession* in the West End, nearly thirty years later.

While Alan was at college we lived in St Alban's Road, Watford, and I went through a couple of weeks of dreaming of my brother Ted. Every night I would have the same dream, and in it he always had a small scar on his cheek. It was strange because I didn't know Ted very well at all when I was growing up, because he'd already left home by the time I came along. He occasionally came to visit when on shore leave. The family remembered him as being a great raconteur. Teddy was a dreamer, a fantasist, imagining himself to be from much grander stock. He was an adventurer by nature, even though as a child he'd suffered from glandular fever which left him with a weak heart. He would perform fearless feats of bravery as if tempting fate. Once Dad gave him some money to go to the shop to buy a packet of cigarettes. When he didn't return a search party was sent out and four days later they found him camping in the country. He'd bought the tent and supplies with the money instead. Another time he stowed away on a boat in the harbour and was discovered and returned the next day. He was a very intelligent boy and loved boats, spending several years on fishing trawlers in the North Sea and Icelandic waters. When I was about ten years old he went away and nobody saw or heard of him for years. However, because of my recurring dreams, I decided to try my luck at tracing him.

It took me weeks to get on his trail. I went to his last known address and asked if they knew of his whereabouts. They didn't. I knocked on every door in the street and showed each occupant a photograph of him. We asked in all the neighbouring streets. When we were almost at the end of our search, a lady did remember Ted and said, 'Oh yes, Ted, lovely Ted. But oh dear, it was such a long time ago and I'm sorry to tell you dear, I think, I'm not sure, but I think someone told me he went to a mental hospital.' I asked her which one, but she didn't know. My resolve to find him was now reinforced. Maybe he needed us if he was sick. I then set about making a list of all the mental hospitals in Greater London and started to phone them. Most were very helpful and checked their records but he was not listed. I finally rang one number and gave all the details of the patient I was trying to find. She asked me to hang on for a minute and I could overhear a muffled conversation she was having with a colleague. She finally came back on to the phone and said yes, they did know him, although he had never been a patient, but for obvious reasons could not divulge his address. If I would care to send a letter to them they would forward it on. Fair enough. So that's what I did.

A few days later I had a phone call at work at British Rail from a man called Nigel saying he was a relative of Ted's, and he invited myself and Alan to St Alban's to meet him and his family. The letter had been forwarded on to Nigel's address and he had opened it. It transpired that this gentleman was Ted's brother-in-law. His wife and Ted's wife were sisters. They were Spanish. He told me that Ted had been working as a psychiatric nurse, had married, had a daughter and was now living and working in British Columbia, Canada. Ted, who had previously lived in this same house, had apparently left instructions to open any official-looking letters instead of forwarding them on. But the weird thing was that his last address in England was only five minutes away from where I was living in Watford. I was a little embarrassed because they obviously didn't know anything about our family. They gave me his Canadian address but I didn't know whether to contact him or not. I reasoned that he hadn't told his wife about any of us or they would have brought their young daughter to visit us at the seaside. I thought perhaps he didn't want to be reminded of the hardship he'd come from and maybe he thought we'd all want a handout. When he last saw us we were all snotty nosed little blighters with little prospect of being anything else. If he did think that he couldn't have been more wrong. In any case if I didn't write to him, his brother-in-law certainly would.

So I composed a letter outlining all the achievements each of us had accomplished. As I read it back to myself I was filled with pride. I was a successful shorthand typist, Martin at that time was doing rather well in the army. Terry was a sales manager for an international company, Bill a research fellow in aeronautics at the California Institute of Technology in Pasadena, Brian a military music teacher, Bernard a chef, Jean happily married with her own swimming pool, and Pam keeping the home fires burning while running an Italian coffee-cum-ice-cream parlour. We were all independent, responsible individuals. Mum and Dad must have got something right. I posted the letter.

Less than one week later Bill phoned me from Pasadena and told me that my sleuthing had paid off. Ted, who was overjoyed at receiving the letter, was at that very moment driving from British Columbia with his family to visit Bill in Pasadena, which was a pretty long way to drive. The upshot was that Ted and his family came back to England to live. Alan and I threw a party and the whole family were overjoyed to see Ted. I had never catered for so many people before in our small flat, and Ted turned up with eight chickens to be cooked. Typical. And he regaled us with the most outrageous stories, and we remembered just what a fantasist he was. We took it all with a pinch of salt. Nothing had changed, except for one thing. Wait for it. On Ted's cheek was a small scar that he'd got only two years' earlier in a minor road crash!

When Alan qualified, we moved back to London, to a tiny flat just off Blackstock Road. It was really grotty but we painted it up, bought some inexpensive wicker chairs, and added improvised blinds to the windows. These were made from pretty pieces of fabric attached to broom poles and suspended from two hooks at either side of the window frame. We had to share the bathroom and loo with the people in the flat below us. But we enjoyed living there for a while, it was ethnic, colourful and cheap. My wardrobe consisted mostly of long pretty dresses and kaftans bought from the many fragrant Asian shops nearby. While on a trip to the West End one evening we met some young American backpackers who were looking for a floor to sleep on. We enjoyed their company so we offered ours. It was only for a couple of nights because they were about to travel to the Isle of Wight for the pop festival and invited us to go along with them. We did. Oh, what an event. While we were there I was offered a puff on a joint.

'Good lord, no thank you. I don't smoke.'

'Go on, Brenda. We're just hanging out! Chill man!'

'Oh, okay then. Just a little puff.'

In two seconds flat I was ten feet above the ground wondering how to get back down again and finding it all terribly funny.

'You okay, Brenda?'

'Haaa HAAA! OHHH HAAAAAAAA, OOOHH YESS THANK YOU HAAAAAAA!!

When I did eventually land I slept for about two hours and missed a couple of the bands completely. I wouldn't try that again in a hurry.

I had forgotten about this incident until recently whilst watching *Saving Grace* on DVD with the actors' commentaries. On it, I said I'd only *eaten* marijuana. I suddenly recalled that flying sensation I'd had and laughed again at the memory.

But the whole Isle of Wight experience was absolutely wonderful despite the dreadful sanitary conditions and the drizzle, which didn't make our makeshift paper sleeping bags any more comfortable. We slept in our paper bags for two nights. We didn't care. We were there to enjoy the music: Joan Baez, The Doors, Donovan, Joe Cocker, Sly and the Family Stone, John Denver, Joni Mitchell, The Who, Emerson Lake and Palmer, Jimmy Hendrix. Joe Cocker was even on our train travelling back to London, and sang some more. Although two of our newfound friends returned home to Florida, our third guest stayed a few weeks longer. She didn't seem to be planning on going anywhere. Secretly I think she had designs on Alan. But the most surprising and thrilling thing about her was the fact that she was totally liberated in every way, and never even closed the door whenever she was using the loo. This was particularly surprising for the residents of the other flat, for while they queued at the open door, our guest would strike up a conversation with them, at the same time smoking a joint and declaring everything beautiful.

Alan was then offered a job with an advertising agency out of town (the southern arm of a London agency) and we moved to Chichester, where I also got a job as a secretary. Before buying our house, we rented a residential caravan in the woods near Arundel. It was lovely, although the idyllic setting was marred by our cat Trampus being killed on the busy A27 only a couple of weeks after we got there. The poor thing had been out on a rampage looking for a mate on the other side of the road. We were really upset. Trampus had adopted us when we lived in London, a lusty ginger tom, and we now regretted ever bringing him with us. We should have known it wasn't a good idea to take him, for when we were moving all our belongings to Chichester in a hired van, on probably the hottest day in summer, poor Trampus was gasping in the back with exhaustion. In desperation, we stopped and I bought him an ice-cream cornet to lick, thinking it might cool him down, but it had the opposite effect. Maybe it was the wrong flavour! In retrospect, I think it's possible that poor Trampus committed suicide. But whatever happened, it wasn't very pleasant driving out of our caravan park to see poor old Trampus squished for ever into the tarmac. I loved little Trampus.

Soon after we arrived in Chichester, I joined the Chichester Players, a local amateur dramatic group, and after a few productions, including *Lady Precious Stream*, set in the beautiful Bishop's Palace Gardens, and *The Prime of Miss Jean Brodie*, the artistic director, Norman Siviter, insisted I should consider acting professionally. What? Was he having a laugh? I told him he was mad. I had a perfectly good job, well paid, and I thought it would be rather irresponsible of me to give it up to pursue a hobby! Even assuming any drama school would want me! Whoever heard of such a thing? I had no qualifications and hardly ever went to the theatre. But he said it so often that I did start to think about it. One thing for sure was that I absolutely loved the stage and so I talked to Alan about it. He readily agreed that I should look into it. He was very supportive, as was my boss. Alan said it was now my turn to study because he was earning enough for both of us.

The Guildford School of Acting was the closest option, only an hour away on the train if we moved just a short distance from

Chichester. I applied for an audition, and surprisingly got one. The audition took all day, and applicants had to perform two pieces, a modern piece and a Shakespeare. I chose Maria from Shakespeare's *Twelfth Night* and Beatrice from Arnold Wesker's *The Four Seasons*, and this was followed by some general improvisation. In the afternoon we had to show our dancing skills, but since mine only consisted of the twist, locomotion and the jive I was a little behind the others. A couple of weeks later I was bewildered to get a letter offering me a place on the course. My first thought was that they had confused me with another applicant! And anyway, I still wasn't absolutely sure it was the right thing to be doing, because it had all happened so quickly, and seemed a little far-fetched. Our house was up for sale and we'd found another in Petersfield, which was ideally placed for both of us, convenient for Alan to travel to work and convenient for me to go to Guildford, but I noticed that he was stalling about committing to it.

He had befriended a beautiful neighbour named Tricia, whose husband was working away from home, and one evening while we were all enjoying a drink at the Fox with its Teeth Withdrawn a quaint little pub near Petersfield, she confessed to me that she was in love with my husband. I didn't immediately take her comment seriously, telling her that everyone was in love with him so it was perfectly all right for her to be, and I put the remark down to the copious amounts of mead that had been drunk. (Why were we all drinking mead? It was like drinking syrup.) It was only on reflection that I realised Tricia had meant it.

I talked to Alan about it, and it became crashingly clear that he felt the same way about her, and when I asked if he would be with her if I wasn't around, he quietly and gently said yes. He felt terrible about saying it, but it was the truth. I could see the attraction. Not only was Tricia very beautiful, she was witty, sexy and fun to be with. I enjoyed her company too. I remember reading

Lucky Jim to them both while they sat on the floor and rocked with laughter. Nevertheless, when Alan delivered this bombshell I lost my head altogether and against his will I went over to Tricia's house and, surprisingly calmly, asked her to come over to ours. When she arrived, I asked her the same question, and got the same answer. There was nothing I could do to change Alan's mind, although I desperately wanted to. He left the house instantly and never returned while I was in it.

Feeling in a vacuum, I then recalled a colleague at work telling me to behave a little more responsibly as far as Alan was concerned or I would lose him. She told me that I shouldn't spend so much time with my theatricals! I told her she was talking nonsense, and that Alan and I would always be together. I truly thought we would be. Perhaps she knew something that I didn't and was trying to warn me. I should have listened because I was again devastated. How naive can you be? It wasn't anybody's fault, Alan's, Tricia's, or mine. It happens and life goes on.

THE GUILDFORD SCHOOL OF ACTING & DRAMA DANCE EDUCATION LTD.

THE BELLAIRS STUDIO
MILLBROOK, GUILDFORD, SURREY.

Principal: BICE BELLAIRS   *Telephone*: Guildford 60701

19th April, 1972.

Dear Brenda Blethyn,

    I am pleased to tell you that we are able to offer you a place on the Acting/Musical Theatre Course commencing Monday, 18th September, 1972.

    I enclose herewith a list of necessary books and clothes required, together with Acceptance Form in duplicate, and I should be grateful if you would return one copy of the form to me as soon as possible.

    Should you require any further information please do not hesitate to contact me, and I should like to congratulate you on a successful audition.

    Yours sincerely,

Constance McConnon,
<u>School Secretary</u>.

Mrs. B.A. Blethyn,
40, Elm Road,
Westergate,
Nr. Chichester,
Sussex.

11

BLOSSOMING

ALONG CAME NELSON EDDIE IN THE SHAPE OF BROTHER BILL to rescue me again and take me back to stay with him and his wife. Coincidentally they now lived in Guildford and so I could continue with my plan to study at drama school. My final act of insanity as I left the house in Chichester was to paper the walls with the topless photographs taken at the camera club – I still don't know why I did that. It was idiotic. I asked them recently if they had a good laugh when they saw them. Worse than hearing the answer 'yes', was their saying that neither of them remembered the photos! The nerve of it! For a while I did wonder if things would have turned out differently if I had protested more to save my marriage. I doubt it. In the circumstances, and since I'd worked to support us both while Alan was at college, he gave me all the proceeds from the sale of our house to see me through drama school. Thirty-five years after the event, Alan and Tricia remain blissfully happy, and I still think of him with great affection.

During a summer break from my course at drama school, I

123

decided to visit Ted and Ana and their 6-year-old daughter Anita at their home in the village of Jimena de la Frontera in southern Spain, which was Ana's birthplace. At a moment's notice I booked myself a flight to Malaga, but not before sending off a telegram to my brother asking him to meet me at the airport. Unbeknownst to me, Ted and his family had themselves gone away for the weekend and didn't receive my telegram. So I was rather dismayed to arrive at Malaga to find nobody waiting for me, especially as I had very little cash and no means of getting any. After waiting a couple of hours and after several fruitless phone calls to Ted's house, I decided I had better go into Torremolinos to find a hotel for the night, and hope that I could contact him the following morning. I simply asked the taxi driver to take me to a hotel, any hotel. I can't imagine why he chose to take me to what looked like the most expensive one, but he did.

The desk clerk wasn't very helpful. I explained that I only wanted a room for one night, a modest room, and asked how much that would be. I counted up my small change, watched by the bemused desk clerk, and found that I had just enough. 'Fist, halet me si eef ey ava rooom,' he stalled. 'Nor, ah dona sink soh.'

'Oh please, any room, a cupboard would do,' I pleaded.

I couldn't bear the thought of traipsing around to find somewhere else to stay. On arrival I had immediately sent another message to my brother's home to say that I was at *this* particular hotel, so I didn't want to have to send another one. I must have appealed to his sense of decency because he barked at me 'PASSPORT!' I handed it to him and he flicked through it as if I were a criminal.

'Aha,' he announced. 'Ramsget! Ah know Ramsget! I lern de Ingleesh in Ramsget!'

'Oh,' I said, hoping to engage him in conversation and then

perhaps get a room, 'whereabouts in Ramsgate?' as if I knew any language schools in Ramsgate other than one.

'It was Rijinsy Skuul,' he said proudly.

'Well I'm buggered,' I thought. 'I know the Regency, my mother works there,' I said casually.

'Oh shee a ticher?'

'On no,' I said, 'she works in the kitchen.'

His eyes went as big as saucers and he screamed, 'NOT LOOLOO?'

I was dumbfounded, and when after a few seconds I finally said 'Yes' he was around the counter and giving me a cuddle in the wink of an eye.

'Looloo fid me win I 'ungry,' he said. 'She slip me fings. You looloo's dotter, yoo av best room in hawtel!!'

I could not believe my luck. My mum, in a crisis, saves the day! And he did indeed give me the best room in the hotel, invited me to the bar and plied me with cocktails. He simply loved my mum.

'She lern me vernaculars,' he crowed.

My brother eventually returned home and got my telegram and when he arrived to collect me at three o'clock in the morning, I was completely pissed. When I woke up in the beautiful Jimena de la Frontera the next morning, I had no recollection of how I got there.

The holiday was glorious. It was fiesta time and I even had a holiday romance. I was completely besotted by a local boy named Pepe who didn't speak English, and as I didn't speak Spanish we communicated in broken French. We corresponded for a while after my return to England, but when writing in French got too much for Pepe he resorted to his own language. Around the corner from drama school there was a Spanish chippy and unwisely I asked him to translate one letter for me. It turned out to be quite an explicit letter and the poor chippy was left finding ways to translate the contents which wouldn't offend the queue forming in front of the counter while the fresh batch of fish fried. Leaving the shop I looked as though *I* had been deep fried, my face was so red. Well, that settled that. I could never go there again! Naturally the relationship didn't survive. But oh, I did like Pepe.

Sadly Ted died in Spain from heart failure at the young age of sixty-one. He is buried at the top of the hill near the castle in Jimena de la Frontera, which was built to protect Spain from the marauding Moors. Considering his lust for adventure there could-n't be anywhere better for him to lie.

Whatever would I have done without my brother Bill? He is the first one I always turn to in times of crisis or celebration. Ever since I was a child he has had my welfare close to heart. He never judges me, and only ever shows pride never disappointment, and this has been the case for as long as I can remember. In fact that's the same with all my family. When my marriage broke up, he and his wife Fran unhesitatingly threw open the doors of their home for me, and were generous in so many ways. I stayed with them for a few months, which was a wonderful time despite my unhappy circumstances. Bill at the time was a lecturer at Surrey University. They were social creatures and had lots of friends and parties and outings and so on. Also, I loved the company of their two sons who are both bright, interesting and interested people.

Once when I was babysitting the 7-year-old, I asked him to help me with my script learning, forgetting that there was a load of expletives in it. His eyes grew as big as saucers when he got to the offending passage and then he got the giggles. So we called a halt to the swatting and played games instead. Naturally after a few months I felt that I should move on and find my own flat as I didn't wish to impose on Bill and his family any longer than necessary, and I rented accommodation nearby. I took a weekend job working in Debenhams' accounts department to help pay the bills. Fortunately my fees were covered by a government grant. But it wasn't easy *then* making ends meet so goodness knows how students manage today to pay their way.

I didn't tell my mother and father that my marriage was over or that I had given up my job in favour of drama school for some time, so that I could feel happy about both events before I disclosed them. When I did tell them they were very surprised, but at the end of the day only needed the assurance that I was happy. A decade later Mum said, 'Brenda, if you do your acting all day long, when do you earn your money?'

I said, 'They pay me, Mum.'

'Do they?' she said, surprised, but as if a little plan was forming. 'Have they got any more jobs going up there?'

Although drama school doesn't really teach you to act, it does enhance any talent that is already there, and teaches you to be observant, and to be aware of what makes people tick. Drama training would be good for everyone, no matter what field of work one intended to go into. Not least it teaches punctuality, reliability, teamwork, observation, camaraderie and trust. I blossomed at the Guildford School of Acting in many ways, for as my self-confidence grew, so did my libido, and I was prepared to enter into sexual relationships if I felt like it. And I did feel like it. I had been liberated from some mental taboo I had about sex. Occasionally I had to see Alan on matters connected with the sale of our house, and couldn't resist trying to get him to come back to me, but it was a no-go area.

And while I kept telling myself that I was okay about it all, I did sometimes get very depressed. I missed him. On these occasions I would call my best friend – my niece Valerie. Once, whilst rehearsing a student production at the Barbican in which I played a hunchback, and a man at that (is it any wonder I got depressed?), I rang Val simply to cheer myself up. She and her husband insisted on driving across London from Ealing to collect me. Spending half an hour in their company is guaranteed to cheer anyone up. I was invited to stay the night.

Chris was a keen and rather good wine maker and on the wall was an impressive display of vintage Winstone crying out for a corkscrew, and from which he chose a bottle to drink with our meal. It was delicious but stronger than I thought, for when I leapt up to give them a little flavour of my hunchback perform-ance, I knocked the lot clean off the wall. After the staggered shattering of the glass on the floor there was a silence as they sat looking at the wine forming a big puddle, with me still bent double like a statue of Quasimodo. Now *they* were depressed! It's a wonder they returned any of my phone calls after that for fear of having to give me another therapy session. Chris gave up wine making following that little episode. But despite this calamity and many others over the years, our friendship endures.

The Guildford School of Acting (now GSA Conservatoire) was the making of me. It was an excellent school and has since gone on from strength to strength. Their musical theatre course is second to none in Europe, and I'm proud to say I'm now a member of the board of governors. But in 1972 four of the tutors, in particular, gave me the confidence I needed to take risks. Ian Ricketts, who is still at the school, was a great champion. His enthusiasm was thrilling. He made me feel I was the most inter-esting person he had ever met. He has the talent to do that to most people, but then he genuinely *does* find most people interesting. Kathleen Frankis commented, on observing me help-ing to make the set for *Cavalcade* while learning my lines, that if I didn't get a job on leaving the school she would eat her hat. Daphne Hawkesworth, with strength and generosity, never laughed whenever I attempted a *pas de chat* in ballet class. The elegance and dedication of Bice Bellairs, who founded the school, was enough to inspire anyone. I worked very hard, attending as many classes as I could.

Being one of the oldest there, I knew I wasn't going to get another chance at training so I didn't want to waste a minute. Every day started with limbering exercises, they were a bit of a stretch, excuse the pun, but I soon saw the benefit. As well as the drama, dance and singing lessons, I enjoyed stage management classes with Derek Melotte, learning how to operate the lighting board, etc. but mainly how to build sets. I was rarely seen without a chisel or hammer about my person and because I was the recipient of the Stage Management Award in my first year, I can only assume it was really for woodwork! Enduring friendships were made. My best friend at drama school, Diana Marchment, took leave from acting for a number of years to devote time to her family but is now enjoying a successful comeback. Anthony Noel, another close friend, is now a deservedly celebrated landscape gardener. Other Guildford alumni not on the same course as me but now good friends include Bill Nighy and Celia Imrie.

While I was in the second year at drama school I was offered an audition with the peripatetic London Bubble Company, which toured the London boroughs in a big yellow tent performing a repertoire of three plays. John Judd, a talented mature actor, who'd been on the same course as me, had already joined the company and recommended me to the artistic director Glen Walford. I turned up for audition feeling rather apprehensive, for this was my first *ever* interview as a professional actress. It also meant that, if I were successful, I would be offered a provisional Equity card. Membership of Equity was hard to come by. In those days you had to have union membership to gain employment, and you had to have employment to gain union membership.

Catch 22. However, some companies were allowed to allocate two cards a year, but these were mostly used up at Christmas time when pantomimes were being cast. So to be auditioning in the spring with the opportunity of a card was quite rare.

The show Glen was casting was *The London Pub Show*, supporting the Campaign For Real Ale. There were to be eight actors. The character I was auditioning for was a young mini-skirted, Donny Osmond enthusiast, who talked too much. And the play was to be improvised. For my audition Glen told me to 'put the case' for the modern plastic makeover pub selling modern plastic makeover beer. In character. I knew there and then that I probably wouldn't get the job so there was no point in being nervous. I launched forth, praising the wonderful music, which was always too loud to hear yourself think, but of course perfect if you didn't want to think. Or couldn't think. And how great it was to be with so many people squashed in together because when you spilt your beer down your clothes nobody could notice it. And when you put your drink down on the bar and elbowed your way through to retrieve it, there were so many other drinks there you could take any one if you couldn't find your own. And you could do whatever you liked without fear of embarrassment because in a modern plastic makeover pub selling modern plastic makeover beer you never saw anyone you knew. And so on.

On the South Bank

12

I'M A PROFESSIONAL ACTRESS!

('*She might think she is!*' *says Mum*)

SEARCH ME! I GOT THE JOB. THE THREE PLAYS WERE *THE London Pub Show*, *Under Milk Wood* and a musical based on *Jack the Ripper* (I lie not). A sample lyric: 'What a star 'tis, what an artiste, what a pipper. An amazer with a razor, Jack the Ripper!' There was also a daytime children's show in which I played 'a lady with a bucket on her foot'. A taxing role, for during one performance 'the lady with a bucket on her foot' danced on a fallen tree trunk and accidentally disturbed a nest of bees. The bees were so incensed they got their own back by stinging several of the children watching. And 'the lady with a bucket on her foot'. Serves her right!

For *The London Pub Show* I had to perfect balancing a full pint of beer on my head while completely lowering myself to the floor, sliding along it, and retrieving a silk scarf with my teeth, which was balanced on a beer bottle some six feet away. Without spilling a drop. I managed it every performance, except one. Someone in the audience was laughing so hard it made me laugh and try as I might I couldn't stop the beer from wobbling over. What a mess it made all over the stage. Beer everywhere. But, of course, I had to attempt it again, but this time I had to crawl through a puddle of beer! It was even *more* nail-biting but there was a huge cheer when I stood up again with the scarf in my teeth, and the pint of beer still intact.

More recently, when I was promoting *Mrs Warren's Profession* in the West End, I was interviewed on *The Frank Skinner Show*. Imagine my horror when halfway through the interview he produced a full pint of beer and asked for a demonstration of the beer-balancing feat. I was gobsmacked. Apart from anything else I was wearing a very nice Escada suit and was reluctant to soak it in beer. Nor did I want to humiliate myself on national television. But I don't know what came over me because I threw caution to the wind and had a go. I couldn't do the whole thing, it would have taken too long, so I just lowered myself to my knees, but the look on Frank Skinner's face on seeing the beer precariously balanced on my head was priceless. I don't think even *he* thought I would attempt it! Imagine doing that while promoting the classics!

It was a blissful six months with the Bubble Theatre Company. I even got my brother Terry on stage one night to dance at the end of the show. While it was difficult to get him on the stage, it was even more difficult to get him off! It was a glorious summer, marred only by a monsoon during the last week. And it was at this venue that I eventually persuaded an agent to come and have a look at my work, with a view to representing me. The immaculately dressed Richard Jackson was the only agent to be so persuaded, the dreadful weather being sufficient to put the others off. I told him to meet me in the pub opposite

London Fields after the show and gave him directions on how to get there from the tent. Unfortunately, I hadn't reasoned that there would be no gate on that side of the park and when I found him thirty minutes after the show had ended, knee deep in mud, clinging to the railings, I felt sure my chances of representation were nil. I apologised profusely, but my mischievous sense of humour got the better of me, and a snigger accidentally slipped out, and then another, and then I couldn't help it, I laughed out loud. To my utter astonishment Richard started laughing too and attempted to climb over the railings. Not a good idea because of the spikes. Although he managed to propel himself to the other side unharmed, the spikes nearly took the pocket off his suit jacket. Despite all this, Richard told me how much he had enjoyed the evening and was very happy to take me on as his client and we often laughed about that evening. Richard and I got along very well and he represented me for a number of years.

My first job in a proper theatre, by that I mean a proscenium arch theatre, was directly after the Bubble. It was to play Spinning Jenny in *The Sleeping Beauty* at the Belgrade Theatre in Coventry, and the character was an accomplice to the wicked witch and had to sell a spinning wheel to the beauty. Again Glen Walford was the director, and for my audition I had to pretend an old chair was a spinning wheel. She told me to sell her the spinning wheel. I turned it upside down and described how the legs act as spindles to wrap the flax around. This particular spinning wheel was an antique and had no wheel attached and was therefore very rare and valuable but I could let it go at a bargain price. Instead of the wheel, the spinner was required to run around the chair pulling the flax until it was fine enough. The rungs at the back of the chair served to store the thread once it had been spun, each one holding a separate colour. This apparatus kept the spinner very fit and therefore removed the necessity for boring exercises on a tread mill. It was compact, portable and durable, and when not in use it could be turned upside down and used as a chair. I got the job. I tell you, if ever acting work dries up I think I'll get a job in sales.

Because pantomimes perform all over the Christmas period, with the exception of Christmas Day, there wasn't time for me to go home to Ramsgate. Instead I got a lift to London to my niece Valerie's house to see her new baby daughter Sarah. The weekend before I had also visited and my mum and Pam were there too. Val had several guests visiting to see the newly born Sarah, and we thought these guests were all rather well to do. Mum was making conversation with Laticia and Hermione, being careful to pronounce her aitches. We were all on tenterhooks in case she dropped a clanger and let a few expletives into the conversation. But she was getting on famously until she was overheard to say 'Ho yees. Hi think breastfeedin' is much better for the little chavvies. Hive always thought so. Hive sed as much to Velry, aint that right Vel? Bout breastfeedin'? Mind yew, when hi hed my Brenda she sucked so hard my tit come up like a pickled cabbage.'

It's a wonder the baby didn't choke on Val's breast. Pam had steam coming out of her ears with embarrassment, but Val and I are still laughing at that one.

When I returned to London I'd sometimes help out in Richard's office if I wasn't working elsewhere. And it was on one of these occasions that a casting call came through for Charles Wood's play *Prisoner and Escort* to be staged at lunchtime at the Open Space Theatre in Tottenham Court Road. Richard named several actresses for the role. After the call was over I tentatively asked Richard if I could be put forward to audition. He had only seen me play comedy roles at the Bubble and was initially reluctant to suggest me, but I insisted I wanted a chance to play in a drama. He agreed to call the director. By the time I got back to the office the next day after my audition, Richard was delighted for he'd already had a call offering me the role. I was so thrilled. And it was playing the woman in this play that landed me in Pseuds' Corner of the *Private Eye* magazine. Harold Hobson, the highly regarded theatre critic of the *Sunday Times*, wrote, on two consecutive Sundays, 'I would not have thought the words as simple as "I have never been to Birmingham before" could be so heartrending or such a revelation of loneliness as they are when spoken by Miss Blethyn.' Well, I had trouble saying the line after that because I'd been ribbed so much by the rest of the company. Despite the ribbing, I was thrilled to get such affirmation from Harold Hobson.

Getting the Open Space Theatre job proved extra provident because the casting director of the National Theatre, Annie Robinson, came to see a performance. She asked to meet me after the show and despite the fact that I spilt a cup of coffee over her, she invited me to come along to the National for an audition. They were casting a play to be included in a season at the ICA Theatre in The Mall. The play was *Bloody Neighbours* written by their resident writer Richard Crane. I was thrilled to learn that I had got the job provided I cleared one more hurdle. Everyone cast in the ICA season had to be involved in a production at the Old Vic Theatre in some way. Tony Harrison's *Phaedra Britannica* after Racine starring Diana Rigg was about to go into production and I was required to audition for the job of understudying Illona Linthwaite. A small part but nerve-racking none the less.

I was at a party at a friend's house when I heard that I'd been offered both jobs at the National Theatre – I was so excited that I jumped into their swimming pool fully clothed, and nearly all the other guests followed me! I couldn't believe it. The National Theatre!!

The first day of rehearsal came and I dressed up in my

smartest garb – high heels, a smart straight skirt, my hair pinned in a neat French pleat as befitted a serious professional actress in my view – and click-clacked up to the rehearsal room at the top of the Old Vic to find the voice coach Kate Fleming surrounded by my colleagues – barefooted and in loose practice clothes, doing breathing and voice exercises, stretching and pulling in, in, in and up, up, up and down, down, down. Let it all go!!! Shake yourself to the floor!!! I was mortified and tried to make as inconspicuous an entrance as possible but all eyes turned in my direction and I managed a feeble 'Good morning'. I thought it prudent to add 'Sorry I'm late', even though by my reckoning I was twenty minutes early. Kicking off my stilettos I joined in the voice class even though my tight skirt made the up, up, ups and down, down, downs a little restricted. I lost my neat French pleat on the second descent to the floor, and when the screaming, barefooted actress to the right of me trod on a couple of hairpins that had been flung loose I wanted the floor to open up and swallow me.

To make matters worse, when I returned from lunch, John Dexter, the director, who had a terrifying reputation, told me to come in, sit down and shut up. But oh how I loved watching the rehearsal. Diana Rigg was mesmerising. In fact, I thought everyone was wonderful and couldn't understand why John Dexter barked his many barbed comments at the actors. I was getting paid to watch all of this, memorise the moves created by my principal, and learn the lines ready for the Saturday morning understudy rehearsal. And try not to catch John Dexter's eye, which was invariably followed by a barb. Once when we were rehearsing at a theatre in Portugal Street, Diana Boddington, the legendary stage manager, passed in front of the stage close to Mr Dexter. He screamed, 'What the fuck is that stink.' Miss Boddington replied indignantly, giving as good as she got, 'If you don't mind Mr Dexter, it's my birthday and this fragrance happens to be a perfume that Miss Rigg has given me to mark the occasion.' 'No wonder she fuckin' gave it to you,' he hollered, 'It stinks!' Charming.

Mr Dexter never spoke to me directly, except for that first day, although our paths crossed frequently, until one day in the green room I was discussing an audition I had been to, which I felt I had no chance of passing, and he tapped me on my shoulder. Fearing another tongue lashing, I could only gape when he said, 'You might well get that, Brenda – there's nothing wrong with you girlie.'

Just before the end of my contract for *Phaedra Britannica* I was offered another understudying role together with a small walk-on part in Ben Travers' farce *Plunder*, and it was during its run that the National Theatre moved into its new home on the South Bank. Only the Lyttleton Theatre was ready for performance at this time. We were to wait another six months for the Olivier Theatre to open with a production of Marlowe's *Tamburlaine the Great*, starring Albert Finney. I was cast to play a vestal virgin amongst other things, and this production must hold the record for the longest rehearsal time – six months.

At this time, I was besotted with an actor/writer named Larry, whom I'd met while at the Open Space Theatre, and he was hot, hot, hot in the sexy department. In fact, he was much hotter than I knew because, during rehearsals for *Phaedra Britannica*, he mysteriously disappeared for a week. I thought he'd got fed up with me and had found another girlfriend, because whenever I phoned him I was always greeted with no reply. I was brokenhearted. Surprisingly, he then turned up with a broken foot and told me that he couldn't see me because he and a friend of his had been arrested, held in custody and accused of conspiracy to sell marijuana. I thought that was the most inventive excuse I had ever heard for ignoring me for a week! But when it dawned on me that he was actually telling the truth I was absolutely astonished. Marijuana? Yes. And it turned out to be quite a lot of it. The broken foot was sustained when apparently jumping from a first-floor window to avoid having his collar felt. The whole scenario seemed a little far-fetched for me to grasp, not knowing the ins and outs of the case, but as a long shot, Larry asked me if I would try to secure the services of John Mortimer QC to defend him. 'What? Rumpole of the Bailey? Are you sure? How am I supposed to do that?' Larry said reasonably, 'Brenda, you just ask him.' 'Oh, right. OK then,' I mumbled, 'there's no need to take that tone!' Fortunately for Larry, I was able to get my request through to Mr Mortimer via a friend of mine who was, once upon a time, a junior assistant at court and who knew him. Miracle of miracles, Mr Mortimer accepted the case and, when I told Larry, he was almost in tears of gratitude to him.

The trial was at the Old Bailey and I was called as a character witness the day after *Tamburlaine the Great* opened. Magnificent Mr Mortimer stood up in court and I was called to the dock. My knees were knocking with the drama of it all.

'Your name is Brenda Anne Blethyn. Is that correct?'

'Yes, sir.'

'And you are an actress. Is that correct?'

'Yes, sir.'

'And is it true that last night you opened in the play *Tamburlaine the Great* at the National Theatre to WONDERFUL notices this morning?'

'Yes, sir. But I only had one line.'

There was laughter and a smattering of applause from the gallery. Afterwards Mr Mortimer told me off. He said I was only to answer 'yes' or 'no' to questions put to me and not to volunteer any more information. However, he said that in this instance it probably did vouch for my honesty. Sadly, Larry was found guilty as charged, but because of mitigating circumstances he got a reduced one-year custodial sentence. The shock caused my legs to give way under me. It felt like I'd had a limb amputated. So God only knows what it felt like to Larry.

I was getting more and more work at the National Theatre, which was wonderful, and I was visiting Larry every fortnight in prison, which wasn't wonderful. It was so depressing. I couldn't understand how someone as talented and clever and, dare I say it, as *honest* as Larry could end up in that situation. Especially as, on the night that the crime was supposed to have taken place, my flatmates and I were throwing a party and Larry was there making savoury pancakes! He must have nipped out for some more eggs unnoticed. While I looked forward to seeing Larry, I hated everything else about the visits. The desperation, the suspicion, the handbag searching, the sadness. It was guaranteed to depress me, and I didn't want to be part of that scenario. But he had no one else. His parents were in Australia and couldn't visit, as much as they would like to have done. I persevered but, as the weeks and months passed, inevitably my affections turned elsewhere.

Mike and me at a picnic at Susan Fleetwood's house,
Stratford-upon-Avon

13

THE PASSION

I HAD BECOME FRIENDS WITH ONE OF THE NATIONAL'S TAL-
ented resident graphic designers, Michael Mayhew, who offered
to drive me to see Larry on occasion if I wanted him to, but it
wasn't necessary because I had recently been offered a regular lift
from the family of another inmate, and in any case my visits were
becoming less frequent as Larry's time was drawing to a close. I
became more and more fond of Michael, his wonderfully dry
sense of humour, his thick dark hair and smouldering Latin looks
were complimented by his great taste in clothes. Michael's best
friend, Sebastian Graham-Jones, was Bill Bryden's assistant,
which meant that when I joined Bill's company in the Cottesloe
Theatre, I saw more and more of Michael.

In the green room one evening, he was standing next to me at
the bar and said 'You hungry?' I thought he was talking to the
barmaid because that's who he was looking at. I was crestfallen.
After a rather long pause he said, 'Well – are you?' I looked sideways to see why she wasn't answering, and I nearly fainted when

I realised he was talking to me. Oh it was lovely. 'Yes,' I chirped, 'I am actually.'

'Fancy a curry?' said the smooth-talking Michael. And that was it, despite the fact that another chap gate-crashed the date and sat between us all evening. Shortly afterwards I moved in with Michael and his mother in St John's Wood. Sebastian's girlfriend was the wonderful actress Susan Fleetwood and the four of us became great friends, spending every birthday and New Year's Day together for many years. Sadly both Susan and Sebastian have now passed away.

It was a privilege working with Bill Bryden. I loved every minute of it. While the company was primarily male there was the occasional female, the only constant woman being Edna Dore, whose Mrs Noah was legendary. Myself and Dinah Stabb practically took turns at playing Mary Magdalene and other characters. While I played the role of the Virgin Mary, it was Dinah who came up with the idea of physically making the baby Jesus, in performance, using sheets of muslin. Fold upon fold of limp muslin was wrapped around a tiny bundle, which eventually created the swaddled infant. It was an ingenious idea and created a beautiful effect. Bill and his company became famous for their fantastic innovative Promenade Productions of Tony Harrison's York Mystery Plays: *The Nativity*, *The Passion* and *Doomsday*, and it was a huge thrill when all three plays were performed on the same day, morning, afternoon and evening. In the first production Mark McManus (Taggart on TV) played Jesus. It was an incredibly moving performance, his rugged workmanlike face suppressing the pain of persecution and crucifixion. When he was nailed to the cross, by the Carpenters Guild, it was done in a workmanlike way, just another day's work to the chippies. But when Jesus was hauled on to Mount Calvary amidst the promenade audience, it was awe inspiring, truly breathtaking. Nuns in the audience touched his robes as he passed by. Some people fell to their knees. Others sobbed openly. There were, of course, other actors who played the part after Mark McManus, and who were themselves wonderful, but it was Mark who truly inspired. We were all deeply shocked to hear of Mark's early death.

It was in *The Passion* when I was playing Mary Magdalene and Percula aka Mrs Pontius Pilate that I was forced to come out with a rather odd ad lib. Pontius Pilate was played by Robert Stephens. Our entrance to our first scene was along a gantry above the audience, Robert entering from one side and me the other, and we were supposed to meet in the middle. The lighting was beautifully subdued, flickering from cheese-graters and braziers and other kitchen implements suspended from the ceiling. I got to the centre of the gantry to start the scene but Robert wasn't there. So to prevent the production coming to a grinding halt, I thought I'd better do his speech for him. Instead of 'Lo, Pilate am I', I said 'Lo, Pilate *lives here*, proved Prince of Great Pride. He was put into Pontius the people to press then Caesar himself, with senators by side, remitted him to these realms, all ranks to redress.'

Then I continued with my own speech.

I am Dame Precious Percula of Princesses the Prize,
Wife to Sir Pilate *who lives here*, Prince without peer.
All well of all womanhood am I, witty and wise
Conceive now my countenance so comely and clear.

After this section we were supposed to start canoodling but I couldn't do that on my own, could I? And since Robert was still not there I had to own up. I turned to the audience and apologised, saying, 'I'm terribly sorry but I'm afraid my Pilot's gone out!' There was a round of applause and laughter from the audience and also from Jack Shepherd who was waiting for his cue to come on as a *brilliant* Judas Escariot, and it was only then that I realised what I'd just said. At that point, on stumbled Robert who explained that his cloak had got caught on his dressing-room door knob. I simply asked the audience if we should start the scene again and to their delight we did so.

Despite the disastrous production of Thomas Bernhard's *The Force of Habit* in 1976 set in a ringmaster's trailer, where he, myself (a tightrop walker), a clown, a juggler and a lion-tamer attempted to play Schubert's Trout Quintet, despite the final note from our director the night before press night saying 'try it differently', and despite Michael Billington's review in the *Guardian*, 'and Miss Blethyn's buttocks in her pink tights wobbled like two plates of warring blancmange', I *was* offered more work.

My big break came in 1977 when Kate Nelligan left the production of Odon von Horvath's *Tales from the Vienna Woods*. The run had been extended for six weeks but she was already committed to another job. I was playing a small part in the production, that of a hat-check girl and a dancer, and when the time came to recast, they naturally wanted another 'name' to take over the role. But Ken Mackintosh the staff director at the time was my champion and implored Peter Hall to come and watch a run-through with me playing the role. Peter did come to see a rehearsal and I was offered the part. I couldn't believe my luck. A leading role at the National Theatre! Kate wrote me a very lovely note wishing me well. Mum and Dad particularly loved this production, with the Strauss waltz and lovely costumes, and me, of course, playing a leading part, but for Dad it was mainly because Elizabeth Spriggs was in it. He was enchanted by her. Mum said he'd be enchanted for ever more if he mentioned her name one more time! With every production thereafter Dad asked if Liz Spriggs was in it and Mum would tease him mercilessly. Because the National was a repertory theatre I was also in other productions.

In 1978 Peter Wood cast me as the maid in Ferenc Molnar's *The Guardsman* alongside Diana Rigg and Richard Johnson. I loved playing this role. Peter is such a dazzling, exciting director and I've enjoyed every single production of his I've been in and seen. I believe I learnt more from Peter Wood than any other director. I've worked with him seven times since. He told me that if I stood on stage for a couple of hours and did absolutely nothing it wouldn't be boring. He really made me feel I had something to offer. The play is the story of a husband testing his wife's fidelity by disguising himself as a guardsman and wooing her. Of course, it backfires. Lisa, my character, had very little to say, but I believed there was another story going on in her head insomuch as I thought her to be in innocent love with the man of the house. So when he returned to the marital home at the start of Act 2 my character was so happy and excited, she burst into tears of joy until (misunderstanding the situation) she remembered that he had been cuckolded by his wife and was then instantly reduced to tears of despair. We got a round of applause after that scene at every performance. And as a reward Peter bought me a bottle of champagne.

Also in this production was the incredible actress Madelaine Thomas. She was ninety-one years old and playing the house-keeper. On her way home from work one night she was knocked over by a motorcyclist and ended up in hospital. I went to visit her and although she was hurt she was more concerned about her false teeth, which she said she had left in her dressing room. I reassured her that nobody would pinch them but she wasn't having any of it. She dispatched me back to the National Theatre to retrieve them. Imagine how difficult it was to persuade the security guard to let me into someone else's dressing room to get a set of false teeth. The biggest surprise of all, though, was Madelaine returning to the production when she recovered.

Other plays with Peter Wood include *Dalliance* (Arthur Schnitzler), *The Double Dealer* (William Congreve), (stage and television) *The Provok'd* Wife (John Vanbrugh), *The Beaux' Stratagem* (George Farquhar), and *The Bed Before Yesterday* (Ben Travers) at the Almeida Theatre. Peter's wit was as sharp as a razor, and just as cutting, and it was no fun being the recipient of one of his acid comments. Although I did notice that whenever I was the recipient of a barb it was usually accompanied by a cuddle, which did soften the blow. During the run of *Double Dealer*, Peter called a full company rehearsal. The reason he said was in order to take out all of Brenda Blethyn's improvements. If I hadn't found the comment to be so hysterically funny I should have been inconsolably embarrassed.

Another time he phoned me in the middle of the night and asked if I would like to play Madamoiselle in his production of *The Provok'd Wife*. I declined, telling him that I didn't speak French well enough to be able to pull it off. But Peter told me that he had asked Tom Stoppard to write another scene in which it would be revealed that Madamoiselle wasn't French at all, it was all just an affectation of Lady Fancyfull to have a *French* lady companion. He said I could do it standing on my head. Oh well, if Peter was that confident in me perhaps it would be fun. Dorothy Tutin was cast as Lady Fancyfull, Michael Kitchen as a suitor, Geraldine McEwan as Lady Brute, the Provok'd Wife, and John Wood as her husband. Dorothy and I were the subplot and as such didn't get as much rehearsal as those in the main thrust of the story. We were as paranoid as each other, and each thought ourselves useless. On top of which, the final scene was set on a frozen River Thames and we were ice skating. We were in fact roller skating but the dry ice hovering over the surface of the

148

stage disguised the fact. Dorothy fell over several times, and each time I would skate on to pick her up. The men in the cast didn't get their capes to wear until the first performance, which meant they had never worn capes and skates at the same time. When we got to the last scene, on the River Thames, they found it was not a good combination as every single actor skated up his cloak and fell over. But most embarrassing of all was the fact that, in production week, Peter decided the play was too long, and guess which scene got cut? The scene revealing that Madamoiselle wasn't French at all. Oh lord! My accent was so bad the stage-hands loved it, and would leave their pints of beer unfinished in the green room to come and watch from the wings. They thought it hilarious. I'm glad someone did! *Mon deux*!! To add insult to injury, the last date of the tour was playing L'Odeon in Paris. When Madamoiselle, observing a lovers' tiff between Dorothy Tutin and Michael Kitchen's characters, said as an aside to the audience, '*Est ce que en fait l'amour en Angleterre comme ça?*', meaning 'Is this the way you make love in England?', there was such a resounding 'tutt' from the audience that all three of us were obliged to turn upstage for fear of corpsing. I've never been so pleased to finish a job as that one.

On another occasion, while rehearsing *The Beaux' Stratagem*, Peter got a bee in his bonnet about one of the actors' voice training and he asked the actor if he had attended drama school.

'Yes,' he replied, 'RADA.'

'Good heavens,' said Peter, 'didn't they have voice classes?'

'Yes, of course, they did,' replied the actor.

'Well, why didn't you go to any?' quipped Peter.

The thing about Peter, unfortunately, is that he is always very funny when he's making some poor creature cringe.

Peter then announced to the assembled cast that the actor would have to go to voice classes every day before rehearsal to learn the importance of breathing properly and of 'carrying a thought right to the end of the line'. It was so embarrassing for the poor chap and the rest of us couldn't see what the problem was at all, he was giving an excellent performance. Actually, I think Peter thought he was too.

Before opening at the Lyttleton Theatre, the production did a short tour of the country. While we were at Oxford, Peter came up from London to watch one of the performances. Unfortunately our hapless actor did *not* turn up for the performance and his understudy was thrust on at a few minutes' notice. Before the next day's matinee, Peter called yet another company meeting to see what this actor had to say for himself.

'Why didn't you turn up for yesterday's performance?'

'I'm so sorry,' he stuttered, 'I'm not familiar with the area and I got on the wrong train.'

'You got on the wrong train?' seethed Peter. 'Why didn't you get off the wrong train?'

The boy had had enough. 'Well Peter, I finally decided to take your advice and went right through to the end of the line!'

Peter exploded, not with anger but with mirth. He thought that was one of the best comeback lines he'd ever heard. To his credit he bought the actor a bottle of champagne, or so I'm told. I'd like to believe he *did* buy him one.

Louisa Kathleen

Mum and dad at Aunt Lil's Christmas party

My first solo photo shoot, aged three

The usual suspects.
Back row, from left:
Brian, Jean, Bill
Front row:
Terry, me, Martin

I'll grow into my school blazer

My school production of
The School for Scandal.
Guess which one is me?

Dad waxes lyrical at my wedding reception.
From left: Bill, his son Danton held by sister Pam,
Dad, Alan's cousin Carol, his father, and Terry

Off on honeymoon
to Poole in Dorset
with Alan

*British Rail Euston Players' Amateur Production
of* Double Trouble *with John Ahern*

*My first professional photo
shoot. The photos were used
to send to casting agents and
theatre directors*

La Pucelle wielding her sword. I'd give her a wide berth if I were you...

My surprise 40th birthday party

Me, Pam and Mum about to do some weeding at my end of terrace house which needed doing up

Mum does the inspection. Excellent. At Ease. Mind the ceiling!

Michael needed a beer after visiting Reno!

2/6/91
Dearest Brenda,
Much love
and happy
tea party
to you,
Lynne

Director Lynne Meadow with the cast of Absent Friends.
Back row, from left: Lynne, John Curless, Gillian Anderson,
David Purdham. Front row: Ellen Parker, Peter Frechette, me

Robert Redford directing the picnic scene in
A River Runs Through It

Chop chop. Love you darling, ok fair enough. The cast of Outside Edge

Having a quick cuddle with Jude Law. One of the perks of the job

'All Tense Who?' As Cynthia in Secrets and Lies

Does gorgeous Nicolas Cage suspect?

Mike Leigh, Simon Channing-Williams
and me having won at Cannes

Off to the Oscar ceremony with
Marianne Jean Baptiste and
Mike Leigh

Queen for a night I was! With Michael Caine in Little Voice

Tomorrow I shall buy Michael one of those shirts

Aunt Fran told me to include a picture of when the Queen gave me the B.O. So here we are at Buckingham Palace

With Craig Ferguson in Saving Grace. *He's Scottish!*

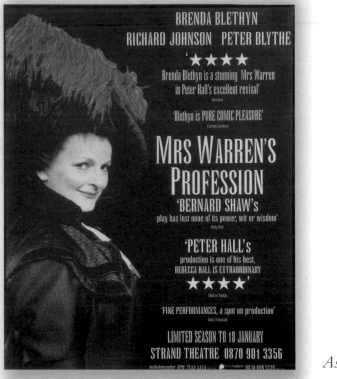

As Mrs Warren

A bundle of Bennetts. Me, Rosamund Pike, Carey Mulligan, Talulah Riley, Keira Knightley, Jena Malone

*Completing my first
London Marathon. Where's
the hospitality room?*

*In 2005, Jeannie
and Herb came home
for a visit.
From left:
Terry, Jeannie, Brian,
Bill and me*

Posing for photographer
Andy Gott's wonderful book Degrees

Georgina Hale, me and Patti Love in *Steaming*

14

ONWARDS AND UPWARDS

W HILE WORKING AT THE NATIONAL I WAS OFFERED MY
first TV film role in a BBC Play for Today. It was Ian McEwan's
The Imitation Game, with Harriet Walter and directed by Richard
Eyre. It was also Harriet's first television film. Coincidentally, the
next time we both worked together was in 2006 on another Ian
McEwan project, *Atonement*, directed by Joe Wright. Maybe we
both have a 1930s/40s look about us. *The Imitation Game* was set
at Bletchley during the Second World War, and most of the
female characters were members of the ATS and engaged in
taking down coded enemy messages intercepted on the airwaves
for the men to decipher. Harriet's character, strictly against all
the rules, decided to have a little go at deciphering herself. But
she didn't get away with it, all the worse for her being a disobe-
dient woman in a man's world. Dear oh dear. While filming it
was cold and drizzly, making the itchy, damp, khaki woollen uniforms and the gas masks almost unbearable to wear. And we
were only wearing them for about five weeks. Imagine wearing

them for five years! Come to think of it, it was probably worse when it was hot.

The process of working was quite different to what I was used to. In theatre, of course, you have the luxury of rehearsal, and the story is told chronologically, and the audience sees the whole action, all the time. Working on film affords very little rehearsal, if any, and is shot in location order and lighting state order, i.e. day or night. Plus more natural projection is called for. It took a little while for me to get used to this new way of working. Learning not to overlap speech during a close-up, for example. I couldn't understand, when every other shot of the same scene had been overlapped, why the close-up shot shouldn't be. Or even when I did understand, I'd forget! Basically it's down to those *not* on camera not to overlap. In fact, I'm only just getting the hang of it now!

In 1980 I was invited to meet Mike Leigh who was making a film for BBC 2 Playhouse. I'd never heard of him before but my agent at the time said it was the best job I had ever been offered. I said, 'Oh great, let's read the script.'

'Oh, for goodness' sake,' he said. 'Where've you been? There is no script. It's all improvised!'

'Oh!'

I met Mike at the BBC and for my audition I had to play out a little improvised scene while he observed from a discreet distance. He offered me the job. It was a three-month engagement to be rehearsed and filmed entirely in Canterbury, just round the corner from where my brother Brian lived. The film was eventually called *Grown-Ups*.

Part of the attraction for me was that in being so close to home I thought I'd be able to get to see my family, but because of the long working hours and I hadn't yet learnt to drive that didn't turn out to be the case. But I made sure I got to Ramsgate when towards the end of the engagement my sister Pam shocked us all, and herself, by having a heart attack. She was fifty-five. She was nursed by Val, who fortunately lived nearby in Folkestone, and thank God she slowly recovered.

But even if I hadn't had this distraction I would still have been overlapping. Mike Leigh's patience wore a little thin with me on one scene. Overlap, overlap, overlap. 'Stop overlapping!' I was concentrating so hard on getting the performance right, even when off camera, that I forgot the rules, that is if I ever understood them. But it all worked out in the end. The story is of a young couple, Dick and Mandy, who move from a council estate into their own council house, which happens to be next door to the private house of two of their old teachers, Mr and Mrs Butcher. There is no love lost between the two houses. Mandy has a lonely older sister Gloria, me, who visits relentlessly, until they get so fed up with her that Dick ejects her from the house, whereupon Gloria runs next door to Mr and Mrs Butcher for protection, and the two households are forced to interact. It's a very funny film, and I've lost count of the times people have quoted lines from it to me. Unfortunately, I was unable to accept an invitation from a family in Essex who invited me to their home for one of their monthly re-enactments of Grown-Ups. However, they did send me photographs of the whole family dressed up as the characters. They were wonderful. And once in the crush of Harrods' sale, a shopper said to me, 'Mind my kidneys, Mandy. Go pushin' people. Lucky I'm not expecting!' Gloria's lines from the film.

Almost immediately after Grown-Ups, Stratford East Theatre sent me a copy of the play Steaming by Nell Dunn. I wasn't at all sure it would be allowed to be staged, prude that I was. Steaming is set in a municipal Turkish bath in the East End of London on ladies' night. The language of the leading character is full of expletives and very colourful to say the least, and she describes in minute detail her sexual exploits of the night before. She is hilarious. The cast consists of six women and one man, whom we only see fleetingly. Five of the ladies are regulars and, on the night in question, a newcomer arrives for a bath. The steam rooms were situated at the back of the stage, and in the centre of the stage was a huge plunge pool. A thick heavy rope was suspended from the ceiling so the bathers could swing into the pool. Downstage were a couple of cubicles for those ladies who desired privacy to change, and also several loungers for those who didn't. Our production starred a terrific Georgina Hale as the central character Josie. Other characters were Mrs Meadow, an elderly working-class lady with the weight of all the problems of the East End on her shoulders, and her daughter Dawn – the character I was to play. Dawn has learning difficulties, a sweet tooth, a tendency towards obesity, and an overdeveloped sense of her own sexuality. (When my agent pointed out to the producers that I only weighed 120 pounds it didn't seem to bother anyone.) The bath attendant, Violet, was the salt of the earth, and there were two middle-class characters, one a relative newcomer and the other a total newcomer. There were scenes of total nudity.

I wasn't sure whether to accept this role or not. I loved Dawn, the character I was asked to play. But when I asked Michael to read it, he loved the play but wasn't sure about the part of Dawn, for he felt she wasn't as well drawn as the other characters and had very little to say. But I thought the character had such a wonderful presence and I felt she had a great journey during the course of the evening.

So adding it all up, I decided to do it. Maria Charles played Dawn's mother, and we had a great working relationship. She wouldn't let Dawn show her naked body, and instead made her wear vest and knickers, plastic trousers, plastic raincoat, flip flops and a shower cap the whole time, reasoning that Dawn would lose more weight that way. Dawn loved coming to the baths each week because she loved to hear about Josie's sexual exploits. Stuart Harwood was the male attendant, who we only ever saw through the frosted glass of the door.

The production was directed by Roger Smith. In the third scene, Dawn is suddenly liberated and decides enough is enough, and when her mother is taking a nap in her cubicle, she strips naked, except for her shower cap and flip flops, and walks around as if she was born to it, serving a Chinese takeaway for the other girls.

Of course, there came the point in rehearsal when we had to take a deep breath and strip off. All the characters were required to do so, except Mrs Meadow and Violet. We'd had two weeks rehearsal without anybody being naked but now we were almost at the end of the third week, and it had to be done. I was the first to throw caution to the wind. It felt very strange to be naked in the small confines of the rehearsal room and I have to say it was much easier once we were on the stage. The play is a drama about the plights of all the characters and the fight to save the baths from closure, and because we rehearsed with no onlookers, we didn't know how it would be received. Also, we didn't have a plunge pool in the rehearsal room and couldn't rehearse with that until we got in the theatre. It would be accurate to say that the water in the pool had had the chill taken off, it certainly wasn't warm, and at the end of the play we all had to leap into it. But for one week during the run, in the winter, the pump malfunctioned and we had to jump into freezing cold water. Fortunately, it was just before curtain call and we were immediately wrapped in warm gowns to take our bow. Although the play was a drama, we all knew that it was also very funny, but would the audience find it so?

We needn't have worried. It was a HUGE success, with sell-out performances at Stratford East. Sometimes the audience would heckle, they were enjoying it so much, but it somehow added to the ambience of the production and the theatre. I read somewhere that sitting *quietly* in the theatre is a modern phenomenon. After the successful run at the Stratford East Theatre, the production transferred to the Comedy Theatre in the West End. I'm someone who absolutely hates being late for anything. I take after Mum and Dad on that score. If they were going anywhere special they'd get ready the day before! Anyway, as far as work is concerned, I always like to get to my dressing room nice and early. All actors are required to be at the theatre half an hour before curtain-up. In the theatre world that means thirty-five minutes. And everyone has to sign in at the stage door. But I like to be there at least an hour before curtain-up because it's a little quieter and I can check my props, costume and so on, and arrange my make-up ready for application. On one matinee day at the Comedy Theatre, I had done all of the above and then realised I was hungry. So I popped out for a sandwich, and *forgot to go back*. I thought it would be rather nice to go up Regent Street and buy a pair of plus fours. Why? Can you imagine the consternation back at the theatre at the half-hour call.

'Where's Brenda?'

'Oh, it's okay, she's here, I've seen her.'

And then at the fifteen-minute call. 'Well, WHERE is she?' demands the company manager.

'She is definitely here. She's signed in, I've spoken to her,' says the stage-door man.

And at the five-minute call, 'Get the understudy ready and send a search party out for Brenda.'

My goodness, my poor understudy, she went on at a moment's

notice. And I heard that she was wonderful, so I made sure I didn't do that again in a hurry! The search party found me strolling across Piccadilly Circus swinging my bag of purchases. They said, 'Brenda, you've missed curtain-up!' I said, 'What curtain-up?' and after a few moments' reflection I realised what had happened and burst into tears. When I got back to the theatre, the concerned producers were very glad to see that I wasn't injured in any way, and advised me to lie down in the fireman's office for the duration of the show. It took me ten minutes to work that one out! Of course, the reason was that my understudy was using my dressing room.

My Mum and Dad came to see the production in Stratford East, and I hadn't told them about the nudity. All they knew was that it was set in a municipal bathhouse and was very funny. Mum used to work in a bathhouse and so did Pam. The night my mum and dad were in, the audience was spectacularly good. They were screaming with laughter, and when I met Mum and Dad in the bar afterwards, Dad was leaning on his walking stick and I could see him wiping his eyes, facing the wall. 'Oh my God,' I thought, 'Dad is really upset.' Mum had her arm around him. Oh well, I thought, I had better face the music. When I got closer I could hear him saying, 'and what about when that other one said about . . .' and they were both crying with laughter. Dad was finding it difficult to stand up straight. They loved it. And they loved me. They asked to come again when it was in the West End. I was delighted to invite them again.

However, *Steaming* wasn't the first time they'd seen me naked on stage. In one scene of *Tales from the Vienna Woods* at the National Theatre I had to strip off and strike a pose in a tableau. But on that occasion I was covered in white make-up and held two huge fans to cover my nakedness.

While performing in *Steaming* and after the reviews had come out, I had a letter from a lady who was outraged. She had seen a review with the word 'stripper' in it, and had assumed the play to be immoral. Her name was Mrs Blethyn. She asked me how someone who was a stripper came by the name of Blethyn and how dare I use it! I told her I probably came by it in the same way as she herself had done – by marriage. I also explained that the play was not immoral, it was about the struggle of ordinary women to stop a vital service in their community being lost, women versus the council, and I would welcome her as my guest if she wished to see it. I can't remember whether she came or not but I do remember having a very nice letter back from her.

My understudy was contracted to play my part in *Steaming* for one week while I was recording a play for the BBC. I continued performing at the theatre while I was rehearsing at the BBC, but when we went into the studio to record I was needed in the evenings as well. The play was *Henry VI Part One* and I played La Pucelle (Joan of Arc). It was great to be swashbuckling by day, and steam-bathing by night. But there was one unfortunate incident that happened while performing a sword fight with the Dauphin of France. And we weren't using pretend swords. No, they were great heavy things. The previous scene had been a Cathedral scene when huge lighted candles were carried, dripping wax on to the wooden floor of the studio, so when we came to our well-choreographed fight, our *fast* well-choreographed fight, I stepped on to the wax and my foot shot away in front of me. This meant I couldn't go into my next choreographed move. Unfortunately, the Dauphin of France could, and walked straight into the end of my sword. Or rather his eye did. I sliced off all of his eyelashes and nicked his eyelid. The place looked like an abattoir. It's a miracle I didn't take his eye out. I think I was more upset than he was. He was taken to hospital, and blow me down if he didn't return to finish the scene. There's dedication. But he was shaken, and so was I, and I was very glad not to have a performance at the theatre to go to.

Steaming won the best comedy in the Society of West End Theatre Awards, and I was lucky enough to win best supporting actress in the awards hosted by Cinzano. And after nine months when we left the production, it was recast, and then recast again.

With Mum and Dad in 1977 – love the wallpaper!

15

LOSING DAD, FINDING MUM

IT WAS TIME FOR A HOLIDAY AND I DECIDED TO VISIT MY sister Jeannie in Florida and I invited Pam to come with me if she was up to it. She was more than up to it. She was now fully recovered from her heart attack but we were all treading very carefully around her. However, she was determined to have a good time on holiday. We'd spend days on the lovely deserted white sandy beaches with picnics of salad and champagne and frolic in the surf like film stars. We kept reciting the phrase 'Drink don't bother me!' We had to put a stop to that after a while though, not because we thought Pam was getting tired, but because Jeannie and I were. On one of the evenings of the holiday, all three of us went to a music bar and settled into a booth for the evening to enjoy the music and to watch couples doing the Boston two-step, and maybe a little line dancing. It was fun. After a drink or two Jeannie and I went to the restroom and told Pam not to venture from the booth unless one of us was with her. Imagine our dismay when we returned to find the booth empty and Pam nowhere in sight. Naturally, we were worried. Where could she have gone? We'd only been away for five minutes and we certainly hadn't passed her on the way back from the restroom. We thought perhaps she had gone outside for some fresh air. We scoured the car park but there was no sign of her. Maybe we should look again inside and check under the tables in case she'd fallen. It was difficult to get to the other side of the bar because of intense activity on the dance floor, where a crowd had formed to watch some kind of display. Jeannie and I nearly dropped dead when we saw Pam tossed to the ceiling in the centre of the circle. She was giving a spectacular jitterbugging display with a very rugged cowboy and having the time of her life. We were speechless. Boy could she jitterbug! We just stood and watched (not with concern but with envy more than anything else) with our mouths hanging wide open. It was a great holiday.

On my return I discovered that Michael Mills, who was casting a new sitcom called *Chance in a Million* with Simon Callow, had been to see *Steaming* and had offered me the female leading part. Remarkably, this is the job I am most remembered for. I can be walking along a quiet lane in Greece, or hiking through the outback in Australia, or visiting caves in Montana, and I'll hear, 'Excuse me, miss, are you Miss Blethyn? We loved that series you did with the guy with the curly hair, that's him, Simon Callow. It was hilarious. What was that called?' '*Chance in a Million*,' I remind them. I think it must have been shown recently on Sky or cable or something, because people are still saying it. Sometimes if I jump in a taxi and say something as simple as 'Waterloo, please' the driver looks into his rear-view mirror and says '*Chance in a Million*! Recognised your voice, dahlin'.'

Our sprightly director Michael Mills was of the old school. He knew everything and everyone. He directed *Some Mothers Do*

'Ave 'Em starring Michael Crawford. I think he must have been ex-navy for at rehearsals and recordings he wore a duffle coat and looked as though he was conducting operations from the bridge of a ship.

'Ahoy there, Simon,' he signalled one day, and gave Simon a walking cane containing two small glasses and a phial of whisky for our use on some of those cold nights filming, but by contrast told one of the supporting artistes to climb up a tree, and on 'Action' to jump out.

'I can't do that,' she said, 'I'll tear myself to shreds.'

'Oh get on with it,' said Michael.

And she did, and she didn't (tear herself to shreds) and she was great.

It was such fun making *Chance in a Million* with Simon. The combination of his intellect, sense of humour and booming laugh was intoxicating. (Literally, when you think of the secret compartment in Simon's cane.) He made my mum and dad very welcome when they came to Thames Television Studios to watch the recording of one of the episodes. The show was successful and a further two series were recorded.

Having made a few appearances on TV, I began to be recognised. One day I was pegging out my washing and my next-door neighbour hung out of the upstairs window and said, 'Oh Brenda, Reg reckons he saw you on the television last night. Is that right? I've told him he's going senile.'

I had never discussed my job with my neighbours, and as they weren't theatregoers, there's no way they could have known.

I said, 'Yes, Gwen, he might have done. Yes', as I pegged up the last of Michael's socks.

'Getaway!' said Gwen and then hollered, 'What was the name of that programme, Reg?'

And from the other room, '*Grown-Ups* or summink.'

'*Grown-Ups*. That was it. Was that you?'

'Yes,' I said, beginning to glow with pride.

'YEAH THAT WAS HER, REG,' she hollered. 'Well I never! We turned it off. Couldn't stand your voice.'

She shut the window and they both emigrated to Australia.

Another neighbour called over the garden wall urgently, 'Excuse me. Excuse me.'

Stopping what I was doing immediately I ran over to her.

'My husband reckons he's seen you on the television,' she accused. 'Is that right?'

'Well,' I said, slightly taken aback. 'He might have done. I have made a couple of programmes.'

'Yeah?' She looked doubtful.

'Yes. Not many. Just one or two,' I said, playing it down a bit.

'Well I never. What you doing living there then?' she said and nodded towards my end-of-terrace, turn-of-the-century house that needed doing up.

'What on earth do you mean?' I asked.

'Well, I thought your types had butlers and chauffeurs and things,' she said. 'You've even got to do your own washing! You sure you're on the tele?'

'Only now and again,' I reiterated.

'Well, never mind dear. Never mind,' she said, sounding a little disappointed, and went back indoors.

In the supermarket I'd wonder why people were staring at me, or nudging one another. At first I thought I was being followed by plain clothes security. I asked Michael why they were staring at me, and he said they were probably wondering why I kept looking at them! Or more probably, they recognised me from *Chance in a Million*.

'Oh yes, maybe that's it,' I thought, wishing I'd combed my hair.

When the second series was transmitted, Dad was in hospital with a fractured hip, and asked for his bed to be wheeled up to the television so he could watch his daughter. He told me that other patients had asked for the same treatment. Not good news for one patient who was a Simon Callow fan, and who was in very great danger of bursting his stitches. But Dad loved a good laugh, and he maintained that laughter was the very best of medicines for any ailment. Although his hip mended and Dad went home, for the next couple of years he was still feeling somewhat under the weather. He was convinced that he had leukaemia, and loads of tests were carried out.

In 1985, I returned to the National Theatre for a revival of the Mystery Plays in the Cottesloe, and on 9 January, I received a 1 a.m. telephone call. Michael answered the phone and before he even broke the news I cried out 'Oh no!! Please, not my dad!' He didn't have to say anything and just gave me a cuddle as I sobbed uncontrollably. I couldn't believe it. My father was dead.

Only a week earlier Dad had been in hospital being treated for anaemia. I had wanted to go to see him, but the weather was treacherous and everyone warned against travelling in such conditions. Besides, the hospital had told us that it wasn't necessary to hazard the journey because Dad was not critical and that he could return home soon. Oh why did I listen? The weather was still very bad but I dressed straight away and got the very earliest train I could to Ramsgate. By the time I arrived Dad's body had already been taken away in the ambulance. I'll never forget the sight of my mother when I walked into the living room. Most of the family were gathered and my mother sat motionless on a chair in front of the fire, turned slightly sideways, her hands loosely clasped around her knee, and her face almost devoid of expression. An emptiness. As if the world was going on without her. She had been with my father for more than sixty years. The house was so cold. How could that be so. We were all successful people, how could their house have been so cold? It was cold because it was January, it was snowing, and despite the many times we offered to install some kind of central heating they firmly declined. Dad said it was a waste of money and got quite cross about it. Mum didn't want it either. They both hated the idea. They spent most of their time in the downstairs living room where they insisted there was a perfectly adequate coal fire to keep them warm enough, and neither of them liked a warm bedroom. And after all those years at the Plains of Waterloo with the bedroom window wide open come rain, snow or hail, they had got used to it. However, on this cold sad morning in January we wondered if we should have insisted.

While Dad was ill he'd slept in the small front downstairs room of the house, which had a two-bar electric fire in the corner. Mum, who slept upstairs, had heard Dad call out for her, but when she went downstairs she found him already dead. He had been reaching out for something for his body was half in and half out of the bed. Mum called Pam immediately and Pam rang the rest of the family. Later that same day Mum went to stay with my brother Brian and his family in Canterbury and she never again returned to the house.

The funeral was the following week and in the morning I went to pay my last respects to my dad in the chapel of rest. I had never seen a dead body before and I was struck by how vacant it was. Dad's spirit had risen from his body, and confirmed me in my belief that the spirit lives on. I kissed him. I became obsessed with the fact that, when the lid went on the coffin, his face would be too near to it, but Pam reassured me that they would first exchange the big pillow under his head for a smaller one. The

168

snow was deep and the procession slow. Dad used to say 'Happy is the bride that the sun shines on' and 'Happy is the corpse the snow falls on.' As the procession entered the drive up to the cemetery, the hearse started to skid on the ice. Not being a main thoroughfare the road hadn't been gritted. Once upon a time it would have been Dad's job to grit the roads. He often went out with the snowplough to clear the roads for the council, so he would have had something to say about that! During the war his job was to clear the runway at Manston of snow and ice. He told us graphic hair-raising tales of having to run for cover as the enemy planes bombed the airfield.

We had to get out of the cars and walk. While we were helping the elderly amongst us to cross the icy path, Michael and Valerie helped to push the hearse up the slight incline to the cemetery gates. Dad would have been saying, 'No, gawd no, don't you get out in the cold, slippin' and slidin'. Leave me 'ere! Get back in the warm of the car. Crikey ay!!' Their feet were slipping as much as the hearse but somehow they got it up the slope. Once at the top we all climbed back in for the short drive to Dad's plot.

I had never been to a burial before and, apart from our hearts breaking, there was an eerie beauty to it. Everything and everywhere was white except for us mourners all clad in black. Everyone was very mindful of my mother. She was such a vital, strong woman living in a tiny, frail body. She loved having her family around her en masse. If only it were happier circumstances. However, hilarity set in even before we reached the wake at the San Clu Hotel. We were all sobbing in the limousine as it very slowly slipped and skidded its way up icy Victoria Hill, until someone said, 'Come on, hurry up, someone will get there first and grab the cream horn.' I think Martin said it.

We roared with laughter. Mum too. Anyone would think we'd been on a pub outing the way we rolled out of the car.

There were lots of people at Dad's funeral, he was considered a gentle, wise, and good man. I had to leave the wake a little earlier than the rest of my family because I had a performance of *Doomsday*, appropriately, at the National Theatre. Dad would have been horrified to think I had missed a performance. Believe it or not there was a funeral procession in the play. It was Mary's funeral. And, accompanied by John Tams' triumphant music, the followers morris danced behind the coffin, and as Mary was symbolically laid to rest, the coffin burst open and a joyful Mary emerged from it and entered into the Kingdom of Heaven. I can't tell you how happy it made me feel on this saddest of days. I rather wished the whole family could have come to it, and perhaps they might have done, had the weather been more fit for travel. It would have been worth it just to see them all doing the morris dance!

A few weeks later, the council announced that they had found Mum a comfortable little flat on the east cliff. She still couldn't bear to return to her house in Nixon Avenue and so my brothers emptied the house for her. Neither did she warm to the idea of us all clubbing together to buy her a little flat. She found the idea rather irritating for some reason and said she simply wanted the council house exchanged for a small council flat. She insisted she wanted independence. Therefore, my brother Brian and his wife Pat completely repainted and redecorated the flat for her and put in new carpets. And ironically, with the installation of efficient flick-of-the-switch heating appliances, Mum very soon got used to them and liked them. Fortunately the flat was situated closer to town and within easy walking distance of the shops and cliff top and didn't seem as remote as the house. It was even close to the Granville Hotel where she could go for a

Guinness if she felt like a little company. She knew a few people who went there for a quiet drink. Eight years later, when Mum died, my cousin Noreen told me that they had loved to see Mum at the Granville not least because she had an endless supply of jokes to tell them. God knows where she got them all from. My brother Brian takes after Mum in that respect.

'Hello Brian, I haven't seen you for ages!'

'Hallo Bren, lovely to see you. Did you read about that bloke who went into the butcher's and asked for a pound of kiddle-eyes?'

'No Brian, I didn't. What happened?'

'The butcher said, "Don't you mean kidneys?" And the bloke said, "That's what I said diddle-eye."'

In 1986 I made another series of *Chance in a Million,* and rehearsals of one episode coincided with my fortieth birthday. I was given lots of gifts including a huge stuffed lion from Simon. Michael was taking me out in the evening, but surprisingly he turned up at the rehearsal rooms at lunchtime. He said my brother Bill had phoned and asked if we could just pop in to say hello before going home. Although it's always nice to see Bill, I thought it might make us late for Michael's treat, but he said he didn't mind the little detour. I got the shock of my life when I got there. A surprise party had been organised by Bill and Fran and lots of my family were there, all hiding in different places. Mum popped up from behind the sofa where apparently she'd been kneeling for about an hour in readiness. Brian and Pat emerged from a cupboard. Terry and Penny popped up through a window. There was family appearing from all directions. It was the most wonderful day. Bill had a huge garden with woodland and a lake at the bottom. On a previous visit Dad had commented that it was very convenient to be able to go for a long bracing walk without actually leaving home. A large and delicious cake in the shape of a script had been made by one of Fran's friends. The logistics of organising such an event without me finding out were mind-boggling. Even Michael had known about the surprise for ages but had kept totally schtum. While recalling this story I was convinced that my father had been there, but, of course, he couldn't have been. I went so far as to check all the photos. His presence was so greatly felt.

It was in Mum's remaining years that I really got to know her and like her as a friend. She would spend lots of time at my house and I would visit her as often as I could. But now that I look back, it wasn't nearly often enough. I have only just realised that when my dad died, and Mum went to live alone, it was the first time she had *ever* lived alone in her life, and I can't bear to think how lonely it must have been for her. However, it is what she wanted or so she insisted. But then what option did she have? Nobody was rushing forward to say 'Come and live with me, Mum', myself included. I think Brian and Pat would have liked her to stay, but again she said she wanted her independence. She certainly didn't want to live in a nursing home. And once when she left the gas cooker on in her flat (the flame had accidentally blown out), and the other residents complained that she wasn't well enough to live alone, I fought tooth and nail on her behalf to keep her flat, and succeeded. We had the gas appliances removed and replaced with electric ones. Mum was so relieved.

And I'm tortured by the times I perhaps got cross with her and shouted at her. She had no one to go home and have a moan to or to console her. But my brothers and sister were on hand, and I'm sure she would have a good old moan about me whenever she saw them! But it's the indignity of it that upsets me so. I wouldn't be best pleased if a younger member of my family took to barking at me, or behaving in a superior fashion, which is what

I did on occasion to my mother. I regret it so much that it's painful. These were only *very* rare occasions, but to me now they are so magnified. Of course, she would often stay with other members of the family and my sister Pam visited her routinely every day, and I know Mum would call me a cranky cow if she heard me going on now. But that's how I feel. Guilty.

But we would have such a laugh when she came to stay with me in London. And she even loved it when I had to go off to work, especially if my friend Gina was coming to the house to do the ironing. Mum would make tea and be the grand hostess with 'Never mind the ironing ducks. I'll do that later.' Gina told me that on one occasion Mum greeted her wearing a full Indian head-dress of feathers, which she'd found in a cupboard, and smoking a clay pipe. Gina insisted on doing the ironing but Mum pulled up a chair and chatted the whole while. Considering her get-up she should have been sitting crossed-legged on the floor. And people ask who I get it from!

I'd take Mum to all sorts of places. She loved coming to the theatre and my friends and colleagues all enjoyed her company. She especially liked it when I did her make-up and hair and we got all dolled up and went out together. And we laughed like drains at the silliest things. We'd go on car trips to visit my brothers or we'd just drive around the countryside and sing songs. 'Cherry Ripe' was a favourite of hers because her father sang it. When she was a girl her mother often commissioned her to go to find her dad to tell him dinner was ready. She'd stand in the street and listen for the melodic strains of 'Cherry Ripe' coming full throttle from some tavern or other and then go and collar him. He always got a free pint for his efforts.

I once took her and Pam on a holiday to Spain to visit Ted and Ana, and although I couldn't really afford it at the time, I booked business-class flights, just in case there were any delays or anything, for I wanted Mum to be comfortable. Looking down on all the fluffy clouds, she remarked to Pam that she was glad she brought her anorak because of all the snow! After our meal the stewardess asked Mum if she would like a coffee. 'Noothenkyou' she said in her poshest voice, we were in business class after all, 'Ay never touch it.'

'Oh well, would you like a cup of tea?' queried the stewardess.

'Thet would be very naice,' said Mum, 'but don't make a pot special.' The stewardess nearly fell over laughing.

Mum really enjoyed that holiday, even though she tripped and sprained her wrist. To our amazement Mum even climbed up to the top of the hill where the cemetery is situated, a trial to even the fittest of us. Who could have foreseen that a few years later I would have the unenviable task of informing Mum that Ted had passed away. I went to her bedroom and stroked her soft grey hair, I can see it and feel it now as clear as day. The grief swept over her like a dark blanket. Ted was buried in Spain, in the cemetery at the top of the hill, and although Mum was not well enough to travel to Spain for the funeral, she reflected that it was a strange comfort to her to know that she had physically been to his resting place.

On one of our many outings, Pam and I took Mum on a day trip to France. Pam packed a picnic lunch containing salad, sandwiches, chicken legs and a flask of tea. We thought Mum might get a little seasick, but not at all. After her picnic she tucked into another meal from the ship's buffet! However, the following week when Pam visited to get Mum's shopping list, she asked her what she would like for her dinner.

'Stumps,' said Mum readily.

'Stumps?' queried Pam.

'Yeah. I liked them,' said Mum.

'I don't know what you mean. What are stumps?'

'Oh for goodness' sake. You know. Stumps. We had them on the boat to France.'

'Do you mean chicken legs?'

'Yeah. That's it. Chicken stumps.'

But I doubt that's what Pam asked for at the butcher's.

16

THE MAN IN THE HOOD

MIKE AND I WERE ON HOLIDAY IN THE WEST INDIES WHEN I got the call from my agent, saying that Greg Hersov of the Royal Exchange Theatre in Manchester wanted to meet me on my return to London. I'd never seen or read Ibsen's *A Doll's House* but I knew the gist of it and was very excited at the prospect of playing one of classical theatre's most famous characters, Nora. We took a bus into Castries, the capital of St Lucia, to buy a copy.

Our accommodation at the hotel was a small detatched bungalow on the beach only yards from the edge of the Caribbean Sea, and on opening the door every morning we were greeted by dozens of crabs, who had claimed the porch as their own. Ah well, I suppose they were there first. As soon as we cautiously stepped out into the sun they all crawled off again. You can imagine, the first time I saw them I *shrieked*, but after a few days we had got used to it and had even christened them all. We were shaded from the blazing sun by two huge coconut trees that would occasionally drop their fruit at our feet. The humidity was extreme. Michael and I loved St Lucia, the laid-back atmosphere, the friendly locals and beautiful scenery, and the delicious cocktails sipped in the evening sun while watching and listening to the tiny hummingbirds as they wrapped up their day's work. We made friends with Sam, a local chap who took us to a neighbouring town to celebrate Friday. A good enough reason. In fact, *every* Friday was celebrated in this little town where the entire population partied in the street. Music, music, music and food, food, food everywhere. It was fabulous. And the lazy days on the beach near our little bungalow were lovely. Perfect for sitting back for a little read. So equipped with my new copy of A *Doll's House*, I sat with my feet in the Caribbean and read it. What a magnificent play!

I desperately wanted to play this part, but now I was worried about meeting Greg. What if he didn't like me? An hour previously I had been remarkably relaxed, but now I was all in a lather. We had another week of our holiday left so I had to try to put it out of my mind. Fortunately, the high humidity gave me a very bad case of prickly heat which did take my mind off it for a few days because we had to scour the shops for prickly heat powder and calamine lotion.

When I returned home I made some enquiries about Greg from people who had worked with him or knew him, and all of them told me how clever he was and what an excellent director they considered him to be. So armed with a lot of hope and a little apprehension I went to meet him as planned at the National Theatre coffee shop expecting to find him a rather serious chap. Hitherto, all of the directors I'd worked for were rather conventional looking, and then there I was face to face with Greg, a friendly, cuddly hippy-type bear of a man. I liked him instantly. And to my great relief he told me straight away that he *did* want me to play Nora.

The Man in the Hood

The Royal Exchange Theatre at Manchester, for those of you who don't know, is theatre in the round, and beautifully refurbished I might add since the devastation of the IRA bomb which shook the centre of Manchester in 1996. I rented a tiny cottage in Whitefield for the duration of the run, about twenty minutes drive from the theatre. David Horovich played Torvald and I enjoyed the rehearsals more than any other. Greg has a great knack of getting to the heart of the matter and of explaining it simply, and is ready to try any ideas his actors come up with, which might deviate from his own. I loved playing Nora, I loved working with David, but I adored working with Greg. I can say for certain, that working with Greg is my best theatrical experience to date.

But a few days before opening I caught Greg with a very pensive look on his face. I asked him if he was concerned about my performance. He said he couldn't quite put his finger on what it was that was bothering him but something wasn't quite right. I said, 'Please don't worry about me, Greg. It will be fine. I hope! Once we're in the theatre it will be fine.' I knew from experience that something happens to me between leaving rehearsal room and stepping on stage. I haven't a clue *what*, but something happens. And after the first preview he came to the dressing rooms to congratulate the cast and was very happy indeed. He said, 'Yes, Brenda, I was worried. But I'm not any more.' Well, thank goodness for that. A *Doll's House* is one of those plays that changes people's lives. One lady I know who came to see it wanted to get up from her seat and hit Torvald for being so unreasonable towards his wife. Another lady was so moved, that she look a leaf out of Nora's book and moved right out of her own husband's life permanently.

But A *Doll's House* was extra poignant because it coincided with the *totally* unexpected break-up of my brother Bill's marriage, and it was time to repay him for all his kindnesses over the years and give him the support he needed to get over the trauma. I couldn't bear to see my clever, capable brother unhappy. But enough of that, we've gone all miserable! Time and laughter, as Dad always said, are both healers, and I'm glad to say all parties are still the best of friends. Bill's current wife Marcy is also beautiful, and generous to a fault to our entire family, and there is always a welcome in their home for any one of us, which is usually accompanied by a banquet! And after dessert Bill and I invariably get stuck into *The Times* crossword, and each week we race each other to finish *The Times* cryptic jumbo puzzle. He usually wins. Bighead! But it's a curious thing, if we are both struggling for hours over one particular clue, and I solve it, he will solve it five seconds later. Or vice versa. It's a sort of telepathy. A human broadband! And it's the same with my niece Valerie.

It was Bill who taught me to jive as a teenager and we actually won a competition at one of the many dances we went to. When Bill wasn't at home to practise with, I partnered the door handle, and spun this way and that. It was only problematic when someone came unannounced through the door and sent me spinning clean across the room.

One night in 1989, I was very surprised to find my brother Bill in my dressing room at the Nuffield Theatre in Southampton, where I was playing the eponymous heroine in Claire Luckham's *The Dramatic Attitudes of Miss Fanny Kemble*. It was the interval and I had a big costume change. His eyes were red and I knew he was about to tell me something I didn't want to hear. Patrick Sandford the artistic director was with him. Bill told me that Mum was very ill and the doctors believed she probably wouldn't last the night. He had come to drive me to Ramsgate directly after the show. Patrick could see I was in torment and said, 'Do what you have to do, Brenda. If you have to leave straight away, so be it.'

I did have to leave straight away. The audience were told what had happened and were given the choice of refunds or tickets for another night. For all those of you who were in the audience that night I give heartfelt apologies, but I never would have got through the second half of the play without mishap. I couldn't stop the flow of tears. Bill drove me home to Ramsgate, a drive of about two and a half hours (for him a round trip of five). But thank God I was in time to see my mother. In fact I was in very good time, because I'm glad to say she recovered and lived for another two years! But each time she had a relapse I thought, 'Oh no, this is it this time.'

When I visited her in hospital, she was in a room off the main ward. She looked very pensive and asked, 'Brenda, is there life after death?'

'Well of course there is,' I said. 'Everyone knows that. Why do you ask?'

'Yesterday there was something in the *Daily Mail* about it.'

'Nothing for you to worry about, Mum,' I said. 'You'll be getting a telegram from the Queen yet.'

And then she said, 'Who's that silly sod standing over there?'

'Over where, Mum?'

'In the doorway, with that bloody great hood.'

My heart stopped beating. I turned to the door. There was no one there.

'I don't know who that is, Mum,' I said.

'Well tell him to sod off,' she said, 'and that priest who keeps wanting to come in.'

There was, indeed, a priest in the ward doing his rounds, issuing last rites, or just having a friendly chat, but I wasn't bothered about him, I was more worried about the grim reaper lookalike.

'Shall I tell them both to leave you alone then?' I asked.

'It's okay now,' she said. 'That bloke with the hood has gone. And I'd better not upset the priest.'

And then all of a sudden she grew radiant and said laughing, 'Hello little soldier. Oh Bren, look at the little soldier dancing.' She could see an imaginary soldier dancing on the counterpane. She laughed and cooed and sang a little along with the soldier.

'Oh look at his old-fashioned uniform. Ah look Bren. Hey up! There he goes. Aaaah, isn't he lovely,' she cried, as the soldier danced in the palm of her hand.

And when the soldier jumped up on to the top of the door, she smiled and pointed and said, 'Look how smart he is, marching', and then she lay back on the pillow and slept with a smile on her face.

And Mum recovered.

I returned to Southampton feeling a little more optimistic. I don't know what medication Mum had been on, but it did her the power of good. And us. They were surprised to see me back so soon. The following week I was paged to the stage door, because there was a phone call for me. Naturally I was apprehensive. But it wasn't the hospital or my family calling me. It was Lynn Meadow, the artistic director of the Manhattan Theatre Club in New York. There was to be a production of *Absent Friends* by Alan Ayckbourn in the new year, and Alan had recommended me for the role of Diane. Obviously I couldn't go over there to meet them because I was working, but she just wanted to hear the timbre of my voice. We chatted for ages about the character and so on and she told me there and then she wanted me to play the part. Thereafter she called me her mail-order bride.

Brad Pitt, me and Craig Sheffer

17

GOING WEST

I TRAVELLED TO NEW YORK VIA SHANNON ON NEW YEAR'S DAY 1990. It was the first time I had ever travelled in first class, and I was the *only* passenger in it. It was really weird. I had about four stewardesses all to myself. I had been to work in America before on a mini-series with Farrah Fawcett, but that was only for a few weeks. This engagement was for almost three months.

An apartment had been rented for me on 51st Street and Seventh Avenue, just a short walk from the theatre on 55th, although rehearsals were down on 16th Street. I walked to work on several occasions much to everyone's surprise, but I had to give that up and take the subway once the snow came. I found living on my own in New York uneasy at first. I didn't even know how to buy a loaf of bread, how stupid is that. There are delicatessens galore, but the procedures are different. If bread is piled up on top of the glass counter, do I just take one, or is the bloke behind the counter supposed to do it for me? Same with soups in the big urns. Should I help myself or should he do it? I used to lurk behind the shelves just to see how everyone else did it. And New Yorkers are great once you get to know them, but at first they seem awfully abrupt. No please or thank you. Straight to the point. No messing. But once I got the hang of it I was fine.

'What can I gecha lady?'

'Gimme a loaf!' See, it's easy.

'Give you a what?'

One of the things I really missed in New York was the sky. The buildings are so tall that I had to take regular trips downtown to Greenwich Village or SoHo where the buildings are not so tall to get a sky top-up.

It was a wonderful experience working with good actors. Lynn the director understood Alan's work well. Mary Louise Parker was to be in it but was unfortunately taken sick in the first week of rehearsal. She was replaced by a newcomer called Gillian Anderson. It was, in fact, her theatrical debut and she was terrific. During the run of the play she had auditioned for a role in some film or other and was disappointed not to get the part. As we strolled through SoHo, I can remember telling her not to be impatient and that I thought she was going to be a big star. Was I right or what?

Absent Friends is about a couple, Diane and Peter, throwing a tea party for an old friend who had tragically lost his fiancée in a drowning accident. Other friends were invited but instructed not to mention the unfortunate incident in case it dampened their friend's spirits again. So while everyone is on tenterhooks trying not to mention it, the guest himself seems to want to talk about nothing else. It's a hilarious play. Meanwhile, lots of home truths are brought into the open about the other guests and the hosts themselves. The production was a big hit, and I was sorry when it came to an end.

The night before returning home, I was at my apartment packing my bags when the telephone rang. 'Hello?'

'Can I speak to Miss Blethyn please?'

'Speaking.'

'Oh Miss Blethyn, this is Robert Redford's office here, and Mr Redford will be directing A *River Runs Through It* and he'd like you to—'

'Oh, leave it out!' I interrupted to this obvious hoaxer. 'Who is it really? I'm trying to pack here!'

'Yes, we realise you are leaving for London tomorrow, but Robert would like to FedEx a script to you. Would that be okay?'

'Ey? . . .'

'Miss Blethyn, are you there? Would that be okay? He'd like you to take a look at the role of Mrs Maclean. You come highly recommended. Our casting lady saw you in *Absent Friends* and mentioned you to Robert. So would that be okay?'

'Um . . . yes. Okay . . . thank you . . . Goodbye then!'

I couldn't believe it.

ROBERT REDFORD!?

First thing in the morning, before leaving for the airport, I called Ken McReddie, my agent. I didn't think there'd be much chance of me actually getting the part, but he thought I had every chance, and within the week he called to say that an offer had been made and the role was mine. I hadn't had to audition and I hadn't had any conversation about it with anyone other than that first call. The film was to be shot in Montana later in the year. Also in the film was Tom Skerritt, Emily Lloyd, and two new young actors called Craig Sheffer and Brad Pitt. Mrs Maclean was the wife of a Presbytaerian preacher, originally from Scotland, and so I honed up on my Scottish accent. I thought this was the reason Robert wanted a British actress for the role. I worked really hard on it and prayed that it would be good enough.

I flew to Montana via Colorado. A unit driver was waiting for me at the small airport, and announced that although I wouldn't be working today, I could go out to location to meet everyone if I so wished. I was so nervous about meeting Robert Redford, Robert Redford, Robert Redford, that I thought I had better get it over and done with. It was such a lovely drive. Montana is a beautiful state. It's called Big Sky Country and it's not difficult to understand why. I was first introduced to the wardrobe department, and as we were looking at some designs for my clothes we could see Mr Redford in the distance just going into his Airstream trailer.

'Let's gecha to say hello to Mr Redford,' said someone.

I walked across the huge field through the unit base towards the Airstream trailer just as he was stepping out again. He turned and saw me.

'BRENDAAAA,' he sang, 'WEEEELCOME!' and he gave me the biggest hug.

Listen, it's not possible for me to describe what I was feeling at that moment, but I don't think I need to, do I? Glorious will have to do. 'Step inside Brenda, let's have a little chat about Mrs Maclean.'

'Right, thank you, yes,' I gibbered.

It was lovely and cool inside and very welcome after the relentless sunshine.

'Now then, Mrs Maclean,' he said. 'She's the wife of a Presbyterian preacher, as you know, and as such is a very hard-working woman. She helps out in the community, doesn't complain, and if there's ever a problem she just . . . um . . . she just um . . .'

'Gets on with it?' I offered.

'Excuse me!' said Robert, seemingly ever-so-slightly miffed.

'She just gets on with it,' I repeated wishing the floor would open up.

'Yes. Right. Absolutely,' agreed Robert. 'She gets on with it.'

When I left the trailer, I realised that he thought I'd said, 'Oh get on with it!'

As if.

I found Mr Redford to be an actor's director. He liked us improvising around a scene. I was a little nervous to do so at first, but he was very encouraging. My reticence stemmed from the fact that on day one he told me he didn't want a Scottish accent after all. Instead, he wanted everyone to be non-specific American. Mid-West if anything. I wasn't needed for two weeks before being in front of the camera so I spent as much time as I could in the town of Livingston chatting to the locals. I really enjoyed it. In any case, everyone else in the film was American, apart from Emily Lloyd, so the accent was easy to pick up. My character had to age from mid-twenties to mid-fifties and so several wigs were made. I was commissioned to have these made in London and to take them with me. They were beautifully made and I was delighted when at the end of the film the producer said I could keep them. I kept two but gave the best one to Bunny Parker, the film's hair designer.

I had lots of time off during filming. My friends and I would spend whole days horse riding through the wilderness, pausing while the horses paddled in a cool mountain stream. Bill Hootkins, a fellow actor, drove me to Meerkat County where hundreds of acres are left undisturbed for the meerkats to make their homes. It was delightful to see them lounging outside their little caves. Some had made canopies to keep out of the sun. In fact, it was just like a town anywhere, where individuals chat idly to neighbours over the boundary fence.

On one occasion Bill and I went white water rafting on the Yellowstone River, in the wilderness west of Livingstone. It was breathtaking, literally, as we tumbled over rocks, tossed from side to side in the rubber dinghy and travelling at about thirty miles an hour. After one particularly treacherous manoeuvre through 'The Kitchen Sink', so named because every skill was needed to negotiate it, we eventually came to a calm but still swiftly moving stretch of river. It was absolutely beautiful. Throwing caution, cowardice and sense to the wind I pitched an inner tube overboard and dived after it, hauled myself on to it and floated in blissful harmony with my surroundings, eyes skyward ahead of the dinghy. I floated, entranced, around the bend of the river, reminding myself that this was a wilderness, and looking up against a wonderfully blue sky, I squinted and saw a bald eagle, perched high on the tallest tree on the mountain side.

Most people have never seen an eagle. With keen eyesight, the eagle can spot its prey as small as a shrew from hundreds of feet in the air and with acute precision, swoop down, claim its victim and soar high up again to its nest. The bald eagle is the national emblem of the United States and is extremely rare. I couldn't believe it – the bald eagle! It was smaller than I imagined it to be, but maybe it was further away than I estimated. I was so excited that I called to the others to look, but the only reply I received was my own voice echoing off the mountains, 'Look, look, look!' It was only then that I realised I had floated out of sight and out of earshot of my companions. I was truly alone with the bald eagle. That's when the beautiful, beautiful calm of the Yellowstone River was disturbed by the white knuckle panic I felt as I tried to back paddle using my hands for oars. Why had I picked up speed? I had visions of a waterfall approaching. Ten or fifteen minutes passed and there was still no sign of my companions. Whose idea was it to come on this stupid trip? Fortunately for me, although my friends hadn't spotted the eagle, they had spotted my absence and propelled their craft around the bend of the river and towards me. I was more pleased to see them than I was to see the bald eagle. There is a God. After I was hauled aboard, the white water guide told us that the day before he had seen two deadly cotton-mouth snakes swimming under the craft and it hadn't been a good idea for me to have dived into the river. WHAT! Hadn't he noticed me go overboard. Why hadn't he stopped me. HELLOO! I can say with certainty that I never will again. I cheered myself with the thought that perhaps those two cotton-mouth snakes will be lunch one day for the eagle. But thank goodness I was safely back on board the craft because only another couple of hundred yards around the bend was another treacherous rapid. A doddle.

Every time I think of that white water incident I get a shiver. Actually, it's a surprise even to me that I dived overboard. Although I grew up at the seaside I wasn't a terribly good swimmer. I was afraid to put my head under water. It's only more recently that I've remedied that by going to the pool every day for six months until I could swim a mile. I can now ONLY swim if I put my head under water! As children we would go to the beach practically every day in the summer months. We especially liked to play in the sea at low tide, when you would have to wade out for what seemed like miles to reach water deep enough to swim in. And because the water was shallow it somehow seemed warmer. My brothers taught me how to do the doggy paddle. Oh, the joy of those first few splattered strokes with your feet off the floor.

My sister Pam was very nervous about us going into the sea, in fact she was very nervous about us doing any kind of physical activity. 'Watch out for the tide!' 'Don't fall over!' Don't go in too deep. Don't run. Don't trip. Look where you're going. Stay on the pavement. Don't drop that. Whatever you do, don't put your head under water! And she'd repeat 'Watch out for the tide!' I can vividly remember those words ringing in my ears when I was trying to teach myself to do some kind of gymnastic feat in the sea. My brothers could all dive down to the sandy floor and pick up rocks and seaweed and crabs and all sorts of weird and wonderful treasures, and I wanted to be able to join in. Of course, I should have waited until someone was with me, but I was impatient to try diving to the bottom. So I did. I hit the bottom with much more impact that expected and winded myself. Swiftly resurfacing to breathe I hit the bottom again, and again and again. I was completely disoriented. 'Don't put your head under water!' I hit the bottom again. 'Don't go in too deep!' My face brushed along the sandy floor. I was praying, 'Please God, I'll be a good girl' and as, thank heavens, I stubbed my toe on a rock I knew I must now be upright and pushed myself to the surface, bursting through and gasping for air. I reminded myself that I mustn't tell anyone of my stupidity but I must never ever try that again unaccompanied.

I never did tell Mum about this childish incident because she would have skinned me alive, but I did tell her about the white water rafting in Montana. However, all she wanted to know was: 'Was Robert Redford with you?' I told her he wasn't and tried to continue telling her about the dangerous bit.

'What was he doing then?' she interrogated.

'I don't know, Mum, working I suppose.'

'Did he know you'd gone on the river. Did you *think* to invite him?' she said, reminding me of my manners.

'No, Mum. He was busy making the film!'

My mum loved Robert Redford. In the early eighties I went to Ramsgate on one of my regular visits to my parents. Although I had a door key, I never liked to startle them by just opening the door and going in, so I always knocked. Besides, it was heavenly to see and hear my dad's surprise when he opened the door. 'Oh gawd crickey ay! Louooooo! Well, look who it ain't. Oh gawd crickey Louoooo! If it ain't our Brender. Well, if this ain't a red letter day. LOUOOOOOOOO, look who's here.' And finally he'd say, 'Well come on in Bren, if you can get in. Well I never. I've won the pools!!' It was so lovely.

Anyway, on this day in question, something told me to use my key and to go straight in. I found my mother and father in the living room in total silence, sitting either side of the fireplace out of each other's eye-line. You could have cut the atmosphere with a knife.

'Is everything all right,' I asked.

'Ask your father,' spat Mum.

OK.

'Is everything all right, Dad?'

'Oh gawd crickey, Bren. Who knows. Who knows,' he lamented cryptically. 'Ask yer mother.'

'Mum?'

'Well, it's like this, Brenda,' she said, and then right out of left field, 'Do you like Robert Redford?'

'Er, yees?'

'Brenda, do you think he's handsome?'

'Oh yes Mum, I don't know anyone who doesn't think so.' I had no idea where all this was going.

'Well Brenda, the other day there was a photo of Robert in the paper and I said to your father, coo look at him, isn't he hand-some, and your father hasn't spoken to me for a fortnight!'

So *that* was it, Dad was jealous!

I was so delighted by the realisation that my 88-year-old Dad was still potty enough about my 78-year-old Mum to be jealous that I burst out laughing, and two seconds later they were both laughing too. Sadly Dad didn't live long enough to know that I actually went to work with Robert Redford, but there again, perhaps he wouldn't have been best pleased about it in the circumstances.

Mum on the other hand did live long enough to know. When I was offered the job she was recovering in hospital and therefore I was quite ready to turn the job down. She was horrified and made me promise to take the job and to give her a daily rundown of what it was like. She was enjoying Mr Redford vicariously through me. She must have driven the other patients mad going on and on about her film star daughter who was working with Robert Redford. And when he sent her a photo signed 'for Louisa' she was over the moon.

Mum would boast about her kids all the time, especially me because I was on the tele. I'd only made one film at that time, *The Witches*, which I took her to see at a cinema in Streatham. I was so proud. My first film. She cooed when my name zoomed on to the screen in the titles but she then watched the film in silence, not even commenting when I appeared. I thought that perhaps she didn't recognise me. 'That's me, Mum,' I said. 'The one wearing glasses.' 'Is it?' sighed Mum. 'How much longer does this go on for?' Ah well, at least she was honest. You can't win them all. But she was proud of me none the less. Whenever I'd come to visit her, before I'd learnt to drive, she would insist on accompanying me on the bus back to the train station. She would wait until I was right at the front of the bus about to get off and she would holler from the back, 'Oh Brenda, are you on the ITV or the BBC tonight?'

I'd cringe with embarrassment, but once I was off the bus I'd have a smile inside me a mile wide knowing that my mum was so proud.

Quite recently I visited the Northwood club-cum-restaurant owned by my cousin Billy Jane. He had landscaped and dedicated a new Thai style garden in memory of his parents and sister Beryl and I was invited to the opening. It was lovely. There were several people there who I hadn't seen for years including a neighbour from the Plains of Waterloo, Mrs Darrington. She approached me and said, 'Brenda, I think I owe you an apology. Or more accurately I owe your mum an apology. She used to boast and tell everyone you were in films and I called her a liar. I'm really sorry, and I wish she were still here so I could tell her myself.' It was so gracious of Mrs Darrington to confess and apologise and I too wish Mum was still here. I wish it every day.

In Montana, the make-up designer Jean Black had a friend visiting from Texas, and the three of us decided to go on a nice long hike up a Rocky Mountain track. It was a glorious day, as was every day in Big Sky Country. We set off early in Jean's car to the foot of the mountain, along with her dog Thurber, a beautiful golden Labrador. Actually, by the time we parked we were already a few thousand feet above sea level. It was completely deserted save for the resident wildlife, which, of course, included rattle snakes, as nearly every public information sign told us. But we were used to this by now and were all equipped with sturdy cowboy boots. Another sign warned beware of bears, but apparently it wasn't often you came across one. I can't describe how beautiful it was with a light breeze whispering through foliage as far as the eye could see. According to the brochure we had brought along with us, there was a lovely waterfall a few thousand feet up the path ahead us, which was our destination.

We clambered onwards and upwards, breathless and exhilarated, only occasionally stopping for a drink of water. We brought no food along because we were warned that it would be attractive to bears. After nearly two hours of climbing, I was getting breathless and decided enough was enough considering the long walk back down the hill we still had to negotiate. Jean and her friend decided it was such a pity to have come so far and *not* see the waterfall. They calculated that they could get to the falls and back again to me within an hour, an hour and a half tops. So it was agreed. They would go on and I would wait. Thurber went with them. It's an amazing feeling to be totally alone. Aside from those two there probably wasn't another human being for a couple of miles or so. Instead of getting frightened I decided to embrace it. Go with it. Learn from it. Finding a big log to sit on, I gave it a kick to make sure there wasn't a snake inside or anything resembling a creepy crawly, because if there was, I would be up at the waterfall before the other two. And I settled down to breathe in the immaculately clean air and to feast on the view. I casually glanced at the brochure and decided the photographs therein didn't do the actual place any justice at all. But how could they? It was breathtaking.

Turning the page, my eyes fell on a typewritten insert that made my blood freeze!! 'ATTENTION LADIES: IT IS INADVISABLE TO ENTER THIS NATURE RESERVE IF YOU ARE MENSTRUATING.' A fine time to find that out!! It went on to explain that the scent could be picked up by the bears for miles around! I knew that I was going to die there, soon, and alone. When my friends returned, all they would find would be the brochure, my boots, and perhaps my 'I Love Yellowstone Park' T-shirt. I was on the first day of menstruation, which every woman knows is the heaviest. My friends had only been gone for fifteen or twenty minutes. I had perhaps an hour to endure. My mouth dried up. Every hair on my body was standing on end. How has it come about that little Brenda Bottle from Ramsgate is up a fucking mountain in Montana (sorry Mum), waiting to be an hors d'oeuvre for a grizzly bear? What stupid fucking clever dick has magicked me here? (*Wash your mouth out!*) Petrified does not come near. I wanted my mum. In the event of a bear attack, the typed insert went on to advise, it is best to pretend to be dead and if the bear believes you, he won't eat you. Fortunately, I was nearly dead with fright. Or alternatively, the warning advised, climb as high as you can up a tree. I think I had lost a stone in weight by the time my friends reappeared and although I couldn't say anything coherent they remarked on the miraculous change of energy in me. I didn't even explain the reason, I just wanted to get down the mountain. An hour and a half earlier I was weak with fatigue but now I was superturbocharged, and so glad to get back to the safety of the car.

At the end of my engagement Michael flew out to Montana, and after a few days we hired a Buick and drove down to San Francisco and Los Angeles, stopping off in various places including Reno. Reno, for those of you who don't know, is a gambling town, a smaller version of Las Vegas. It was a very leisurely drive, the maximum speed limit never exceeding fifty miles an hour. In Reno, while enjoying a drink in the bar of a casino one night, we noticed there was a party of some sort going on in a private room next to us, with very smartly dressed guests mostly in black tie garb.

The doors were open. There were gales of laughter coming from the room and the sound of coins falling into a metal receptacle. Through the open door we saw able-bodied people crossing to go to the other end of the room, but when each of them returned in the other direction they looked really decrepit and finding it hard to walk. It was puzzling. We took a closer look. Peeping around the door, what we discovered was a game called 'Bum Darts'. I kid you not.

Bum Darts is a form of gambling. A receptacle is placed on the floor at one end of the room. Each contestant has to cross the room and deposit a coin in the receptacle. Sounds easy? Here's the difficulty. They each had to carry the coin, clenched between their buttocks, for the length of the room, poise themselves over the receptacle and release it. If the coin fell into the pot, the contestant won the pot. More often than not though, the coin missed its target, in which case the coin would be *added* to the pot. No wonder these smartly dressed people looked decrepit as they returned past the door. The concentration needed was extreme. Especially from the ladies because their flowing gowns were trying to loosen the coin from its firm grip, and in some cases *not* so firm. There were lots of different styles. Some shuffled zombie-like with their arms doing a sort of breaststroke action. Others shuffled along with their arms poker stiff at their sides, their chins tucked into their chests. Some felt it easier to walk on tip-toe like a ballerina. Another like Charlie Chaplin. It was hilarious. A great party game and we've played it often. You should try it.

Lovely Louisa Kathleen

18

FAREWELL, MY SWEET

W HEN FINISHING A FILM, ESPECIALLY WHEN FOLLOWED BY A holiday, it's always nice to have another spell in theatre. Or vice versa. So it was a pleasure to return to the Royal Exchange Theatre in Manchester to play Mrs Cheveley in *An Ideal Husband*, directed by James Maxwell, and the male lead (or the *chief* actor as my mum would say) was Robert Glenister. What a fine actor he is. I had never been in an Oscar Wilde play before, and it was like playing in a treasure trove. Mrs Cheveley is such a clever devious character, and not the sort of part I would normally be offered. Hitherto I had usually played sympathetic characters. I was struck by the fact that when this play was written in the late nineteenth century, my Dad was already in the world. He was one year old. And as a small boy he might have heard his parents talking of the scandal of Oscar Wilde and of his death just into the new twentieth century.

It was during this production, on the Friday of the third week of rehearsal, that I got the dreaded call I hoped I would never get.

Mum had been taken to hospital again. The last time, and the time before, she had rallied, but something told me it wasn't going to happen this time. I was inconsolable. James gave me leave to go home. Mum was in Margate hospital and looked so frail that I could feel myself falling apart inside. But my best performance to date was not showing it. Although she was covered with a blanket she complained of being cold, especially her feet. I wrapped them in my cardigan, sat on the bed and tucked her feet up inside my jumper so that my body would keep them warm, and massaged her legs. She ticked me off for taking time off work to come to see her 'all the way from Manchester', but she also said how pleased she was. I had to move from the bed when the nurse came to rearrange the covers, and I whinced when she trapped Mum's leg in the railings at the side of the bed. Mum screamed in agony. I bounded around the bed and released her leg, telling the nurse that I would take over. She mumbled an apology and moved on to the next patient. I know the nurses were over-worked and underpaid, but on that occasion I could willingly have throttled her. When Mum recovered she asked me about the play, and I described in detail the lovely costumes and told her the story. I could tell from her line of questioning that she knew she wouldn't be seeing it.

When I visited her on the Sunday, my brothers Brian, Bill, Terry and Martin and my sister Pam were also there. Brian was a grandfather of one week and had brought along a photograph of his new grandson Peter to show Mum. Mum was fading and I could see she was a little uncomfortable on her pillows, so I plumped them up and sat behind her on the bed in order to support her better. She had her head nestling into my right shoulder.

She said, 'Thank you, Bren. That's much better. It's so lovely to see you all.' And then without moving her head, she looked as far right as she could, and then as far left, and she gazed at me with a mysterious look in her eyes. My brother called a nurse. The staff sister came and held her wrist, and announced 'She's going.' And with her head cradled in my shoulder, she died. Oh what loss! Oh what terrible monumental loss! We were all silent. The nurse methodically pulled the curtain around the bed and we were asked to leave while she laid Mum out. All I could think of was that the nurse had said 'She's going' because I'd read somewhere that, at the point of death, hearing was the last faculty to go. Had Mum heard those words? Had the man in the hood been standing amongst us at the bed? What would become of her now? Who did her body belong to now? And although my brothers' sense of loss was as heartfelt as mine, I was also filled with an unreasonable anger. I felt I was the victim of theft. We were told by the doctor that she had suffered a massive heart attack. Is the word 'massive' really necessary, even if it is the correct medical term? I went back to the cubicle, kissed my mum and stroked her hair. I was devastated, and filled with the conviction that Mum had died on a Sunday so as not to inconvenience anybody. The nurse gave me Mum's small hoop earrings and wedding ring, which I had bought for her a few years earlier, when she'd lost her own. I thought of that occasion as I looked at her. I'd taken Pam and Mum to a performance of the musical Me and My Girl in the West End. During the interval Mum asked me to pass her the catalogue.

'What catalogue?'

'That one, in your hand, with all the names in it. I want to know the name of the chief actor. I've seen him somewhere. He's ever so good.'

'Oh, this is called a programme, Mum,' I said. 'Michael designs programmes. The chief actor's name is Robert Lindsay.'

And as she reached for it, she noticed her ring was gone. She thought she must have lost it in the ladies' room when she washed her hands. I went straight to the ladies' room to search for it but it was nowhere to be seen.

And now, as I looked at her in the hospital cubicle, my mum was nowhere to be seen either. Her spirit had risen from her body.

The funeral service was at St Ethelbert's Catholic Church in Hereson Road the following week. As the solemn cortege proceeded from the undertakers, the first car behind the hearse containing my brothers, my sister and myself stalled, and we watched helplessly as Mum disappeared into the distance, travelling solo to the church. As soon as our driver got the car started again, after several long grinding attempts, it was necessary for him to put his foot down in order to catch up with Mum. It was a bit like a 'Carry On' film. Mum would have rolled up laughing had she been witness to it. Although we could see the humour of it we could only manage a smile. After the service, Mum was buried in the same plot as my father, and their grave has been meticulously tended by my brother Brian and his wife Pat ever since.

Although I probably could have walked away from the play in Manchester in the circumstances, I thought of all the people I would be letting down. The play would have had to be cancelled or postponed putting the entire season out of sync, and in any case Mum would most certainly not have approved. I returned to Manchester after the funeral with a heavy heart and dedicated my performance in *An Ideal Husband* to my mum. I would *make* myself cheer up and try not to be weepy and, against all the odds, I did manage it. It was a performance I was proud of and I was very disappointed that my agent at the time didn't travel to Manchester to see it.

But most of my family did. While having an after-show meal with Terry and Penny, we reminisced about the first time he came to see me in Manchester. It was in the late 1960s when the

Euston Players had entered *Fumed Oak* by Noel Coward in the British Rail amateur dramatic festival at the Lesser Free Trade Hall. We had won the competition, and I had won the best actress award. Terry had loved the play and said he thought me good enough to act professionally. He was the first person to say this but I told him he was doo-lally. Actually, after he saw *Fumed Oak*, he himself took up amateur dramatics and was a leading light for a number of years at the Enfield Players in Derby, and of which I am now a patron. I'll never forget when I went to see him in the pantomime. Terry was the dame. To tell you the truth, I was a little apprehensive about going because I didn't know how good the drama group was. What would I say if Terry forgot his lines, or if the scenery fell down? I was more nervous than being on stage myself. But I needn't have worried at all, because the 'little box of tricks' was fantastic. He had the audience eating out of his hand! 'The cunning little whelp!' In fact, the whole production was fantastic and was very ably assisted by Penny, who had helped to make the costumes, their daughter Amanda, who was a fairy, and their son Gary, who operated the lights. I was so proud. And in 2006 the Enfield Players celebrated their fiftieth anniversary.

We played *An Ideal Husband* for six weeks, after which time, when I would normally have gone to see Mum, it really hit me that she was no longer there. My brothers and Pam had dealt with the emptying of her flat and so on. But because they didn't know without consulting me what to throw away and what to keep, they had stored everything in a little seaside flat I had at Folkestone. It was heartbreaking to go in there and to see Mum's life packed in boxes and suitcases, and to have to decide what to do with it all. Opening a suitcase I could smell the soft sweet powdery scent of Mum. I buried my face into her clothes and the floodgates opened.

Cynthia Rose Purley

19

RED CARPETS

I WOULD HAVE LOVED MUM TO HAVE SEEN *A RIVER RUNS Through It*. The premiere was held in New York and I really wanted to attend. However, I did not know the protocol involved. I fantasised that I would be invited along with Michael, and my fare and hotel would be paid as I'd heard that was the norm. I got that wrong. I *was* invited but at my own expense. We bought a pair of economy tickets and booked into the cheapest hotel we could find on Broadway. You could hear people stirring their coffees in the next room the walls were so flimsy. But that didn't matter, because we were going to the premiere. I phoned the production office to say that we were attending, whereupon they announced that they would be sending a limousine for us. The driver must have thought he had the wrong address. The stretch limousine looked incongruous outside this very modest hotel. But who cared. This was my first red carpet event and I didn't know what to expect. The cinema was thronging with onlookers and photographers awaiting the arrival of Robert

Redford, Brad Pitt, Craig Sheffer, Emily Lloyd and Tom Skerritt and the young boys Caleb Schiff and Vann Gravage, and when Michael and I arrived the flashbulbs blazed because they didn't know who was inside the car. As we emerged it became clear that all cameras were pointed at Michael, I don't know who they thought he was, and I was totally ignored. When we got to the other end of the carpet and were greeted by the press officer I was introduced to the journalists (who had already seen the film) as the boys' mother.

'Aren't you so proud to have your little boys in this film,' asked one.

'Oh, I'm not their real mother,' I said.

'Oh no,' she continued, 'you're English. I'm sorry, I thought the lady said you were the mother of the boys.'

'Well yes I am, but only in the film.'

'That was you? How can that be? You're English and the mother in the film is American?'

Doh? Um? There's no answer to that is there really.

'She was doing an American accent,' explained the press officer. 'She was acting.'

'Oh really?' said the journalist not convinced. 'But you don't even look like her.'

'That's because she was wearing a wig, a corset and period costumes,' clarified the press officer, pulling me along to the next journalist who was a little more on the ball.

We really enjoyed the film, and I kept thinking throughout how much Mum would have relished it, remembering how she didn't go a bundle on the first film she saw me in.

One of the most rewarding premieres I've been to was at the Sandwich Technology School, near Ramsgate. In the winter of 2005 I was invited to open a small fifty-seater art deco-style cinema that the school had saved up for and had built, supported by a government initiative. While at the opening ceremony one of the teachers outlined an idea that he and Bruce Partleton, a friend of his, had come up with, of making a film at the school, called *The Drama Room*, starring the pupils, administration staff and teachers. His friend Bruce would direct the film. It was such an exciting idea and was supported wholeheartedly by the headmaster Richard Wallis, Secondary School Headmaster of the Year, 2005, in a national poll. Bruce tentatively asked me if I would consider playing the headmistress. I readily agreed, and a couple of months later I was summoned to Sandwich for my one day's filming. I was so nervous! Apparently the pupils weren't terribly keen on the idea of 'acting' at first, but soon warmed to it. The story concerned a drama group rehearsing a stage production of John Steinbeck's *Of Mice and Men*, but the underlying theme concerned bullying. I was taller than the camera and boom operators but they overcame this problem by standing on chairs, and I was terribly impressed by the standard of acting, and work ethic, from everyone. The premiere of *The Drama Room* was held nearly one year later at the school when pupils, parents and teachers were invited to see the fruits of their labour. The time, effort and enthusiasm put into the project was inspiring, and I was so proud to have been involved. But as a headmistress, I don't think I'd be any threat to Richard Wallis.

But Mum would have loved the third film I made, which was *Secrets & Lies*. Working with Mike Leigh was a godsend. As I'd worked with him once before on the BBC film called *Grown-Ups* sixteen years previously, I knew his approach to screenwriting was unique. The script is arrived at through a lengthy process of improvisation and consultation with Mike, a process that would take too long to go into here, and in any case since the process is very personal to each actor and Mike, it's possible I don't have the whole story, I only know about my own experience. Suffice it to say that each character is created in the minutest of detail, chronologically, from infancy. It is a painstaking process. In the case of *Secrets & Lies*, it took six months to arrive at what was eventually filmed. I didn't know entirely what the film was about until I saw it in the cinema. But it's a great discipline and at the end of it all the actors come away with a wonderful sense of achievement that perhaps they wouldn't have with a ready-scripted piece.

Although the work was intense there were lots of laughs along the way. Timothy Spall is not only a magnificent actor, he is also the cleverest and funniest man, and the research we did together as brother and sister, walking the streets of London finding inspiration for our characters, deciding where they lived, where they worked, where the doctor was located, the dentist, their school, etc., was joyful. But however much I liked the character I played, Cynthia Rose Purley, creating her could be very depressing at times. At the end of my working day, I'd drive home in my Mercedes, through an area of London inhabited by lots of people of Cynthia's means, to my cosy house, loving partner and delicious meal. It was sometimes emotionally confusing. I didn't know whether to be happy or sad. Cynthia is a woman who struggles on a daily basis to make ends meet, for little reward. And although there are very few similarities between her and my mother, I was reminded of my mother's struggle to bring up her family in post-war Britain and I came to understand things I hadn't understood before. Cynthia taught me that no matter how hard you try in life, sometimes the die is cast against you.

And sometimes you get a windfall, as my mum would say. An unexpected treat. The following year we were told that *Secrets & Lies* was to open the 1996 Cannes Film Festival, and of the actors, Marianne Jean-Baptiste, Timothy Spall and myself were invited. At the time I was rehearsing *Habeas Corpus* at the Donmar Warehouse with Jim Broadbent and Imelda Staunton, directed by

Sam Mendes, and I had to ask permission for time off from rehearsal to go to France, to which Sam readily agreed. Everyone was thrilled for us. It was very exciting because this was the first film festival I had ever been to. However, the excitement was lessened considerably by learning that at the last minute Tim wouldn't be coming with us for personal reasons. I missed him.

I have to say it was all a little scary being at such a high profile event. The festival aside, Cannes is a highly fashionable, super-smooth, suave, seaside holiday resort, full of sophisticated Europeans. And during Film Festival time, the streets are also filled with famous film directors, actors and celebrities, most being trailed by the world's press, and some *hoping* to be trailed by the world's press. It is also a film market where experienced filmmakers and novices alike hope to sell their film, or their idea for a film.

Secrets & Lies received a standing ovation that seemed as if it would never end. The following morning we were congratulated by film-makers and holiday-makers alike. Despite the super sophistication of the event, the working-class centre of Mike Leigh's film had been taken to heart. The baptism of press junkets in the gardens of the Metropole Hotel on the seafront was extraordinary. Dozens of interviews with journalists from all over the world had to be done, moving from television to press from press to television, and all were enthusing about the film, and openly predicting that it would win the Palme d'Or. But Mike Leigh told us not to let it go to our heads and to take it all with a pinch of salt. Wise words, but nevertheless it was exciting. The next day, I left Mike, Simon Channing-Williams and Marianne to enjoy more films and sunshine and returned home to London where my thoughts returned to *Habeas Corpus*.

A week later Mike Leigh and myself were invited back to Cannes. Did this mean that *Secrets & Lies had* won the Palme d'Or? Nobody knew if that was the case or not, it was such a closely guarded secret. Sam Mendes gave me leave of absence yet again. It was all very last minute and the dress I was to wear was the same one I'd worn the week before and was still in the boot of my car. 'Oh what the heck,' I thought, 'I'll give it a shake out when I get there.' But I did have a rather expensive pair of Manolo Blahnik shoes to wear. I could hear Mum's voice saying, 'She's got more money than sense!'

We were met at the airport and driven to our hotel but surprisingly we were shown through the back entrance, past the kitchens and up to our rooms in the service lift. Security men reported our every movement as if it was a top secret military exercise, and it seemed more and more likely perhaps that our film *had* won. But when we got to the presentation, I saw that several other contenders were there and realised my optimism had been somewhat premature. The legendary Francis Ford Coppola was chairman of the jury and presented the awards. I was on tenterhooks. Lars von Trier won the Grand Jury Award for *Breaking the Waves*, Joel Coen won the Best Director Award for *Fargo*, Best Actor was shared between Daniel Auteuil and Pascal Duquenne for *Le Huitième jour*, and heavens above, I won Best Actress for *Secrets & Lies*. And the *pièce de résistance*, Mike Leigh won the Palme d'Or. I danced the night away with Simon Channing-Williams, producer of *Secrets & Lies*, even though I had a very early flight home the next morning. I have a bleary recollection of standing on the beach drinking champagne and chatting to Baz Bamigboye, as my Manolo Blahniks slowly sank into the sand.

Just before Christmas 1996 I got the shock of my life to learn that I had been nominated for a Golden Globe for my performance along with Marianne Jean-Baptiste and the film itself. The ceremony was to take place in Los Angeles in January. I'd never been to any such event before and the prospect was very exciting for all of us. But my excitement was almost immediately overtaken by my concerns of 'what to wear'.

I'd hired a publicist, Nancy Seltzer, to help me through this film promotion period and she organised for me to visit the Armani salon in London. But I wanted to talk to someone who'd previously attended this type of ceremony, so I called Tom Rand for his advice. Tom was Oscar nominated for designing the costumes for *The French Lieutenant's Woman*, and he agreed to come shopping with me. I'd recently worked with Tom at the Royal Exchange Theatre in Manchester where he'd designed the costumes for Oscar Wilde's *An Ideal Husband*. The costumes were beautiful. Tom took me to several exclusive salons but most of the gowns I looked at I thought a little over the top for the occasion. I now know differently, of course, that all of those flouncy gowns would have been perfect. However, as I was feeling a little more conservative we went along to Armani in Sloane Street. Everything I saw was lovely, but when Tom pulled an all-in-one black Tuxedo suit from the rail, I thought he was having a funny turn. I told him I wouldn't be seen dead in it. Tom said, 'Trust me, Brenda. Put it on' and handed it to me.

I said, 'Tom, firstly it's going to look ridiculous on me, and secondly I shall die of heat. I'm going to be wearing this in Los Angeles!'

'You're forgetting about the air conditioning, Brenda. Most people are *cold* at the ceremony but you will be comfortable in that. Try it on! Please trust me.'

With less than good grace I disappeared into the cubicle to try it on. Of course, it was made for someone a foot taller than me but otherwise it fitted. I stumbled out of the cubicle standing on the bottoms of the trousers.

'See I told you,' I said, 'it doesn't suit me. I look ridiculous.'

'What are you talking about?' said Tom. 'Its fabulous. It just needs shortening. AND the addition of this brooch I've just found.' He produced the biggest brooch I've ever seen in my life. It made me laugh.

'Are you serious?'

'Deadly serious,' he said as he came at me with the brooch and held it to my shoulder. The seamstress magically appeared and pinned up the hems of the trousers and Tom pinned on the brooch. I couldn't believe it. Yes, it really did look lovely. Plus it looked very dressy without being over the top. Tom then pulled from the rail a fuchsia-coloured suit, skirt and jacket, and said 'Now try this on.' I just stared. From the look on his face I knew there was no point in arguing this time, so I just put it on to humour him. Who'd have thought? 'What a lovely rig-out,' as my mum would say. We decided it was perfect to accept my award from the Los Angeles Film Critics Association for Best Actress. Tom is a godsend and is the first person I turn to whenever I have a wardrobe emergency.

In Los Angeles most nominees are inundated with offers of gowns and jewellery to wear for big occasions, but we were not due to travel there until the day or two before the event and so there was obviously not enough time to arrange wardrobe. A hair and make-up artist is hired by the distributors of the film to come to the nominee's hotel room on the day of the event to make him or her look their best. I hadn't met the particular artiste allocated to me before and on such a big occasion I was rather anxious as to whom I was going to get. Anyway, at the appointed time there was a knock at our door. I opened it and there was Colin Booker wearing shorts and eating a sandwich.

'Let's have a look at what you're going to be wearing,' he demanded with a Lancashire accent, bustling his bags of make-up into the room, 'so I'll know what I'm dealing with.'

I showed him.

'Right, just sit here and we'll get started,' he said with a smile.

He sat me in what I thought was the darkest corner of the room with no mirror and *very* quickly applied the make-up. And with a swish, swish, swish of his fingers through my hair and a squirt of this and a squirt of that I could tell that he considered he was nearly finished. He'd only been in the room about fifteen minutes. My make-up had been applied so quickly, and as for my hair, I never even saw a comb! The biggest moment of my career and I was going to look like a scarecrow! I could feel my eyes filling up so I made my excuses and said I had to use the bathroom. I needed to look in a mirror and estimate how I could make the best of a bad job. Behind the closed door of the bathroom, with a sob in my throat, I hazarded a glance into the mirror. And I DID cry. I was absolutely astonished because I thought I had never looked *BETTER*. How did he do that with so little fuss.

Now whenever I'm at a function in Los Angeles I *always* ask for Colin Booker to do my hair and make-up. He was so good the distributors hired him to come on a tour of about ten US cities with me to promote a film called *Saving Grace*. It's amazing how much easier it is to do all those interviews if you have a make-up artist you can trust. Anyway, I dabbed my eyes dry, being careful not to smudge my make-up, and emerged from the bathroom. It was lovely to see the look of approval on Michael's face. On with my tux and with a little assistance the brooch was heaved to my shoulder and pinned, and I was ready.

Outside the Four Seasons Hotel there were stretch limousines galore, a constant bumper-to-bumper stream of them. My publicist's assistant made sure I was deposited into the right one and off we slowly went to the ceremony where I would be greeted by Nancy Seltzer. The logistics of organising such an event must be mind-boggling. All of the nominees and the hundreds of celebrities and their guests process up the long red carpet, thronged on both sides by journalists and cameras, each trying to catch the eye of one famous face or another in order to get an interview. Nancy would advise which ones to stop at and which ones to pass. Not only is this a celebration of film, it is also a celebration of haute couture. Every single journalist wants to know 'What are you wearing?' In other words, who designed the dress? the shoes? and the jewellery? Joan Rivers and her film crew were situated about halfway along the parade. Apprehension set in. Her angle on the proceedings is totally concerned with fashion and style, who is the best dressed? who is the *worst* dressed? who looks ridiculous? and who looks like mutton dressed up as lamb? She doesn't pull any punches. I do find her programme very funny despite cringing at some of the celebrities' discomfort. And as we approached her I couldn't help re-analysing what I was wearing. Oh dear, perhaps I should have worn a dress, I hadn't seen any other women in trousers. Ah well, here goes.

'That is a *beautiful* brooch!' Joan enthused

'Oh thank you, Joan, yes it is.' I agreed, perspiring, while trying to second-guess what her punch line was going to be. But there wasn't one. She really *did* like it *and* my tuxedo. So with Joan's seal of approval I felt a little more confident and relaxed as I progressed down the red carpet.

It really was surreal walking shoulder to shoulder with all those famous actors and actresses. But stranger even than finding myself staring at *them* at close quarters, was finding them staring at *me*, and then saying how much they had enjoyed *Secrets & Lies*. Faye Dunaway also said she'd enjoyed seeing my work on the London stage.

Unlike the Oscars, the Golden Globes guests have a meal before the ceremony instead of after. There's a lot of table-hopping and the atmosphere is very friendly. It's a long ceremony, because it celebrates television as well as film, and since I was nominated as Best Actress in a Drama, I had to wait for a couple of hours before my category was announced. As the time approached I got very nervous and went to the ladies' room to check my make-up. Win or lose the cameras would be trained on all the nominees. While I was there I thought I had better spend a penny.

But I hadn't anticipated how difficult it was to get in and out of an all-in-one tuxedo without it dragging on the floor or without taking it off altogether. Carefully holding it all around my knees as I took a leak, the weight of the giant brooch took it crashing to the floor. With a reflex action I dived after it but then *urgently recoiled* when I realised I was peeing on my collar! Oh no. Oh NO. The Golden Globes and I've peed on my collar! And I gazed at my lovely big brooch on the floor, which was now, to my horror, two medium-sized brooches. And while I was wondering what to do, I heard two girls outside talking about the next category.

'Best Actress next. Who do you think will win?' asked one.

'What about that Brenda Belthling,' said the other.

'No waaaaaay' sang her friend. 'Nobody has ever heeeeeeard of heeeeeeer! And anyway, I don't know anybody who can pronounce her name,' she laughed.

I was crestfallen. 'Oh well, that's that then,' I thought, trying to be instantly philosophical. Just as well really, what with my wet collar and broken brooch. But nevertheless I told myself I had better hurry back to my table for the announcement. I rinsed and dried off my collar as well as I could, and scoured the floor for a missing part of the brooch so that I could try and fit it all together again. Gillian Anderson found me doing this, and wearing her exquisite gown got on her hands and knees to help me search. Alas, we couldn't find the missing link, so I just pinned the biggest piece of the brooch to my tuxedo and hurried back to my table.

I got there just in time to hear Nicolas Cage reading out the names of the nominees and I related to Mike Leigh what I had just overheard in the restroom. Clips from each of the films were shown and then it was time for Nicolas Cage to open the envelope. 'And the winner is . . . Brenda Blethyn.'

There was a wonderful roar coming from somewhere. Embraces all round. Mike Leigh was kissing me. Marianne was kissing me. Simon was kissing me. Everyone was kissing me. I wended my way through the tables of applauding guests to get to the stage. Nicolas Cage kissed me. Oh my goodness! And as he handed me the trophy I wished that I'd prepared a speech. But I was so happy it didn't worry me for long. It didn't worry me that there was probably steam rising from my collar. It didn't worry me that I was only wearing half a brooch because it was gorgeous anyway. And I told myself that it's better to give the worst acceptance speech ever, than to have the best acceptance speech never given. And my mind was filled with thoughts of my family at home and in Florida and how happy they would be to hear the news. I gave many thanks to everyone involved, but especially I gave heartfelt thanks to Mike Leigh. And as we celebrated into the night I said to Mike Leigh. 'That'll teach me to go listening to other people's conversations in the toilet.' Mike laughingly replied, 'You only *got* the part because you listen to other people's conversations in the toilet.'

My friend James Ulmer and me salsa-dancing

20

IN FOR A PENNY

W HILE THE PROMOTION OF *SECRETS & LIES* WAS GATHERING
speed in Los Angeles prior to the Oscars, I was offered a film
called *Music from Another Room* with Jude Law, to be shot in
Pasadena. It was a three-week engagement and fitted in just
nicely. Pasadena is only a forty-minute drive from Los Angeles.
Halfway through the filming schedule the day came for the
Oscar nominations announcement to take place live at 5.30 a.m.
Pacific time on national television. Because I had won a Golden
Globe, it was organised that I was to be interviewed live by Katie
Couric on breakfast television in Studio City. It just so happened
to be on my way to work. Also on the programme being interviewed were several members of the O. J. Simpson jury, the trial
having just ended. It was nerve-racking and potentially embarrassing if *Secrets & Lies* didn't get any nominations. But I soon
felt justified in being there because one of the first categories to
be announced was Best Supporting Actress, and Marianne Jean-
Baptiste was one of the five. I was delighted. It was Marianne's

221

first feature film and it was also the first time a British black actress had been nominated. After the nine months or so she and I had been promoting the film worldwide it was such a wonderful payday.

Still on the programme with Katie Couric we waited while all the other nominees were named. It was a very satisfying morning indeed because in total *Secrets & Lies* got five nominations. I nearly fell off the sofa when my name was announced. Again I had a mental image of all my brothers and sisters receiving the news. It made me smile because I knew that they would be even more pleased than I was, if that was possible. Best Director (Mike Leigh), Best Original Screenplay (Mike Leigh), Best Film (Simon Channing-Williams), Best Supporting Actress (Marianne) and Best Actress (me).

When my interview was over and I returned to the green room I got a round of applause from the jury members. It was surreal. Only in America, I thought.

I called my sister Pam with the news of my nomination. She was thrilled. As she hadn't been too well lately, I asked her if I could treat her to a trip to Hollywood for a two-week holiday. The suggestion left her breathless. She said she was just going to set down the phone for a moment while she went to ask her husband John for his blessing. She was back on the phone again within seconds.

'It's okay, Bren,' she gasped. 'Yes, I can come. How do I get there?'

I explained that Bill would take her to the airport, her ticket would be waiting there, and I would meet her at this end. No worries.

'Oh dear,' she flustered, quite breathless. 'What do I need to bring with me?'

'Just yourself, Pam.'

She was excited and so was I. The journey was scheduled for the end of the week. Only five days to wait.

I arrived back at work, and words of congratulations were coming from all directions. But now the big question reared its head again. 'What to wear?'

By the time I got home from work my closet was stuffed with tempting gowns from various designers offering to dress me for the Academy Awards. Armani had left a message, saying they would love to dress me for the occasion, and since they had dressed me for the Golden Globes I wanted to stay with them. All I was required to do was to go to the salon on Rodeo Drive, approve the design and be measured. It was as easy as that. The vaguely oriental design showed a full-length gown covered with a full-length loose coat. It was gorgeous. The fabric sample was golden citrusy yellow and beautifully soft. Meticulous measurements were taken, and when I went for my final fitting, I was amazed to discover that the gown was so well made that I didn't need to wear any undergarment, and, believe me, that is quite rare for someone with an ample bosom. It was so comfortable and easy to wear. A long lemon chiffon shawl complemented the dress and coat together with beautiful golden sandals.

Harry Winston had also contacted me inviting me to his salon to select which diamonds I would like to wear for the occasion. We chose necklace, earrings and bracelet all with yellow and white diamonds, valued at something like $2 million. How much? Yes, $2 million! They would be delivered to my hotel by a security guard on the day of the event. I broke out into a sweat! Can you imagine! Michael had better be on his toes on that day, keeping an eye on my neck, wrist and ears. I was all set.

At the end of the week I was so excited to be seeing Pam. I called an American friend of mine to ask his advice on where I could hire the best stretch limousine to meet Pam at the airport.

'Hell, you don't need to *hire* a stretch, Brenda, take mine.'

'Well, thank you, Robert,' I said, 'how generous.'

And he was true to his word. Not only did he send the stretch limo, he came along with it for the ride.

On the way to the airport I explained to him that my sister was a little frail, only recently recovering from a second heart attack and the long flight would have tired her terribly. The flight was due to arrive at around 4.30 p.m. but on Pam's body clock it would be half-past midnight already. She emerged through the immigration door looking radiant, and draped across the arm of a very handsome young man who had apparently been her next-door neighbour during the flight. My friend was a little taken aback because, after my description of Pam, he was expecting to have to carry her to the limo. But this was good news because he now felt justified in insisting he should take us all out on the town. And did.

First stop Santa Monica for cocktails. Then came a stroll past the roller-bladers and cyclists displaying their skills along the promenade at Venice Beach, and the purchase of obligatory souvenir T-shirts and a baseball cap. Pam's knowledge of Venice Beach was gleaned only from TV shows, mostly with gun-toting policemen chasing villains. She looked a little apprehensive until our friend reassured her by informing her that his 'pal', who had also come along for the ride, was 'packing a piece'. I will never as long as I live forget the look on Pam's face. We laughed about it many times afterwards. Her body clock now said 3.30 a.m.

'How's about another cocktail at Marina Del Rey,' chirps our escort.

'Oh well, in for a penny,' answers Pam.

'What's that?' queried our American friends.

'In for a penny,' said Pam, 'means in for a penny, in for a pound. We've started so we'll finish.'

'Oh that is so cute,' they sang. 'In for a penny! How about that? I'm gonna use that. Okay. Gotcha. Let's go. In for a penny!! Oh, you English girls! In for a penny!! Ha ha ha.'

He was having such a good time showing us the sights. And we were grateful. Pam and I were finally delivered home, tired but very happy.

A day or two later I was invited to be a guest at the premiere of David Lynch's film *Lost Highway*. Pam had never been to a premiere before and I wanted to make it special for her. We spent the afternoon shopping at the Beverly Centre, a huge mall in West Hollywood, and despite resistance from Pam, I bought her a new outfit. Top to toe. Pam was actually a bit like me in that she didn't like anyone spending money on her. But I was determined. I forced her to let me buy her a new outfit just for the fun of it and we both got all dolled up for the occasion. I warned her that when we emerged from the limousine there would be dozens of photographers lining the red carpet, waiting for the stars of the film to arrive, and to just stay close to me. Sure enough, as the door of the limo opened we were almost blinded by the blaze of flashbulbs. Miss Blethyn, Miss Blethyn, over here Miss Blethyn, Brenda to the left, to the left, Brenda straight ahead. Over here Miss Blethyn, thank you, to the right.

And then, 'Who's the dame with Miss Blethyn?'

'It's her sister.'

'What's her name?'

'Pamela.'

'Pamela, Pamela, over here, thank you Pamela. Lovely that's right. Over here Pamela, Pamela. You're beautiful. Miss Blethyn stand together now. Lovely.' We were shrieking with laughter.

I really enjoyed the film but Pam enjoyed it even more than me. Patricia Arquette was great in it. I wasn't terribly familiar with David Lynch's work but Pam was, so she had more to say to him at the party afterwards than I did. I can remember sitting in a booth with him, marvelling at his fuzzy hair, with Pam chatting away to him nineteen to the dozen. I was astonished by her self-assurance. We danced and laughed and had a jolly good time until the limousine took us back to our hotel. We were just in time to catch the late news, including an item covering the premiere, and there was Pam being photographed on the red carpet. You couldn't see me.

Imagine my sister Jeannie's reaction on watching the news in Florida. She didn't yet know that Pam was in America. Her eyes apparently nearly popped out of her head. More than that, imagine my cousin Beryl's surprise watching CNN in Bangkok, because Pam was supposed to have been looking after her house in Ramsgate while Beryl was away on holiday. But don't worry anyone, Pam wouldn't neglect her duties. Her husband John was meanwhile keeping a very diligent eye on Beryl's house.

Pam's trip to Los Angeles coincided with my birthday, and some newly acquired friends of mine held a special birthday party in my honour. They took over an entire restaurant and invited many of their friends and my own. It was extraordinarily generous. I just happened to mention to them in passing sometime earlier than I liked salsa dancing, and to my astonishment, aside from the many gifts the guests had brought for me, they had also hired champion salsa dancers. If I had mentioned that I liked ice-skating, no doubt Torvill and Dean would have been there. They had also commissioned, and had made, a wonderful red salsa dress, which I was required to wear in order to dance with one of the champion dancers. It was fabulous. I was enjoying myself enormously. I had three or four dances and then thought I'd better return to Pam, only to find her waltzing with a very elegant gentleman, who it transpired was a very very very very rich single chap who had taken a shine to Pam. He asked if we had ever

226

been to Las Vegas, and when we said we hadn't he offered to fly us both there the following morning in his Learjet. Well, can you imagine, Pam and I got the hysterics, we thought it was the funniest thing we'd ever heard. I don't think he actually wanted me to go, just Pam, which somehow made us laugh even more. It was as if we'd fallen asleep and woken up in the TV series *Dallas*. We couldn't possibly accept, tempting though it was, because I was working the next day. Pam came on set with me.

A few weeks before the Oscar ceremony was the Screen Actors Guild Awards. I'd been nominated for *Secrets & Lies*. Pam and I were on the same table as Frances McDormand and her family, and again we were both nominated in the same category. Frances won. But she did let me hold the trophy for a couple of seconds and I was surprised at how heavy it was. I congratulated her, and Frances said jokingly, 'Sure, I bet you mean that!' and I expect I would have jokingly said the same. But my sister, not spotting the humour, piped up and said, 'Yes Frances, actually Brenda does mean that.' I said, 'It's okay, Pam, it was just a joke.' I thought I'd better get Pam a little glass of something cheerful, like champagne, before there was an incident! I said, 'I'll only be a moment, Pam, and when I get back I'll introduce you to some people.' I had only left her for something like three minutes when I heard Pam calling across the room, 'Brenda, Brenda come over here, I'd like to introduce you to the cast of *ER*.' She didn't need my help. She had got friendly and chatty already, and had introduced herself.

Pam had thoroughly enjoyed her holiday and went home laden with lots of stories and gifts for her husband, daughter and friends.

The day of the Oscars arrived. Despite trying to be blasé, this was a huge event for me. Here was Brenda Bottle of Ramsgate walking up the red carpet for the Academy Awards, and nominated as Best Actress to boot. It was amazing. But it was too much of a leap to hope that I would actually win, even though the Las Vegas betting odds had at times been in my favour. The preamble was pretty much the same as for the Golden Globes, save for the fact that the ceremony takes place in a theatre. The host for the evening was Billy Crystal and he was hilarious. Practically every famous face in Hollywood was there. Faye Dunaway complimented me again on my performance. I met Alec Baldwin. Robin Williams gave me a big smacker on the cheek. To tell the truth I can't remember if these people were at this event or one of the other events I attended during this period. It all merges into one. But who cares.

During the Oscar ceremony Michael went to the rest room and he was gone for ages. A seat filler took his place next to me meanwhile. These are people hired by the Academy so that the television viewers don't see any empty seats. When he returned he apologised for being so long and explained that on the way back he had got into a long conversation with Shirley MacLaine, as if it was the most natural thing in the world. Again it was Nicholas Cage who opened the envelope. We hadn't won in any of the other categories and I held my breath as he pulled the name from the envelope. I was so proud of *Secrets & Lies* that I wanted it to win *something* even if it was me. It wasn't. And the Oscar goes to Frances McDormand for *Fargo*. No surprise there then. It was a great film, and she was great in it.

But now, here we were at the Oscars, and we hadn't won. After our meal, I had arranged to meet my nephew Liam to go to the Elton John party, which is considered to be the best after-show party, so we were required to take a small detour in order to pick him up. We gave the driver instructions of where to find Liam and sat back in the limousine, chatting and sipping champagne. After about half an hour, I looked out of the window and discovered we were driving up a back alley somewhere!! I panicked! I said, 'Driver, do you know where you are?' He looked at me in his rear-view mirror and said, 'No, mam.' 'No, mam? What does he mean no mam? For goodness sake!' I was convinced it was a ploy to nick the diamonds. I broke out into a sweat. Until he explained, 'Pardon me, mam, but I'm from outatown. The Academy hires hundreds of drivers for this event, cos there ain't enough of 'em in Los Angeles to cope. I sure am sorry, mam. It's cos I took the detour.' Michael had to get out the road map to direct him. That was OK so long as the diamonds were still in place. We finally found my nephew and got to the Elton John party which was already in full swing. It was so crowded and everyone was having the time of their lives. His parties are always to raise awareness of the Elton John AIDS Foundation. When leaving any of the parties, each guest is given a goody bag, the contents ranging from the sublime to the ridiculous. After the Oscar ceremony I was given a watch worth somewhere in the region of $2000.

We drank quite a lot of champagne going from one party to another and when we returned to the hotel and I took off my diamonds I decided it would be prudent to hide them somewhere safe. I found the perfect hiding place, where *no one* would find them. And in the morning, neither could I. Talk about panic. I couldn't remember where I'd hidden them. I was convinced a burglar had come in during the night and lifted them. I turned the room inside out. Eventually I found them, literally two minutes before the security guard came to retrieve them. I should have followed the lead of one famous actress and refused to give them back! You probably all want to know where I hid them. Well I'm not telling you. That is for me to know and for you to find out, as my mother would say. But the saga of ceremonies and haut couture wasn't over yet.

Look behind you!

21

HONOURS EVEN

ONE OF THE BENEFITS OF WINNING HIGH PROFILE AWARDS and nominations is that it opens the door to the international film market. Suddenly I was on casting lists that I would never have been considered for previously. As well as *Music from Another Room*, I was also offered a role in a film to be made in Australia. The film was *In the Winter Dark* from Tim Winton's novel.

Although there were other interesting projects on offer at that time, I was more interested in *In the Winter Dark* than my agents were, even though it was a small independent film. Weeks after I had read the script I was still thinking about it. It haunted me. The story is set in a remote farming community in the Megalong Valley in the Blue Mountains. Ray Barrett, who played my husband, and myself lived in a small farmhouse in this vast open space, and the nearest neighbours were about a mile away. Those neighbours were an odd couple, townies recently moved to the area, and played by Richard Roxburgh and Miranda Otto.

The story concerns the mysterious killing of some of their livestock, and in trying to solve the mystery the two households are brought together.

I loved Australia. I was expecting to find an arid country but instead found lush vegetation. In the Blue Mountains, so called because of the blue haze given off by the eucalyptus trees, there were forests as far as the eye could see. I witnessed a couple of bush fires on the escarpment while we were filming, and the helicopters dropping gallons of water over the inferno seemed totally inadequate. There were wallabies galore, and many colourful wild birds, cockatoos, parrots, and the laughing kookaburras. On the downside, there were red-bellied snakes, funnel-web spiders and worse, but I was longing to see a wombat. Every night one of the crew would drive me slowly back to the hotel, keeping our eyes peeled in the hope of catching sight of one. In the last week, joy of joys, lumbering across the road in the car headlights was a wombat. I don't think it was badly hurt when we hit it because it had scampered off whimpering by the time we'd got out of the car. I was suicidal, and I didn't know whether to laugh or cry, so I did both alternately. My wails of grief turned effortlessly into gails of laughter. I know it's not funny, it's tragic, but hysteria had set in. Poor little wombat, out on his little nightly stroll. My driver assured me that there was no sign of blood so the wombat was probably just a bit miffed instead of badly hurt.

There were two scenes in the film which made me feel uncomfortable. One was having to feed a real leg of kangaroo to our dog. It stunk to high heaven. The frozen leg had been bought from an abattoir, but by the time we came to use it, it had thawed out and it was HIGH. The leg was about two and a half feet long, and quite heavy, and I wasn't wearing gloves. We did the scene several times, and when James Bogle, our director, called CUT, the leg was snatched away from the dog, so that we could have another go. The dog was used to it. He was an actor too! I was glad to see the back of that leg.

Another scene I was uncomfortable with, was when all four characters were at our farmhouse having a meeting about strategy to find out what was killing our stock. Remember that we were in a very remote farmhouse. The walls were thick, the windows small, to keep out the heat of the sun, and it was dark in there. Obviously we had to use some lighting for filming purposes but it was still dark. The four of us were sitting around the table, waiting for the crew to be ready, when Ray leant over to say something to me. I leant forward to hear, and he said, 'No, it doesn't matter. I'll tell you later.' Curious!

So later, when we had finished lunch and were about to go back inside to finish the scene, I said, 'Oh Ray, what was it you wanted to tell me?'

'Oh yes,' he said, 'it's all right, I can tell you now, it's gone.'

I said, 'What are you talking about? What's gone?'

He said, 'There was a tarantula right above your head!'

I turned white.

I said, 'Ray, when you say "it's gone", what do you mean exactly?'

He said, 'Oh it's okay, it's moved off somewhere.'

'Jesus, I can't go back in there!' I said. 'Where's it gone?'

'It won't bother you,' said Ray cheerfully, wishing he hadn't mentioned it.

Oh no! I don't believe I've got to go back into that dark dismal room, I thought, but I've *got to* unless I want to bring the entire film production to a halt. If only the next scene wasn't Miranda and me crawling about and laying on the floor. It's no good, I thought, I shall have to tell them. They are going to have to find our little hairy friend. I don't want them to hurt it or move it, just locate it, and keep an eye on it. So before shooting every scene from then on, there was a make-up check, a wardrobe check and a spider check.

The next day, after a lie-in to recover, Ray and his wife Gaye took me out for a late Sunday lunch to get the colour back into my cheeks. We went to a quiet restaurant up in the hills with a splendid view of the valley. I shall never EVER forget it, not because of the view, but because the waitress when serving us our starters said, 'Who's having the soup? . . . Right . . . And who's having the prawns? . . . Right . . . Diana's dead, and who's having the pâté?'

'I beg your pardon?' I said, 'What did you just say?'

'Diana. She's a goner.'

'Diana who?'

'Princess of Wales – been in a car crash – well they reckon she's dead.'

We were stunned. And when the waitress returned to take our plates we hadn't even touched our food. 'Yep. She's dead all right,' she said. 'Are you going to eat that, or shall I clear it away?'

We were absolutely speechless. Literally. How could she have been so casual? We and the few other diners just sat there for a couple of hours, finding it very difficult to accept.

Of course when we got home and turned on the TV there was wall to wall coverage of it. When something as momentous as that happens, my goodness it makes you sit up straight doesn't it. And there was me worrying about a little tiny spider. Well, a little tiny spider as big as a dinner plate, but it all seemed so unimportant all of a sudden.

It was while I was in Australia that I finally agreed to play Mari in *Little Voice*. I had turned the role down twice already during the previous six months because I thought the actress who had created the role should have been considered for the part. But that was not to be and when push came to shove, I decided to do it. It would have been daft not to. A couple of days later I heard that Ray Say was to be played by Michael Caine.

The film was shot in Scarborough. I was apprehensive about working with Michael because I'd never played close contact scenes with such a huge star before, and there were a few raunchy scenes. I also thought he might want the total focus of attention. But I found that not to be the case at all. Like me, he wanted the scene to work, regardless of who was in it. Mark Herman, the director, cleverly decided that the first scene to be shot was the one where Mari rushes from the house and pounces on Ray Say and smothers him with kisses. Well, that certainly broke the ice!!

It was a pleasure working with Michael. I think everyone thought the same. He took the trouble to remember everybody's name in the cast and crew and never at any time pulled focus. Encouraging Annette Badland to favour camera while shooting one scene he said, 'Get yer face in girl', which gave Annette and me the giggles. And watching Jane Horrocks give such a stunning performance as Little Voice gave all of us a thrill.

When a few of us had an evening off work, we went to a pub along the seafront in Scarborough where an Elvis impersonator was performing. The place was packed to the gunnels because he was really good. We thought it would be great if he could perform at our cast and crew party before starting filming. But Elvis indignantly said, 'If Michael Caine wants to see me, he can come here!' So we told him.

A few nights later we revisited the pub and it was equally as crowded. About halfway through Elvis's act, the door opened and in squeezed Michael Caine wearing a flat cap and anorak. Elvis and the other customers couldn't believe their eyes. But they could see that Michael had just come to enjoy the act the same as everybody else and chose not to bother him. He sang along with the rest of us. Elvis was really chuffed.

Michael quite rightly won a Golden Globe for his performance as Ray Say, and his magical rendition of 'My Way' at the end of the film will probably go down in history!

Jane and I were both also nominated for a Golden Globe, so the vexing problem of 'what to wear' reared its head again, and then yet again when I learned I had been nominated for another Oscar.

Little Voice also brought an increase in fan mail. Early in my career, when I first started to receive such mail, I was deeply flattered and resolved to answer every single letter, until I received one too many that read: 'Dear Sir or Madam, You are my favourite actor . . .' Most letters ask for a signed photograph, and I usually obliged, but as time went on I was being asked if I would send several photos 'for their friends', but undedicated, and I came to realise that they were then being sold on the internet. Do they know how much those photos cost to have printed? I decided to take a page out of Mum's book and 'pull in my horns'. Or better still, to give my photos to a charity, and if anyone wants one they'll have to apply to them and pay a nominal fee. Any requests sent to me will be forwarded on, but then it's probably too much bother even for a charity.

Most actors also get dozens of letters from students who are looking for assistance to cover their tuition fees. Or even if their tuition fees are paid they need money to live on. I don't understand why young people have to pay for their education. It's a false economy. I think we should be investing in young people not putting them in debt. These people are our future. I especially think that a lot more investment should be put into primary education. If learning was made more attractive in the early years maybe there wouldn't be so many problems later on. I don't suppose it'll ever happen, though, because you wouldn't see an immediate benefit. Anyway, if I was at No. 10 that would be a priority for me. Although my parents were Conservatives, I have always been a Labour supporter. I didn't like the way my dad always called the doctor or anyone in authority 'sir'. I liked the courtesy, of course, but it went much deeper than that. And there's another thing I'd put on the school curriculum – courtesy.

I had a letter from No. 10 once. As I ripped it open I joked that the Prime Minister had heard of my views and was demanding an audience! Imagine my surprise when I read that, confidentially, Her Majesty the Queen might be offering me an OBE in her 2003 New Year Honours List, and if that were the case, the letter asked, would I accept? 'Well! There's a turn-up! What a windfall!' I didn't utter a word to anyone, except Michael, of course. I rang him before I'd even finished the letter. I didn't think I would EVER be awarded anything like that, despite the fact that Craig Ferguson insists on calling me Dame Brenda followed by a celestial fanfare!

I replied to No. 10 immediately and said, of course, I would accept.

A couple of months later another letter arrived confirming the award and told me that I was to report to the Palace on such and such a day and that I was permitted to invite three guests. I chose Michael, Auntie Fran and my brother Bill. I was a little concerned that walking around for a whole day might be too tiring for my fragile 86-year-old aunt, so I suggested taking the wheelchair and enquired if there was wheelchair access at the Palace. There was, and moreover I was informed that people confined to wheelchairs were positioned right at the front. Excellent! The day came and I got myself and Auntie Fran all dolled up, she in a navy blue suit and my mum's treasured navy hat, and me in an Albert Nippon suit from the series I was currently working on. A limousine whisked us off to the Palace.

On arrival we were greeted by liveried ushers, one of whom, named Liam, was to be Auntie Fran's personal escort. He pushed her right to the front of the hall. Meanwhile, I had to go to be briefed about protocol. It was great to be honoured alongside theatre directors Trevor Nunn and Michael Blakemore, but even better for us to be counted amongst dozens of people who were nothing to do with showbusiness at all.

The presentations were in alphabetical order and therefore I was fortunately near the front of a very long line and I could see into the hall. When Prince Charles entered to a trumpet fanfare, Auntie Fran shot up from her wheelchair and stood to attention. I tried to signal to her 'Sit down, sit down, everyone will think you got to the front of the hall under false pretences!' But she stood erect until the music had stopped. Prince Charles gave every single recipient the exact same amount of time while presenting the medal. I wondered if he would recognise me from my association with the Prince's Trust. A smile did play on his lips as I approached. He asked if I was surprised to receive the envelope with the announcement.

'Surprised and very relieved, sir,' I said, 'because at first I thought it was a tax demand.'

He congratulated me and asked what project I was working on at the moment.

Blushing I told him I was working on a series called *Between the Sheets*.

'My goodness,' he said. 'Really? But is that something that I would watch do you think?'

'Oh I think you'd love it, sir.' I said, engaging my mouth before my brain.

Auntie Fran spent the morning like a princess, and as we swept out of Buckingham Palace's gates, she waved regally to the cheering crowds.

Desperately missing Whoopi

22

FIRST-CLASS TREATMENT

I HAD A FITTING FOR A BEAUTIFUL GOWN AT A HAUTE COUTURE salon in New York. For about three hours I stood on top of a box while the length was adjusted and the bodice was pinched in and tucked and folded and pinned. Cinderella came to mind. It had miles of beautiful lace with a delicate golden-coloured metallic thread weaving through and was breathtakingly lovely. Having satisfied everyone that I was going to be the most gorgeously dressed guest at the ceremony I returned to my hotel in order to pack because I was leaving for Palm Springs, California, via LA, early the next morning. The weather had been bad all week but overnight, as luck would have it, there was a severe blizzard threatening to halt most transport.

After an early morning call at 5.30 a.m. I took a shower. Accidentally I glanced in the mirror and didn't recognise who was looking back at me. I was covered from head to foot in the most appalling rash, which at that very moment started to itch. Oh no.

Despite the blizzard my limousine sat waiting for me at the appointed time of 6.30 to take me to John F. Kennedy Airport and although it took twice as long as normal to get there we did manage it, only to find pandemonium. Dozens of flights cancelled or delayed. Thousands of people, shoulder to shoulder, trying to switch flights or get refunds or even trying different destinations. The passengers on my flight were told hourly that departure was delayed for yet another hour at least, and tempers were frayed. The blizzard worsened.

After I'd been squashed in the airport for about eight hours (no exaggeration), itching and scratching and swearing at the least provocation, I gave up all hope of ever getting to Palm Springs, where I was expected to introduce a film at the film festival. I gazed into the middle distance and thought I was hallucinating. James Bond was approaching!

It was like the parting of the Red Sea. The crowds magically and magnificently made an aisle for him to walk through, and as the space widened for his companions, my eyes came out on stalks. Better even than seeing James Bond, walking at his side was Nancy Seltzer, his publicist, but also MY publicist. I had never been so pleased to see anyone in my life.

'Nancy!!! Nancy!!! Over here! Nancy, it's Brenda!'

'Brenda? Is that you?' queried Nancy. 'You look different. I thought you were in Palm Springs. What's the matter with your face!'

I grabbed my case, and the stranger who was sitting on it fell to the floor.

'Oh Nancy, I've been here for ever. I should be on my way to LA. I'm going out of my mind. Are you just arriving or leaving?'

She told me that she was accompanying Mr and Mrs Sean Connery to LA and was reliably informed that their flight was due to leave in one hour.

'Why don't you come with us,' crooned James Bond, not yet having noticed the spots.

'Because I'm booked on a different flight and everyone is trying to change and all the flights are full and I expect your flight is already full, and a million other reasons,' I gibbered.

'Nancy will make enquiries,' said 007.

And Nancy did make enquiries and when she returned she handed me a new set of tickets and told me to accompany her and James Bond to the first-class departure lounge. Oh heaven. Nancy was like a guardian angel. It wasn't long before we stepped on board the aircraft. You know, it's not cheap to hire a publicist to look after you during all these endless rounds of press junkets, but as I sunk into my spacious seat I realised it was worth every penny. However, it wasn't all going our way. We sat comfortably on board for upwards of two hours waiting for takeoff. At least I wasn't being poked in the ribs every five seconds as I was while sitting on my suitcase.

A passenger 'in the know', sitting next to Nancy, patted the side of his nose and told her conspiratorily that President Clinton's plane was scheduled to take off soon and nothing was allowed to take priority over it. So we simply had to wait. But waiting presented another problem. After another sub-zero hour, one of the gauges or dials or clocks or whatever it was in the cockpit, which was needed to navigate us across North America, had frozen so we had to wait for a spare part to be delivered which might take some time. The PA system apologised to passengers for the delay! Fortunately those of us in first class were served with cocktails to help pass the time, but Sean said that, in the circumstances, it was unfair if the people in coach class weren't also served cocktails. The stewards agreed and proceeded with the trolley down to the back of the plane.

Wined and dined we eventually took off for the West Coast.

Because of the extended time to enjoy the hospitality of the airline, a few people had got a little merry and unfortunately one lady passenger from the rear of the plane had stumbled and broken her ankle. She was carried by two stewards along into first class and it made my eyes water to see one of her feet pointing completely backwards. It must have been excrutiatingly painful and the lady was so brave. Another announcement was made over the PA system to the effect that we would be making an unscheduled emergency landing at Colorado in order to get the lady to hospital, and because we were landing sooner than expected we would have to eject all our surplus fuel prior to touchdown. And we all knew what that meant. It meant another wait at Colorado while we were refuelled. The journey now seemed to have lasted a fortnight and my itching wasn't getting any easier. But here's where Nancy helped again. While we were on the tarmac at Colorado, she telephoned the film company in Palm Springs and organised for them to send a stretch limo to LAX and to simply wait there until I arrived. While on the phone she discovered to her dismay that a news item had been shown on the television saying that the aircraft carrying James Bond was missing!

Eventually we arrived at LAX and the crowds and reporters waiting to greet Sean Connery were enormous. From here on the journey was as smooth as butter. It was warm, the limo was waiting, the driver cheerful and off we whizzed to Palm Springs. Of course I missed the screening I was supposed to have introduced but there was another the following day, which I did attend. Meanwhile a consultation with an allergist had to be arranged. It was out of hours and the surgery was closed, but one of the organisers managed to ring the allergist at home. Would you believe it? Apparently I was allergic to Cinderella's frock with the golden-coloured metallic thread. So although I only looked like

Cinderella for the duration of the fitting, I felt like Cinderella when I was being whisked away by James Bond. I sincerely give many thanks to Sean Connery and his wife and to Nancy Seltzer for saving me. And to Escada for coming to my rescue with a beautiful green silk chiffon gown, to replace the offending one.

More recently I met the now *Sir* Sean Connery in Berlin at the European Film Academy Awards Ceremony, where he was to receive a Lifetime Achievement Award. I had been allocated a seat in the same row as his, and as he progressed along the row, accompanied by a standing ovation, I said, 'Oh how lovely to see you again, Sean.' He graciously replied, 'Oh heeelooo, good to shee you', but it was quite obvious to me that he didn't have a clue who I was. It occurred to me that if I'd put red dots and welts all over my face, and had a good scratch, it might have rung a bell.

During a visit to Los Angeles in 2000 I was lucky enough to be invited to a BAFTA LA Steven Spielberg tribute being hosted by Whoopi Goldberg. Mr Spielberg was to be presented with the Stanley Kubrick Britannia Award for Excellence in Film. There were dozens of glittering guests, including Ronald Neame, Jeff Goldblum, Robert Zemeckis, Craig Ferguson, Lynn Redgrave, Alan Cumming, Ben Kingsley, Russell Crowe, Ridley Scott, Joan Allen, Michael Crawford and HRH Prince Andrew, and, of course, Steven Spielberg himself. I had been asked to introduce one of the guests on to the stage, who would then give their own personal tribute, and thereafter I could sit back and be entertained by Whoopi. I was really looking forward to it. Escada again dressed me for the occasion in a lovely black slinky dress with a fur-like trim. As taught by Mum and Dad, I was ready in good time and waiting for the arrival of my car.

The phone rang in my hotel room. It was reception. I told them I'd be right down, thinking my car had arrived. They said,

'Oh no, Miss Blethyn, would you please stay in your room. A representative from BAFTA would like to come up to see you. Is that okay?'

I said, 'But I'm ready, I can come down.'

'No please,' said the voice from reception, 'the lady *insists* on coming up to see you.'

That's odd I thought.

Three minutes later I opened the door to let her in.

She said, 'Brenda, will you sit down a moment please,' and then added, 'Oh how lovely you look.'

I sat down. She continued, 'You do know that Whoopi Goldberg is hosting this evening, don't you, Brenda?'

'Yeees,' I said, not at all sure where this was leading.

'Well,' she said, 'she's not! Unfortunately she's just phoned in sick. Could you, would you, Brenda, please, will you *please* take over and host the evening?'

I was dumbstruck. I couldn't *possibly* host the evening. I said 'This is a wind-up, isn't it? Because in any case it starts in half an hour!'

'Yes it does start in half an hour, Brenda. You are our only hope. *Please* help us out of this difficulty,' she said, and then the inevitable, 'We're desperate!'

My stomach did a somersault. Where had I heard that phrase before? But this is more than one line I thought. If *ever* a woman suffered!

'Is there an Autocue?' I asked, seeing no way out, short of taking a taxi to the airport.

'There *is* an Autocue,' she said as if that settled it and opened the door.

'Just a minute! Just a minute!' I said. 'What about the presentation I was supposed to have made?'

'That's okay. Lynn Redgrave has agreed to read that part. So you'll do it then?' she asked, swiftly followed by, 'That's marvellous. Thank you SO much, Brenda.' She was relieved.

Dear oh dear!

And off we went. I felt as though I'd been hit by a ten-ton truck. When we arrived I asked to at least have a look at the script that would be projected on to the Autocue, but there was no time because I was immediately required to go to a photo shoot. And suddenly there I was in front of dozens of photographers posing with Mr Spielberg and HRH Prince Andrew and wondering what on earth I was doing there. It actually made me laugh. Half an hour earlier I'd just been minding my own business in my hotel room and all of a sudden I'm in a huddle with British royalty and Hollywood royalty as if it was the most natural thing in the world. I thought of Dad. 'Just take it in your stride, Bren, and if all else fails, sing a song!'

Well, I did manage to get through the evening without major mishap, although I was a nervous wreck. There was another presenter on the other side of the huge stage but he'd had time to study the text. Although the video presentations got out of sync because a page had been skipped in the Autocue I was able miraculously to steer the evening back on course in time for us to invite Prince Andrew to the stage. And when he presented the trophy to Mr Spielberg to tumultuous applause, he commented that it was the heaviest award anyone from the Royal Family had ever lifted. My reward was standing in the wings and hearing Michael Crawford and Dale Kristien perform songs from *Phantom of the Opera*, and when Michael sang 'Music of the Night' I was in floods. It was so beautiful. At the end I had a very large cocktail, courtesy of BAFTA LA, and they also relaxed and had one with me.

23

STRANGE TIMES

Anyone on the outside of the film industry looking in will probably think it is terribly glamorous. Mostly it's the opposite. The only time the public really see the actors is when they're done up to the nines on a red carpet, or scrubbed up nicely for the endless rounds of publicity interviews and photo shoots. But that all happens *after* the film is made. *While* the film is being made, it's early mornings, long hours and, often, unsavoury conditions. It's sometimes nerve-racking, it can be lonely and sometimes deeply embarrassing.

I was thrilled to be offered the part of Mrs van Pels in the HBO mini-series *Anne Frank – The Whole Story*, which told her story including before and after the attic. It had a multinational cast including Hannah Taylor Gordon, Ben Kingsley, Yoachim Król, Tatjana Blacher and Lilli Taylor, and was directed by Rumanian Robert Dornhelm. The project was shot in Prague both in a studio and a specially made set built along the side of the Vlatava River to represent Amsterdam. The only actor I had worked with before was Ben, and I was quite excited and full of anticipation when I arrived at the Prague Hilton to meet everyone else. However, it transpired that most of the actors had opted to stay in accommodation at the bottom of the hill by the river. In any case, Tatjana had brought her dog along for the ride and needed special accommodation. In my room I discovered a lovely bouquet of flowers with a card saying 'Welcome from your own dear Curly.' This was, of course, the actor Yoachim Król who played Mr van Pels. What a delightful man Yoachim is.

Working on this project was a very emotional experience. Costumes and jewellery were authentic and I couldn't help thinking that some of them could conceivably have been confiscated from the victims of the Holocaust themselves. The women in the cast had all agreed to have their heads shaved in performance on camera, including myself. Shaved isn't the right word. Hacked is more accurate. It was a very cold winter and when filming the Auschwitz scenes our costumes were so flimsy that we were freezing cold. However, as soon as they heard 'cut' from the director, the wardrobe department bundled us all into lovely warm duvets or thick warm coats, and served warm drinks, while the next shot was being set up. The torment endured by the original inhabitants of the camps is unthinkable. There was one particularly harrowing scene, when we were herded out of the cattle trucks to be met by snarling, salivating Alsatian dogs and violent screaming guards. It was freezing cold and many people slid and fell on the ice while the women were separated brutally from their sons, brothers and husbands. We were tattooed with a number, and jewellery, spectacles and all other belongings confiscated. We were ordered to strip and in front of male officers we were unceremoniously herded into the shower rooms to be disinfected. To say it was a very sobering experience is totally inadequate, and as a mark of respect Mr Dornhelm forbade us all to bring any food on to the set.

But despite the sombre subject matter, it was a happy shoot and about halfway through, Robert invited us all out to dinner at one of the best restaurants in Prague. I knew it would be special because apart from being wonderful to work with, Robert is a fantastic cook, a gourmet, a wine expert and has very fine taste. To make the occasion even more special I thought I would ride down the hill to the restaurant on the tram as I hadn't experienced them yet. It didn't matter that it was winter, icy cold and dark, I waited, shivering, for about fifteen minutes for the tram to arrive and climbed on board. There were only a handful of other passengers and I found a seat easily and settled down to enjoy the ride. It was lovely and warm on board and I was soon lulled into a reverie, with 'Lara's Theme' flooding my mind.

When I came back to the present I was astonished to realise I was the only passenger left on board. Where had everyone gone? I hadn't noticed anyone leave. I looked at my watch and my eyes nearly came out on stalks! I'd been on the tram for more than forty-five minutes and the journey should only have taken seven or eight minutes. Cupping my hands round my eyes I looked out of the window only to see blackness looking back. No street lights, no moon, no anything! I hauled myself along to the driver to enquire where on earth we were, but I couldn't make myself understood. I didn't speak Czech and he didn't speak English. But then he sighed, put his hands together as if in prayer and laid them under the side of his head indicating that he was on his way home to bed. Oh heavens! Please let me off the tram. I have to get back to Prague. I had absolutely no idea where I was and couldn't see a hand in front of my face as I alighted. The only lights I could see were on the back of the disappearing tram. I didn't even know if I was in the road or on the pavement, but since there was no other traffic it didn't really matter. I could feel my eyes filling up. It was scary. I decided to call my friends at the restaurant thinking hopefully they would come to fetch me. I groped around in my handbag for my phone, only to find that I'd left my special Czech mobile at the hotel, and in any case, how could I tell them where I was, because I didn't know. I was lost, confused and frightened for what seemed like twelve hours but was in fact only twenty-five minutes and was scared witless when suddenly my inside pocket started to vibrate.

My *London* phone! I didn't know I had it with me. Oh what joy! It was Michael calling from London.

'Oh Michael, thank God. Thank God. Michael, I'm in the middle of nowhere, I'm absolutely totally, completely and utterly lost. I'm frightened and don't know what to do.'

'Never mind all that,' he said. 'I'm locked out. I know you buried some spare keys in the front garden. Where are they?'

I couldn't believe my ears.

'But Michael, I'm going to be murdered, I just know it!'

'Are they on the left- or the right-hand side of the path?' he queried.

'Oh for God's sake Michael, stand with your back to the door, take three paces forward and one to the left. Dig between the rhododendron and the hebe. Oh Michael, whatever shall I do?' I waited.

'Nope. They're not there!' Beep beep the battery was going.

'All right then, take six paces forward and four to the right and dig between the roses and the lavender.' A long silence. Had I lost the signal.

'Nope they're not there either.'

So while I was waiting to be murdered and my front garden in London was being demolished my battery died along with my hopes of ever being rescued. An eternity passed, during which time I resolved never to hide keys in my garden again!

I could see two tiny red specks. Were they glow-worms in a

hedge? Was it something caught in my hair? It was so dark I had no idea of distance. The red spots seemed to be moving. Wait a minute. It was a car! Was it? Yes it WAS a car, approaching at some speed, and it was at that precise moment that I discovered I was indeed in the middle of the road and the driver had to swerve wildly to avoid killing me. I'd taken him so by surprise I'd scared him half to death. But 'never mind all that' as Michael would say, THE CAR WAS A TAXI. Saved. In the back of the car I pulled myself together and dug into my handbag for some money and found I hadn't enough to pay even the smallest fare. So with sign language I asked the driver to take me to my hotel, the Hilton at the top of the hill by the castle.

After what seemed like an hour and a half, we arrived at our destination, he'd obviously taken the pretty route, but it took another thirty minutes for him to let me out of the car because I hadn't paid him. 'Money inside hotel. Money inside. Me fetch.'

'Okeeeee,' he threatened. 'Bring monies queek.'

But it just wasn't my day. Inside my room I discovered I didn't have any money there either, and that I needed to go to the hole in the wall just up the street. But how do I explain that to the assassin waiting outside in the taxi. Better to just dodge out the door, nip up the road and hope he doesn't see me. No such luck. He legged it up the road after me, hollering and screaming and this time I knew exactly what he was saying.

Another fifteen minutes of mime explaining what I was doing. He accompanied me for the rest of the way and suddenly metamorphosed into an angel when he saw the readies issuing from the machine. I was so happy the nightmare was over that I gave him a huge tip. Much bigger than I had planned actually because I discovered later that I had made a whopping great miscalculation and he could probably afford to have the rest of the week off!! It was only after he had gone whistling back to his car and disappeared around the corner that I realised I still didn't have transport to the restaurant to meet my friends. It took me only twenty minutes to walk down the hill to the restaurant, where I found them all very merry indeed and downing brandies after a delicious meal. Robert, however, did loan me his phone to call Michael in London to tell him I was safe and to make sure he was all right. He had long been tucked up in bed, having found the keys, and was rather miffed that I'd woken him up!

Poor Michael, I also woke him up on another occasion when I phoned him in the middle of the night from Las Vegas. I was in two minds whether or not to relate the following story but as I think most people will identify with it, I have thrown caution to the wind.

I made Kay Mellor's 'Girls' Night' in 1997, with Julie Walters and Kris Kristofferson. Girls' Night was inspired by a friend of Kay's who sadly died of cancer, and concerns the friendship between two women dealing with generosity, selfishness, loss and discovery in the face of death. It is a celebration of life rather than a lament. Written without melodrama or self-indulgence, the script was funny, compassionate and a joy to work on.

Most of the filming was done in a studio in Manchester (for studio read shed), but also a great deal of it was filmed in the casinos of Las Vegas and the Nevada desert. I had never been to Las Vegas before and was astonished to find wall-to-wall casinos, gambling and showgirls. Blinking, blazing, flashing, winking lights everywhere you go. And that's just in the streets. Inside the casinos you can multiply the aforesaid a hundredfold. Open twenty-four hours a day, people would sit at slot machines in the hope of winning a car, and sometimes did!! There was not a clock in sight. From the entrance of the casino to the elevator, which would rocket us up to our suites on the twenty-fifth floor, was a good five or ten minute walk. So our call times in the mornings had to be adjusted accordingly to accommodate the hike to the exit. Most of the scenes were shot in the casino, at around 3 a.m., which was the time when they were least busy, and while they were setting up the shots Julie and I would sometimes fall asleep at the tables with our faces laying down on the green baize. The first assistant director would wake us with a start, shouting through a megaphone 'OKAY PLACES PLEASE, TURNING OVER.' We'd leap to attention, HAIR, MAKE-UP, READY AND ACTION.

Apart from the gambling, Las Vegas is also famous for its many marriage booths, where a wedding can be booked and carried out almost at a moment's notice. I had been with Michael well over twenty years and I was lulled into thinking that perhaps it was time to tie the knot. I gave it a lot of thought and finally plucked up the courage to pop the question. Hence the phone call. Forgetting the eight-hour time difference I telephoned him in London, inadvertently waking him up. It was only 3.30 in the morning. 'Hello Michael' I crooned, pausing for dramatic effect. 'Shall we get married?' There was a long long pause while the question seeped into his sleepy brain and then another long pause before he indignantly enquired 'Who is this?' Cut to the quick, I decided that maybe it wasn't the time to tie the knot after all!

Some scenes of *Girls' Night* were shot in the Nevada desert. Now, for someone who never, EVER thought they would EVER be an actor and certainly never ever EVER be in a film, can you imagine how I felt to suddenly find myself riding a horse across the desert with Kris Kristofferson? It was an unbelievable thrill. Although I enjoyed the occasional horse-riding session when I was growing up, at the stables at Bromstone, Broadstairs, I am not an accomplished rider. But Julie is. I remember when I was about eleven years old I was thrown from a horse but I refused to let go. I ended up sliding round to the front of the horse hanging on to its bridle and staring it in the face while it galloped into a cabbage field.

But enough of that, back to Las Vegas. The script demanded that my character *could* ride and that Julie's could not, and because the director Nick Hurran needed a two-shot of myself and Kris riding past camera, I had to have a much bigger horse than Kris, so that we would be more or less the same height over-all. I was practically doing the splits on this huge horse. And when Nick directed that as soon as we had passed the camera we were to gallop off into the desert, I put my foot down firmly in the stirrup and reminded him that I'd probably die if I galloped off anywhere unless they super-glued me to the saddle. I particularly didn't want to fall off because we had just been told of the colonies of thousands of tarantulas that cross the desert at just about that time of year. A wind-up surely. Also, the day before I had seen a creature that looked exactly like a scorpion scuttle over my boot. It wasn't black but a sort of transparent creamy colour. When I described it to one of the crew, he said with utter conviction, 'Ah yes, that'll be the vinegar scorpion.'

'Leave it out,' I said.

'It's absolutely true,' he said, 'if it bites you, you'll taste vine-gar for a week.'

Now can anyone tell me, was he having me on?

Gallop off into the desert indeed. I couldn't get over it. The hot and dusty, cacti-filled Nevada desert.

Actually, what I didn't know before embarking on this lunatic horse-riding venture, and was very shortly to find out, was that I am allergic to the Nevada desert. I got terrible hay fever. Quite recently someone suggested that I might have been allergic to my horse, a possibility I hadn't even contemplated. I hope that's not the case because, despite my lack of equestrian skills, I love horses. Anyway, to counter the allergy problem one of the make-up artists gave me a reliable antidote in the shape of some little yellow pills. If I remember correctly, they contained pollen, and I was told that I'd be as right as rain tomorrow. Excellent, because tomorrow was a day off and afforded me the time I needed to go to the mall to buy Michael the cowboy shirt he'd requested. Couldn't have worked out better. Not that he deserved a treat after the 'Who is this?' quip.

So at about 10.30 the following morning, dressed comfortably and casually in white T-shirt and pale blue jeans, I hopped into my limo and was driven to the mall. And what a magnificent mall it was too. Gleaming marble, light, sparkling clean, bright, welcoming shops and department stores, uncrowded, leisurely, lots of choice and, most importantly, COOL. The temperature outside was about 95°. Yes, Brenda, you're going to enjoy yourself. I ambled around, browsing here and there to find the nicest shirt I could for Michael, there was so much to choose from. What fun. I eventually found a very nice (Roy Rogers type) maroon check shirt with leather piping and leather frill along the seams and bought it. Terrific. (What was I thinking?) When browsing through another gents' outfitters I espied a cowboy shirt with a variation on the first one and decided to push the boat out and get that one too. Lucky Michael.

I was beginning to feel pretty hot. Just a minute, I thought to myself, has the air conditioning been turned off? Perhaps it was because I was carrying all my purchases. Phew, never mind. I continued to browse through the shops, having all the time in the world, but it was definitely getting hotter. Actually I was beginning to sweat quite badly and feel a little light-headed. I decided I needed to sit down. Just at that moment a group of tourists were crossing the mall and shouted, 'Oh my God, is that Brenda Blethyn?' and came rushing over to ask me. ' Excuse me, love, are you Brenda Blethyn?' My God, fancy seeing you here. Are you on holiday? Are you working here? Oh this is fantastic. Could we have your autograph, love? Would you mind? Thanks, love.'

I wasn't quite sure what was happening because by this time I was feeling decidedly queasy. I signed my autograph, and was just about to go and sit down when they asked, 'Could we possibly have a photograph?' Certainly, it was easier to be courteous than to make a fuss. They all gathered around and the photographer went about 5 yards off to take the snap. I asked them if they were hot, and I distinctly remember one saying '*Au contraire*' and complaining that the air conditioning was a little too efficient and she'd been obliged to put ON her anorak to keep warm!

Oh really? Curious? 'READY,' cried our photographer, 'Say CHEEEEEEEEESE' . . . and just as she pressed the button I was almost shaken off my feet by an enormous explosion. We were all visibly shaken. Where had that terrible sound come from? And as I pondered the whereabouts of the explosion I became aware of a seeping warmth creeping up my back and my circle of fans backing away from me. I realised with a terribly terribly horrifying clarity that I had shat myself. The explosion was me. I had shat myself in the middle of the light, sparkling, marble mall. Oh my God. Oh my God. Oh my GOD . . . The STENCH. I backed away from my adoring fans, forcing a smile, pretending to be totally unaware of the fog forming around my middle. I had to find a ladies' room. A what? A ladies' room. A toilet. A bathroom. Oh for goodness' sake, what is the correct term! A RESTROOM. Eureka. Up and down escalators, up and down, up and down, do you think I could find a RESTROOM. What with so many dazzling lights I found it enormously difficult to locate the sign, and I was absolutely NOT going to approach someone to ask, for obvious reasons. I was nearly gagging with the stench and I certainly wasn't going to inflict that on someone else. So trying to keep my back to the wall and draping my shopping bags around me, I skulked through a department store (attracting suspicious stares from security guards) until I finally found a lavatory. Do bear in mind reader that I'm wearing a white T-shirt and pale blue jeans. Suffice it to say that I cleansed myself as well as I could but there was nothing to be done with my jeans. Time to improvise. Out came Michael's leather tassled cowboy shirts. Both of them. I ripped off the cellophane and tied them neatly around my waist to cover the unmistakable accident. Oh God, the stench.

Now then, I thought, give me strength, I have to get back to the hotel. My smiling driver was waiting in the limo with its lovely cream leather seats, with all the windows shut as requested and the air conditioning full on. I wanted to die. He saw me approaching and leapt out of the car to open the door for me. 'Good to go?' he cried cheerily. 'I'll tell you what,' I called from a distance of twenty yards, 'could I have all the windows open please to let the warm air in – I'm a little cold.' 'COLD?' he queried wiping the sweat from his brow. 'You need to see a doctor, Miss Brenda.' 'You've never said a truer word,' I mumbled to myself and thinking I CANNOT sit on his lovely cream seats. Miraculously, I came up with the idea that I had met a friend in the mall who was going to be following us in her own car and that I would kneel on the back seat to make sure we didn't lose her.

'Okey dokey' he said very slowly, screwing up his nose and putting his handkerchief over his mouth as I approached. 'Let's getcha home.' The dividing window between driver and passenger, which had hitherto been open all the while I'd been in Las Vegas, swiftly closed as I knelt in the car. The journey back to the hotel was only about fifteen minutes, but it felt like five years. Courteous to the end he more than aptly told me to 'hang loose' as I crawled out of the car and backed away from him. 'You have a good day now.' I thanked him, and he told me he had decided to take the rest of the day off! Now that I was safely deposited back at the hotel, all that remained was for me to negotiate the crowded casino and the ten minute walk to the elevator. Which, as sod's law would have it, was full of people as I entered. I was now so embarrassed I was past embarrassment and I smiled at everyone as if nothing had happened. As I stepped out of the elevator I turned, winked, and chirped, 'I feeeeeel lucky! Have a good day now.'

I was fully recovered the next day for filming, save for my vanity and even that was saved by my sense of humour. Curiously enough the make-up artist who had given me the magic pills had gone on to another job, which is just as well because she would have been mortified to know just how effective her remedy had been. It was certainly no surprise to find that my limo driver had suddenly gone on to another job. When I related my ordeal to Julie she wept, nay sobbed, with laughter as did Kris Kristofferson. In fact, as did everybody. The shirts, of course, had been swiftly disposed of, and when I had returned to normality I realised that Michael wouldn't have been seen dead in them anyway. But thank the Lord for those shirts with the leather piping and tassels. It's interesting to note that nearly every person I relate this story to has had a similar experience, and many even more embarrassing and funnier than mine. And those people who profess that it's never happened to them, quite frankly I don't believe.

While filming the Manchester scenes of *Girls' Night* I had a visit from Mark Crowdy and Craig Ferguson, producers and co-writers of *Saving Grace*. They had previously sent me a script, the tale of a widow who grows and sells marijuana, and it had gone through several rewrites since, but they now needed to know of my interest. I loved it and committed to it there and then. I said that I thought the first part of the film should be dealt with seriously and shouldn't be milked for laughs. I didn't find the woman's plight funny at all, but the way she solved her problem hilarious. Both Mark and Craig agreed. And then Nigel Cole came on board to direct. The perfect choice, so inventive, kind and funny.

The film was shot on location in Port Isaac, Cornwall, and a happier time couldn't be imagined. Many of the villagers played supporting parts, including Mark Crowdy's mother, and despite the great disruption to the village, holiday-makers and locals alike all seemed to enjoy the experience. There would have been some noses out of joint I expect. The unit trucks were almost as wide as the pretty little streets, so there was the odd traffic problem, but they were soon overcome. I'm told that a special dispensation had to be obtained from the Home Office to allow us to show real marijuana plants, the ones closest to the camera. All the other magnificent plants were made in the art department by Marko Waschke. These imitation plants looked really authentic, and when my character was obliged to go to Notting Hill to try to sell her wares, a few other people thought they looked authentic too.

It was a normal busy market day in Notting Hill. All of our cameras were hidden so that the scene would carry on as naturally as possible. However, I was taken to a nearby pub and introduced to forty or so extras who would mingle with the shoppers, and these were the people I was to approach to sell the marijuana. I couldn't possibly remember forty strangers who were mingling with hundreds of other strangers, so inevitably I approached the wrong people and invited them to look inside my handbag and asked if they would take me to their dealer. The looks of astonishment on their faces were amazing. Not just because I was asking them to buy drugs, but because of the *size* of the marijuana bud hidden in my bag. Two of the people I approached got over excited and said they were *very* interested in taking me to their dealer, and on each occasion Nigel came crashing out of hiding to rescue me. He also had to save me from one incensed punter who tried to do a citizen's arrest. We explained that we were making a film and we were only pretending and he said, 'You don't get out of it that easy. POLICE!' Frankly, I take my hat off to him.

I was so nervous playing that scene, not just because it was totally improvised but because I felt like a criminal. Real criminals must have nerves of steel and a really strong heart. Mine was pounding so hard I'm sure everyone could hear it! I was so glad to get that day over and done with. But it's remarkable that everyone who comments on the film says that that is one of their favourite scenes.

My favourite scene is when the policeman, played by Ken Campbell, catches us red-handed in the greenhouse with a huge pile of marijuana buds, and he says 'But Grace, that's a HUUUGE amount?' Craig and I thought Ken's portrayal was so funny that he couldn't get to the end of 'It's not so much me, Grace, it's the officers on their way from Coldock HQ which worries me' without us folding up laughing. Eventually after about ten aborted attempts, Nigel got cross with us, because time was running short, and the light was going. Suitably reprimanded we tried to shoot the scene again, and we used every ounce of effort not to laugh. This was more than Nigel could bear and *he* burst out laughing instead. So Ken had to do it yet again. I seem to remember that eventually Ken could only do the scene with Craig and I facing the other way.

Another scene that got us all corpsing was the opening funeral scene. Grace simply had to toss an orchid bloom into the grave on top of her husband's coffin. Easy. But it was a windy day and every time I tossed the bloom, no matter how forcefully, it was lifted on the wind and carried away. The art department came up with the good idea of weighting the orchid. Nobody would notice if a six-inch nail was inside the stem. It's not something you would automatically think of is it? The moment came and I tossed the flower. Well, it was as if I had scored a bullseye in darts, for the flower speared into the coffin and stood vibrating upright for about five seconds and, coupled with the DOIOING noise it made, caused all the solemn mourners at the funeral to weep with laughter!

But we weren't laughing during the scene where we were smoking a joint. Neither Craig nor I are smokers. I hate cigarettes. Of course, we weren't really smoking marijuana, just the weakest kind of tobacco you can get, made to look like a joint. We thought the scene would be covered in one shot but we were wrong. Nigel shot it from several points of view and each time we had to smoke a joint. I'm sure Nigel was getting his own back because Craig and I took so long over the other scene! We felt thoroughly sick at the end of it. Fortunately the following scene was Grace feeling ill, so no acting required for that one!

It was so lovely working in Cornwall, we felt as though we were on holiday. And on an afternoon off work I went across to Padstow to revisit the lovely bay there. When I was nineteen Alan had taken me to Cornwall for a two-week camping/touring holiday. My very first holiday. He and his parents spent two weeks there every year and I had heard from all three of them what a wonderful place it was. Alan had described to me so accurately the sensation of seeing Padstow when approaching from over the hill after a five- or six-hour drive from London. Well, I should think any place would look nice after a five- or six-hour drive, but Padstow was magical. Only a couple of weeks previously he had answered an advertisement in *Carmart* and bought a Consul Mark II Convertible from someone in Ladbroke Grove for £200. We were royalty. Although I doubt royalty would have slept in the car as we did. We'd pick a farm, any farm, and ask the farmer if we could park in one of his fields, and mostly we were given permission. The farmers would give us fresh milk straight from the cow, although it was a bit lumpy for my taste.

We found some beautiful places. Although I got a little sunburnt, it was all absolutely idyllic. Until it rained. How could we know that there were little pinholes in the canvas roof of the car. Everything got sodden wet. All of our belongings had to be laid out on the grass the following morning to dry. We were very surprised to find a handsome crop of mushrooms growing from the carpet, caused by the heat of the sun and the interior dampness. The weather had changed for the worse, but by this time we had moved around the coast veering east. We found it necessary to go into a launderette in Plymouth to wash and dry all of our clothes and blankets, but mostly to get ourselves warm. Nevertheless it was a lovely holiday, and we could see the humour in most of our mishaps.

And now, Craig and I walked aimlessly on the beach as the sun sank low in the west. It is such a huge bay and at low tide you can walk out for quite a way. We were each in our own thoughts. Remembering that first holiday, the bloom of romance, coupled with Kelly's ice cream, made my skin tingle. Or it might just have been remembering the sunburn! Whatever, it was a nice feeling. And I also thought of Michael and counted my blessings. After reading this book, people who don't know him personally will perhaps think he sounds an uncaring, hard-nosed, selfish, humourless chap with very little to recommend him. They'd be so wrong. Those people who *do* know him personally will know, without a shadow of doubt, what a kind, caring, sexy, clever, loyal, funny, talented, generous, low-maintenance, deadpan, adorable little git he is. Michael makes me laugh more than anyone else in the world. The 'Who is this?' response I received when I phoned him to propose marriage made me laugh for a fortnight.

He also buys me flowers. Secretly I think they're for himself, but he says they're for me. When I first met him, his swarthy dark looks made me buckle at the knees almost, and I got such butterflies, I was sometimes rendered speechless. Perhaps my difficulty in speaking was the quality he found most attractive in me! I asked him once, what one thing in life could he not live without, and fluttered my eyelids. 'Music,' he said without hesitation.

One of the most wonderful qualities about him though is his honesty. He never ever bullshits, even when I sometimes want him to. If I ask him if he likes a new outfit I'm wearing, for instance, and he doesn't like it, he says quite frankly, 'No'. Some of you might find that harsh, but I don't, I admire straightforwardness so much. I wish I were more so. If someone asked me the same question I would dance around the answer to find something a little more ambiguous. Imagine how the world would be if we never had to second guess, if everyone told the truth. But when Michael pays me a compliment, I know that he means it. At least I think I do, it's so long since I got one! I'm joking. The very thought of Michael makes me smile.

He makes an effort to come to see me at every location I'm working at, especially if I have an extended stay away from home. He's travelled all the way to Australia twice to spend just a few days with me. He phones me several times a day. He's a first-rate cook. He does the shopping: in fact, he won't let me go with him any more because he says I read too many labels! He helps me research, buys me reference books whenever I need them, and sometimes before I even know myself that I need them. He is so incredibly reliable. He does all the foregoing whilst holding down an extremely responsible job as art director at the National

Theatre, and has done so ever since we met thirty years ago. It's a little known fact that he's been headhunted three times, and if he'd been tempted would have earned three or four times the money he earns now, but not only is he loyal to me, he is loyal to the National Theatre. But it's his dry wit that has the greatest magnetism for me. If I'm feeling down, he lifts my spirits. If I'm deluded, he points out the truth. And for all the foregoing he doesn't charge very much at all, just the flat regular weekly rate. And just when I was thinking what a bargain it was, and how much I loved him, a small wave rippled over my shoe and I noticed that the tide was quietly coming in around us, as if not to disturb our reveries. I yelled to Craig, 'LEG IT!!' And we both sprinted like mad back to the top of the beach, wading through ankle-deep sea, lest we should be cut off completely by the tide. And I heard Pam's voice, loud and clear, 'Watch out for the tide!'

Oh Pam, I do miss her. She died in the early hours of 2 January 2001. She and John had spent Christmas at Val's home in Stratford-upon-Avon. My brother Terry had collected them from Ramsgate before the holiday, and I had agreed to collect them after the New Year celebrations to drive them home again. Pam especially was in no hurry to go home. In fact, she and John wanted to sell up home in Ramsgate and move to Stratford so they could see more of their daughter, and they probably would have done if fate had taken a different course. On New Year's Day, I drove to Stratford, arriving just in time for lunch. Val's daughter Charlotte, a newly qualified physiotherapist, was also visiting. We had a lovely relaxing day, and in the evening enjoyed a board game of *Who Wants to Be a Millionaire*. There was a great deal of hilarity, a glass of wine or two, and lots of photos were taken. Pam said she didn't like having her picture taken because she thought she wasn't photogenic and frequently commented, 'How come you always look good in photos, Brenda?' What a giggly bunch we were, practising silly smiles for the camera. I told Pam to pretend the photographer was a dentist asking to see her teeth, which she did, and we got some really nice photos. Just before midnight we all went to bed, and the plan was to rise fairly early in the morning to set off for Ramsgate even though they were rather reluctant to go home. At three o clock in the morning John called desperately from their room. Rushing to his aid we found that his wife, Val's mum, Charlotte's nan and my sister, had died. It was incomprehensible. Only a few hours earlier we'd been practising smiles for the camera. Charlotte gave mouth-to-mouth resuscitation even though she knew it was futile. Pam was gone. The centre had fallen out of John's world. The ever-capable Valerie dealt with the situation and with her devastated father with a remarkable, heroic, quiet dignity. In private, I know she would have fallen apart. The paramedics took Pam's body from the house like a piece of furniture. We could only gape with tears in our eyes as the black bag carrying Pam was tilted this way and that, 'down your end a bit' 'up your end a bit' and raised completely above their heads to clear the newel post. It's a good job Pam hadn't seen it! She would have been telling them to mind the paintwork! How quickly it had all happened. She was here one minute, then she was gone. No more.

Have I passed the emergency stop?

24

STAMINA

ACTORS NEED TO BE REASONABLY FIT AND SOMETIMES HAVE to *physically* prepare for roles. Actors need more than just mental agility. Look at Hilary Swank in *Million Dollar Baby* for instance, Robert De Niro in *Raging Bull*, or Ben Kingsley in *Gandhi*. Or indeed Brenda Blethyn in *Bob the Builder*! If I need to get mind and body in shape I generally take myself off for a week of exercise and pampering at a health farm, preferably Forest Mere or Henlow Grange, where the grounds are beautiful, the accommodation luxurious, the food fabulous and the treatments are all sublime. The perfect place for a hedonist like me to enjoy all of the above, plus regular long bracing walks through the countryside. And it's worth the trip alone just to experience the mineral rich thalassotherapy pool. As well as a workout, it's a holiday.

But those of you who have ever suffered with a frozen shoulder (adhesive capsulitis) will know about the extreme pain you have to endure and that the *last* thing you want is a holiday unless you're allowed to moan and swear all the time (*Swearus nonstopus*).

I had a frozen right shoulder for twenty months and for six of those I was playing Mrs Warren in Sir Peter Hall's production of *Mrs Warren's Profession* in the West End. It was agonising. In the last act I made an angry gesture, raising my arm to shoulder level, pointing, and accusing my daughter of being ungrateful, and at every single performance I forgot that I had a frozen shoulder. The pain took my breath away. Each time I had to turn upstage and lower my arm as slowly as I could without drawing attention to it. It was agony. Fortunately it was a very emotional scene so I got away with it. The relief I felt on waking up one day to find that my shoulder was miraculously back to normal was short-lived. Less than one week later I felt the early telltale twinges in my left shoulder. After enduring more agonising pain for six months, and succumbing to cortisone injections, I then resorted to surgery. On waking up in hospital, with my arm strapped over my head, I was told that it hadn't been fully successful, insofar as any more manipulation could have resulted in a fracture. Moving my arm was still painful. Suicide wasn't far from my mind.

At the same time as I was offered Mrs Warren, I had also been offered a part in the film *On a Clear Day*. I'd had the script for over a year but I didn't know if it would ever get made or not. It depended, of course, on the funding, so it didn't take up much of my thinking time. All of a sudden, the director, Gaby Dellal, asked me to come along to meet her and her producer Sarah Curtis at the Hilton Hotel for tea to discuss the project because it had now been green lit. The role was Joan, the bus driving wife of Frank, played by Peter Mullan.

The fact that I was committed to the project came up on me by surprise. I hadn't yet actually made a decision to do it. But somehow, by osmosis, I *was* doing it. Gaby just totally assumed

270

that I was on board and didn't actually bother to ask me. But that was OK by me. I liked her. I liked the script and it didn't seem to clash with anything else that I could think of, so I just went along with it. I heard later that in sending the script to Peter Mullan, Gaby said that if he didn't do it she would kill herself!

And then the Chancellor in his wisdom decided to close a loophole which allowed investors in film production certain tax advantages. The film came crashing down along with many others, including some that had already started filming. But good old Isle of Man Films came to our rescue and we were buoyant again and it was all systems go. Drastic action was needed. So I told myself, 'Come on, Brenda, you've got to drive a bus soon and your shoulder has to be working properly.' And then someone uttered the magic words: Shrubland Hall!

I've already mentioned I was in no mood for a holiday, and an onlooker could be forgiven for thinking I had Tourette's syndrome. But now that Shrubland Hall Health Clinic had been planted in my mind I gave them a call. And blow me down with a feather, they had a room available, so I booked in for a two-week visit before I could change my mind. At the same time I also booked a daily session with the resident physiotherapist Sylvia Webb, who pulled and manipulated and vibrated and stretched and coaxed and scolded and corrected and ultimately cured my shoulder. God bless Sylvia Webb.

My appointments with her were always straight after the water aerobics first thing in the morning, and immediately before the heat treatments which were either a sauna or Turkish bath. Ladies were ushered in groups of six or less into the various rooms and were ushered out again at the appropriate time by an ever-watchful Valerie who has been ever watchful of her ladies for the last twenty-seven years.

Then came the pilates session recommended by Sylvia Webb.

Michael, the very knowledgeable instructor, gave me all the best exercises to increase mobility in my shoulder, and it was fascinating to see the small daily improvement, and to feel each day the slightly reduced pain. And all of this was followed up by the massage. Oh, oh, oh. Take your pick, George, Peter or Arnie, all fabulous masseurs. Which was just as well as I've had some dodgy experiences with massages.

Like the time in Rio I was lying on the massage table, face down, arms at my side, palms facing upwards. The masseur entered wearing a white cotton suit. He looked every inch a surgeon. However, after manipulating one side of my body, instead of walking round to the other side of the table to do my other half, he decided to lean across my body, thus letting his entire bunch of tackle nestle in my upturned palm. I was suddenly very awake and as tense as a cheese wire. What should I do? Should I ignore it? Did he know? When he started to jiggle about I came to the conclusion that he was very skilled in the art of tackle targeting and promptly put my hands under my head, although I was momentarily tempted to give his tackle a mighty squeeze.

Or another time, at a health spa in California where I had a blind masseur. I was told how good he was by several other guests, who suggested his sense of touch was probably better than that of sighted people. And, indeed, he *was* good and as I jumped naked and carefree off the table at the end of the session and couldn't find my key, he pointed to a dark corner on the floor and casually asked, 'Is that your key over there?'

Or my experience in Sydney, where the physio was correcting the small of my back. I was lying face down on the table, and he asked me very sincerely if I would like to see his reptile! I nearly swallowed the pillow.

In any case, Shrubland Hall was starting to feel like a holiday after all. On alternate days you could opt for an underwater massage where a high-powered water jet hit you all over the body and was particularly effective when massaging my shoulder. And if you add to all of this a daily salt rub, a long walk around the estate and award-winning gardens, a swim, lovely fresh salads and fruit and an early night and a mended shoulder, you have all the ingredients for the perfect relaxing holiday. I returned home after two weeks feeling great and ready to tackle my next job and the double decker bus. And do you know what? I even stopped swearing. There was no need to any more because everything in the garden was wonderful.

But now that I was physically fit, I needed to be vocally fit, for the film was set in Glasgow.

To find a decent accent it seems you have to overaccentuate each vowel and consonant sound until you have discovered all the differences and then try to forget about them altogether, not pronouncing them at all. That's what I do anyway and it seems to have worked so far. If you haven't got the accent under control by the time you start filming you end up playing the accent rather than the character. All you do is listen to yourself instead of the person you're playing the scene with.

Vocal training is needed more often than you would think, and is usually standard if the film budget will stretch to it. For instance, in *Pride and Prejudice*, under the alert ear and guidance of Gil McCullugh, it wasn't just Donald Sutherland's Canadian accent that needed disguising, because all the people in the Bennet household needed to sound reasonably similar. The same went for all the people in the upper echelons of society. Donald Sutherland was wonderful to work with. The whole world knows what a good actor he is, but us Bennet girls all found him to be such fun too. He's kind and although a bit of an intellectual he's also mischievous and a bit saucy. Joe Wright our director thought it was vital to get a good family atmosphere in the Bennet household, so prior to starting filming, he invited us down to Groombridge Place, the setting for Longbourn, to play hide and seek. It was heavenly. We had bought bags of cherries on the way to Kent and childishly had them draped over our ears, and rouged our cheeks with the juice, as we scrambled under stairs, down dusty corridors, and climbed into cupboards, waiting to be discovered. It was a brilliant idea, because in one afternoon we'd learnt the geography of the house like the backs of our hands. If only we could have lived in the house while filming.

As an actor one is often required to work away from home, living out of a suitcase. Hotels of all descriptions are booked by the production company to accommodate everyone concerned. Actors are usually accommodated in the best hotel available, depending on budget, and the crew, drivers and everybody else in a moderate hotel nearby. A happy cast and crew makes for much better working relations especially when it comes to the odd bit of overtime.

The filming of *Pride and Prejudice* called for several hotels to be found and booked and the logistics of this operation alone makes the mind boggle. Our first location work was near Tunbridge Wells in Kent and, although it was only an hour's distance from my home, the very early morning calls made it necessary to stay at the nearby Ashdown Park Hotel, a converted convent. Set in lovely grounds it was also fortunately next door to a llama farm, which of course I visited several times along with one or other of the Bennett girls, and where I bought each of them a soft alpaca shoulder bag for carrying personal belongings around on set. There was one particularly feisty, saucy-looking llama named Donald that, of course, made us all shriek and we couldn't wait to tell Mr Sutherland. As lovely as the hotel was, it wasn't home. We weren't there on holiday, or for a quick business trip. We were there for over a month to relax and sleep after a very long day at work. It was the sort of place where jackets were needed for dinner, but if we didn't have one, they politely found one and placed it on the back of your chair. They were courteous and put up with us rather well I thought, unlike one or two other hotels we stayed in.

The rooms in the hotel I shall name as Pretentious Park Hotel had names instead of numbers and while it would probably make it difficult for burglars looking for a particular room to plunder, it also made it difficult for the guests to find their rooms, and an impromptu chat with one of your workmates was out of the question because you wouldn't know where to find them. But that's by the by. The problem arose on returning to the hotel after wearing corsets and eighteenth-century costumes and wigs for twelve to fourteen hours when we needed to slip into something a little more comfortable. But no, that wouldn't do at the Pretentious Park Hotel. Not even in the bar. Oh, no no no no no. Oh no no no. That wouldn't do at all. Jeans were absolutely FORBIDDEN. No exceptions! Not even Talulah's chic designer jeans nor, surprisingly, Jena's jeans with the stylish rips in the knees, thighs and arse. Even though both girls looked absolutely gorgeous. Has the Pretentious Park duty manager no sense of style at all?

'But why are jeans forbidden?' enquires one from our guilty circle.

Our accuser fell to his knees conspiratorily and slowly and carefully explained, 'Because it is offensive to our other guests.'

'What other guests?' asked our incredulous director. 'You 'aven't got any other guests!'

'Beside the point,' parried the Pretentious Park duty manager as quick as a flash. 'You have been warned once and now I am warning you again. These are the rules of the Pretentious Park Hotel.'

'Has anybody complained?' I asked.

'No,' he returned.

'Well . . .' I said in such a way that meant all was mended.

'But they will tomorrow,' prophesied the Pretentious Park duty manager. 'We have one or two other guests arriving tomorrow, and I don't want to embarrass you in front of them, do I.'

He smiled thinly, his nauseating aftershave curdling the air. And by way of solving this potentially sticky situation he cryptically suggested that we dined in the billiard room.

'Or.' He paused. 'The pavilion.'

'A tent!' cried Carey, outraged. 'A tent!'

'The cricket pavilion,' sneered the Pretentious Park duty manager tired of this conversation, 'out the front door, turn right, around the building and along the gravel drive. You can't miss it.'

'That sounds quite nice,' interjected our director optimistically. 'Let's Bren and me go and do a recce.'

'Just a minute,' someone added. 'Is it a different kitchen at the pavilion. A different chef?'

'Yes,' said the Pretentious Park duty manager standing up, glad that the situation was satisfactorily resolved.

'Well let's be thankful for small mercies!' said a ravenous actor.

The Pretentious Park duty manager spun on his heel so smartly that he sent a huge waft of his nauseating aftershave into the circle.

'What on earth is that pong?' queried someone at the back.

'You lot!' quipped the Pretentious Park duty manager under his breath as he left the room.

Well! I needed a whisky after that, and on returning to my table with a Black Label on the rocks and my purse £15 lighter I made a snap decision not to have another one, not for fear of being drunk but for fear of being bankrupt.

Other hotels were much more accommodating. But the courtesy shown to me at a hotel near Weybridge, while filming *Belonging* for ITV, was more than I needed. Hitherto I had been going home after a day's filming, but on this particular day we had gone into overtime and I had a very early call the next morning. The simplest answer was to stay at a nearby hotel. But I hadn't come prepared. So I pinched some clean clothes from the wardrobe department and toiletries from the make-up department and checked in. It was a modest hotel but perfectly adequate. I was tired and went straight to bed. Having no nightclothes I slept as naked as the day I was born.

My heart nearly stopped beating at about three in the morning. The fire alarm had gone off. Usually when that happens, you always think, 'Do they mean it?', but when I heard dozens of feet running down the hall I thought I had better follow them, and quickly. I'd been wearing my contact lenses at work and had forgotten to bring my specs. There was definitely no time to put my lenses back in. I grabbed the hotel bathrobe, which was old and paper-thin and put it on. There was no belt. EVACUATE. EVACUATE. Tousled, barefooted, and clutching the robe around me I followed the sound of the other guests fleeing down the corridor. Everyone had congregated in the car park as instructed and, trying to be as inconspicuous as possible, I squinted my way towards the back of the cars.

'SORRY TO INCONVENIENCE YOU, MISS BLETHYN,' came the voice from the megaphone on the other side of the car park. 'WE'LL GET YOU BACK INSIDE AS SOON AS WE HAVE THE ALL CLEAR.'

I wanted the ground to open up. 'CAN I GET YOU SOME REFRESHMENT OR ANYTHING, MISS BLETHYN, WHILE WE'RE WAITING?' came this disembodied voice. I pretended I didn't know who this Miss Blethyn was and kept my head down, but when the voice came over with a fold-up chair for me to sit on while everybody else had to stand, I had to own up. After declining to pose for a couple of mobile phone photographs, while still clutching my robe about me, I mercifully heard the 'all clear'.

'SORRY TO HAVE INCONVENIENCED YOU, MISS BLETHYN,' said the voice. 'IT IS SAFE TO RETURN. LET MISS BLETHYN PASS PLEASE. (If ever a woman suffered!) THANKYOU. LET MISS BLETHYN PASS. SLEEP WELL, MISS BLETHYN! THANKYOU.' (I've never been so shown up in all my life!)

How much further is it?

25

ENDURANCE

LONG HOURS, SLEEPLESS NIGHTS AND HEAVY WORK LOADS take their toll. In 2001 I made a mental note to have a medical check-up. It was a good thing that I did because I discovered I had high cholesterol, and not the good kind at that. I learned that a low fat diet would bring down the overall cholesterol level but it was exercise that would transform it into a better kind of cholesterol, i.e. high density lipids as opposed to low density lipids. As a consequence I lashed out and bought myself a Tunturi treadmill and a Health Rider. The treadmill I used nearly every day for about forty minutes first thing in the morning and contrary to expectations I found I really enjoyed it, and each year when the London Marathon was on, I would get on my treadmill with the television in front of it and set off when the whistle blew, and I stayed on it until someone crossed the finish line, about two and a half hours later. I didn't stop for anything. Michael would hand me beakers of water and I would lob the beaker over my shoulder whether I'd finished the drink or not. Just like the runners.

Who did I think I was? What you must remember, however, is that the marathon runners had run over twenty-six miles, I had only walked about seven or eight. And was exhausted. But I soon saw the results of my labours at my next blood test, for I now had HDLs.

It so happened that shortly after the 2001 London Marathon I was invited to do a television interview on Southern Television with Twiggy, and the subject of cholesterol came up, so I told her what I have just told you. By the time I got home my answerphone was flashing like mad with messages to call my agent. I thought, oh goody, lots of lovely job offers coming up. Wrong. The messages were mostly from charities, who had seen the interview or had heard about it and were asking me to run the London Marathon for them in 2002. They were all having a laugh surely. I had trouble running up a bill never mind running twenty-six miles. Of course, I had to say no. What was I? Mad? I was already a supporter of CHILDREN with LEUKAEMIA, and I knew Eddie O'Gorman, the founder, from helping out at various fundraisers and so on. Eddie phoned.

'Eddie, don't even ask,' I said before he'd opened his mouth.

'Well no one can do it to start with,' he said reassuringly. 'You'd have to train for it.'

'Eddie,' I said, 'do you know how old I am? It's tiring me out just having this conversation.'

It transpired that Eddie's wife, Marion, had also seen the interview and it was her idea to call me.

'But we still haven't got a team leader,' said Eddie, as if that made it all right.

The fact of the matter is that I admire Eddie O'Gorman so much. He started the charity CHILDREN with LEUKAEMIA at the request of his dying son Paul. They had been on a boating holiday when Paul announced that he wasn't feeling very well. They returned home immediately and, to the entire family's dismay, leukaemia was diagnosed. After a very short time Paul died and Eddie and his family set about keeping their promise to him to help other young sufferers and the charity was born. Their main helper and fundraiser was their daughter Jean, who tragically lost her life to cancer only nine months later. I can't even begin to understand the heartache that the O'Gormans went through, but undeterred they carried on. The more I thought about what they had endured, the more churlish of me it seemed to not even try this small thing he was asking of me. *Small* thing?

I said, 'Eddie, listen. Here's what I'll do. I'll have a go at this training lark. And I'll try. I promise you I will really try. But if on the day I feel I can't do it, you will have to understand.'

Eddie said, 'Brenda, you're a star.'

What had I let myself in for? Had I taken leave of my senses? A *fucking marathon*! I needed help. Enter Paul Smith, personal trainer. I'd heard about Paul from a friend of mine who needed help to recover from a hip operation. Paul was just the ticket. The first time we went out I was puffed out by the time we got to the end of my road. We rested and then we just walked around the park. The second time we trained we walked a bit faster around the park.

Already I needed a month's holiday. But very, very slowly, I gradually got a little less tired. I had a few months to get in shape and each time we went out I ran either a little faster or a little further. In between sessions with Paul I would use the treadmill, but I got bored with using it with all that walking and not going anywhere. I also got bored of walking in circles around the park although I did persevere. Instead, I got Michael to drive me to all sorts of places in the centre of London and just leave me there.

(*He* enjoyed that!) I would then have to jog home again. I started to enjoy it. I thought to myself that I would get a little more enthusiastic if I learnt the *route* of the marathon, so that when it came to the big day I would be able to judge distances.

For one session Paul met me at Blackheath and we set off on the first leg. Blackheath to the Cutty Sark. Six miles. Almost a quarter of a marathon. By this stage I was doing a sort of jog, which was more of a silly speed walk really, you know the one, with hips comically exaggerated. But I could whizz along and by way of resting I simply walked for a couple of hundred yards. Anything just to keep moving. I was so pleased to see the masts of the Cutty Sark.

So far so good, but now I had to walk up that bloody great hill through Greenwich Park to get back to the car. The next time we went out we did the same route but tried to go a little further and blow me down if we didn't reach Tower Bridge, THE HALFWAY MARK. I was on cloud nine. I could walk, stumble, jog after a fashion a half marathon, so if I could at least do that on the day I'd be well pleased. Surely nobody is expecting me to do the whole thing.

You see, the problem with all this training was that I sometimes had to go off to do a bit of grafting and because of the long working day when filming there was little time for training. My energy level plummeted. So when the job finished it was back to square one. Oh heavens, I can't do all that again. Nobody in their right mind would really expect me to. But I *promised* Eddie, I thought. So start again I did. I was stunned at how quickly my stamina returned. Because of my cholesterol problem I thought it prudent to wear a heart monitor to keep a check on my heartbeat. According to the chart listing my age and weight, my heartbeat shouldn't go over 160 and that's when I'm exerting myself the most. If it inched over 160 I was to slow down or rest.

I got so familiar with it that I could tell what my heartbeat was without looking at the dial. Paul suggested we try the third leg of the route, from Tower Bridge to the Isle of Dogs, which we did a couple of times. The big day was approaching and I still hadn't done the last leg but this was the section I was most familiar with, the Isle of Dogs to Buckingham Palace. But was I ready?

The closer the event came the more publicity I had to do to raise awareness for the charity. Letters were sent out signed by me asking for sponsorship. I even sent letters to friends, producers and directors and distributors I'd worked with in America to try to raise more support. There were over a 1000 in my team all collecting money from friends, families and colleagues for so much per mile.

Michael took me to the Nike shop in Toronto whilst we were at the film festival to buy some special trainers for the event. I took such pleasure in explaining to the shop assistant that I needed the trainers for long distance running! I was hoping he'd say 'pardon' so that I would have to say 'long distance running' again. And he did. Bloody cheek. He produced a pair that looked like indoor slippers and explained that they were for long distance running and 'that they were able to breathe'.

'I just hope she'll still be breathing,' said Michael, the full import of what I was about to do suddenly sinking in.

The trainers were great. I put them on straight away in the shop and, as we crossed the street, some trendy teenagers stopped me and said they thought my trainers were 'really cool' and asked where I'd bought them. I was thrilled.

The day before the event I collected my number and CHIL-DREN with LEUKAEMIA vest from the Isle of Dogs, along with special pouches of energy-giving drinks, and set off home for an early night, after having pasta for dinner as recommended in the official literature.

The day arrived. I smothered my legs in white horse oil, vaselined anywhere that might rub, i.e. between my toes and under my bra straps, the top of my legs, etc. I stunk of liniment. I had oatmeal and banana for breakfast as recommended by Paul and I was ready to leave for Blackheath. My stomach was in my mouth along with my heart as Michael opened the passenger door of the car to drive me to the start line. Surely I must be dreaming. A marathon!?

The closest Michael could get me to the start line was Blackheath station, about a mile distant. There were throngs of people in various states of undress wending their way to the top of the hill, and everyone reeked of liniment. The feeling of high anticipation and camaraderie filled the air.

There were three starting points on the heath. I was to report to the enclosure allocated for all the celebrities, people off the tele, and so on, and where television interviews were to take place. This was simply to raise awareness of all the individual charities being sponsored. The other starting points were for professional competitive runners and for the great multitude of fun runners. As the minutes ticked by and the start time came closer and closer, everyone was limbering up, doing knee flexes and adding more lubrication. And as I was wondering if I should seriously think about having myself committed, I went to the line.

I was positioned in the front now amidst actors from *Emmerdale* and *EastEnders*, newsreaders, etc. Live TV cameras focused on our faces as the countdown started. HRH Prince Andrew was to fire the starting pistol.

TEN, NINE, EIGHT, oh lord, courage Brenda.

SEVEN, SIX, FIVE, I'll just check my heart monitor is working.

FOUR so that I don't exceed my 160 maximum. CHRIST, 220!!

THREE (I'M GOING TO DIE ON NATIONAL TELEVI-
SION).

TWO, I'VE GOT TO MOVE, THERE'S 45,000 PEOPLE
BEHIND ME!

ONE. WE'RE OFF!!

I'm going to die. I'm going to die. I'm not going to make it to
the edge of the bloody field. I was swept along on a tide of liniment like a little tadpole in a tidal wave, and as the wave crashed
on to the tarmac of the surrounding road, I saw a lamppost in the
distance beckoning me towards it. I had run all of 200 yards and
was now gasping and clinging on to a lamppost for dear life. So,
as soon as I could stand up straight, I did the only sensible thing
one could do in the circumstances and pretended there was
something in my shoe. I removed my shoe and examined it very
carefully and did an elaborate mime of shaking out a stubborn
pebble. I then checked my heart monitor and to my relief it had
gone down to 170. So I thought I'd better remove the other shoe
just to give myself a little more time and I shook out another
imaginary pebble. When the monitor read 150 I gave myself
another five minutes rest and then thought it safe to continue
provided I didn't exert myself too much. I told myself it didn't
matter that a runner dressed as a chocolate bar had just overtaken me. It didn't matter if everyone overtook me. I was doing
this for Eddie and for CHILDREN with LEUKAEMIA.

And as I got into my stride I started to enjoy myself. Although
most were accomplished runners, there were lots of people running with the same ability as me. Actually, there were some who
were worse than me. But everybody was cheering everyone else
on. The crowds lining the streets were cheering, and handing out
fruit slices and sweets. Some recognised me and shouted words of
encouragement. Come on, Brenda! You can do it, Brenda! It
doesn't matter what you look like, Brenda! Swing those hips,

Brenda! But as I ran down the steep hill in Woolwich, it was disturbing to see a gentleman runner, dressed in a pink tutu, lying on the pavement and being given artificial respiration. I said a little prayer for him and wondered how many more casualties there would be. And I reassured myself that it didn't matter how many lampposts I clung to.

Reaching Tower Bridge was a triumph, especially as Michael was there to cheer me on. I never dreamt he would fight his way through the crowds to champion me. I was delighted and thought *anything* after getting this far was a bonus. Not long after Tower Bridge, approaching Poplar High Street, a young female runner named Sara ran up alongside of me and said that it was *my* fault she was running.

'How do you make that out,' I gasped.

She said that she'd seen an interview I'd done when I said I was going to find the whole thing very difficult. She thought, if Brenda can have a go against all the odds, so can I. This young lady was herself suffering from leukaemia and she and her family had had much support from the charity CHILDREN with LEUKAEMIA. Just after the halfway mark she was struggling a little and finding it very difficult to go on, but I'm pleased to report that both she and I *did* finish the run. And on the second and third marathon I did for the charity, although she wasn't running herself, she and her family were there to cheer me on, popping up at various points along the route, and feeding me with bananas to keep my energy up. But on this first occasion I was mostly grateful not to have been overtaken by the chap in the deep sea diving suit who successfully completed the course in seven days.

Crossing the line was absolutely exhilarating. Although I'd run the marathon for charity, crossing the line was for me. I had set myself this challenge a few months earlier and I had succeeded. I didn't matter that it had taken six and a half hours. In fact, I maintain that it's a much more heroic feat for people who are less fit than for the athletes who run it in two or three hours. Dogged determination had got me round.

However, when I took on the second marathon I hadn't had time to do any training at all because I had been so busy working. On this occasion I wasn't the team leader but I had agreed to take part. Obviously I couldn't go the distance this time so I managed to persuade my trainer Paul to come with me. The plan was that after a few miles he could help me off the course and get me into a taxi home. However, when we reached the Cutty Sark I suggested we do a few more miles and perhaps bunk off at Rotherhithe. Let's do a couple more. At Tower Bridge we didn't seem to be flagging too much so thought perhaps we could make it to the Isle of Dogs despite the fact that the front runners were already running *under* Tower Bridge on the final stretch, and before we knew it we were ourselves leaving the Isle of Dogs on the homeward stretch. Paul said I had residual fitness, left over from last year. Now Paul, who is as fit as a fiddle, hadn't anticipated doing any of this. I'd only asked him to do a couple of miles with me. Twenty-six miles later there we both were sitting with Eddie O'Gorman with medals around our necks. We both had a wonderful sense of achievement. But Paul, left to his own devices, could have run the marathon in half the time.

Come marathon three, Paul gave me a wide berth. Can you blame him? He was unexpectedly very busy, because (guess what) again I hadn't done any training and since I was team leader I had to turn up and have a go. Not normally a good idea, but I wouldn't have had any qualms about stopping if I thought it wise.

Waiting at the start line, the heavens opened. Everyone was absolutely wet through before the race even started, and on top of everything else I had brought the wrong trainers with me. It was bucketing down. I took my mobile phone from its little water-proof bag and called Michael. 'Emergency Michael, I need my other trainers.'

'What's the matter with the ones you've got on?' he reasonably asked, not wanting to venture out in a monsoon.

'They've got no bounce – I need bounce.'

'Well, how the hell am I supposed to find you amongst 45,000 runners.' I gave him a landmark somewhere along the Jamaica Road, Rotherhithe, and I said I'd phone him when I was approaching it. As luck would have it, I'd kind of got used to my unbouncy trainers and thought it prudent to keep them on, but unfortunately I was unable to contact Michael to tell him to stay at home in the dry because my mobile was waterlogged. I could see the landmark in the distance, and as I pounded towards it, into focus came an utterly drenched Michael with a carrier bag containing my bouncies. But I was now in my stride.

'Can't stop, Michael,' I splattered as I streaked past, 'I'm on a roll.'

'Oi,' he hollered. 'Come back here.'

'Only joking,' I said as I emptied my plastic pockets of rain-water and returned to swap my useless mobile for his unwaterlogged one. He was so soaked that I thought it wise to swap shoes whether I wanted to or not, simply to save our rela-tionship.

'Ooooh thank you Mike. You're a godsend,' and I sprinted off.

Because of the terrible weather conditions, it was more ardu-ous to get around the course than in previous years and, after what seemed like four months had passed, I approached Big Ben on the final mile. I could hear the announcement from the other side of the park that they were closing the finishing line in three minutes. With my hand on my heart I can say that I reckon I broke the speed record in that final mile, so determined was I to be within the time frame. I crossed the finishing line with only seconds to spare but I can now say that I'm the proud owner of three London Marathon medals.

CHILDREN with LEUKAEMIA isn't the only charity I support. I am an ambassador for the Prince's Trust and also for Barnardo's. When I was first asked to attend a fundraiser for the Prince's Trust, I didn't actually know what the charity did. I thought it was something similar to the Duke of Edinburgh Award, given to adventurous youngsters. I was wrong. The Prince's Trust helps young entrepreneurs, who aren't able to get help elsewhere. If an applicant has no business acumen or good credit but does have a good business idea, the Prince's Trust will find a suitable mentor and loan enough funding to get him or her started on their venture. For instance, one young man, with no qualifications whatsoever, was a good wallpaper hanger and decorator, so the charity bought him a ladder, brushes and all the other accoutrements, a second-hand van, had business cards printed, allocated a mentor, and he was all set. He now has a flourishing business. Over the last thirty years, the Prince's Trust has helped to start over 50,000 small businesses. Other programmes help young people, the majority of whom are unemployed, to develop their confidence, motivation and skills, and there's a schools-based programme to help pupils at risk of truanting and underachievement, to raise self-esteem and cultivate a sense of worth. There's even a programme to assist young people in music or the arts. In fact, several youngsters from the programme appeared in an award-winning film I made for ITV with Kevin Whately (also an ambassador) called *Belonging*. And very good our supporting artistes were too.

I had a very old-fashioned view of Barnardo's when I first became involved with them, having images of old Victorian workhouses and of poor miserable children. The modern

Barnardo's couldn't be further from that. They don't, in fact, have any 'homes' nowadays. They try to adopt a more holistic approach to childcare, working with youngsters and families in their own community. I have visited several of their projects to help keep abreast of the work they do. It's a very worthwhile charity.

One project I visited in Glasgow provides help, accommodation and hope for 16+ teenagers who are coming out of care. Perhaps they've previously been fostered or in prison, or in any case where their lives have been managed for them. And the accommodation provided isn't some makeshift impersonal room in some lodging or other. No, the flats are decent, well furnished, well equipped and tasteful. And every single tenant I met valued the help given and was well on their way to becoming confidently independent.

I visited a refuge in London for young girls striving to turn their backs on drugs and to escape adults who have prostituted them. This is a 100 per cent safe haven for girls. Men are not even allowed in the building. And here the girls are given help and advice to hopefully enable them to recover from situations we can't even imagine and eventually to make their prospects brighter.

One project in Edinburgh provides comfortable homely respite care on a monthly basis for six or so children with physical, mental, educational or emotional difficulties. The children each visit for two days per month, at the same time allowing a little respite for family or carers. This one project provides care for some forty children. At the time of my visit I met a delightful young boy who was a *Big Brother* enthusiast. When it was time for me to leave, he took great pleasure in going into the next room and announcing, THIS IS BIG BROTHER SPEAKING. BRENDA YOU ARE EVICTED. YOU HAVE TEN SECONDS

TO LEAVE. TEN, NINE, EIGHT, SEVEN, SIX, FIVE, AND NO SWEARING, FOUR, THREE, TWO, ARE YOU PACKED? ONE. EVICTION, and then showed me the door! It was terribly funny.

Terry, Brian, me, Martin and Bill

26

COUNTING MY BLESSINGS

IT GIVES ME PLEASURE TO HELP OUT WHENEVER I CAN, BUT I'M not a saint by any means. All this charity work has to fit in with my own work, and sometimes I get so bombarded by requests I wish I'd never got involved with any of them! But knowing how charities have an uphill struggle to raise funds, I start to feel guilty and remember the hardships some people have to endure, often through no fault of their own, and I count my blessings.

In writing *Mixed Fancies*, my childhood has leapt into such sharp focus that I have started to understand things I'd never understood before. The best vision of all is hindsight. The hardships my mother and father overcame in bringing up nine children in what could only be described as poverty were heroic, and to do so with such humour and a clear idea of what our goals should be set us all on the right course.

When I was growing up, we went through some really tough times, and while us children had some hard lessons to learn we were also shown a lot of love. And in writing this memoir I've come to realise that I'm haunted by my parents in such a comforting way. The simplest everyday tasks bring them to mind. For instance, at many of the parties or buffets I'm obliged to attend, I can tuck into my stumps with a smile, or in throwing away a ribbon or piece of string I hear Dad saying, 'that might come in handy'. Whenever I comb my hair, Dad will advise me to, 'start at the ends and work your way to the scalp to ease out any tangles'. And if I'm feeling greedy I'll hear Mum's voice reminding me, 'There's another day!' I'll eat my vegetables, Dad, just in case I have to wrestle with a black mamba. On every airline when asked if I would like tea, I'm tempted to say, 'Don't make a pot special.' If any of my family spend too long on the telephone, one or other of us only has to say 'I'm having that cut off!' and we know it's time to wind up the conversation. And whenever I sign an autograph, I remember the time I was once stopped in the street to sign some, making me a little late for my appointment with Mum, and she asked, 'Well who did they think you were?' Mum and Dad taught us right from wrong. And we laughed. They taught us the importance of humour. That was their legacy. If you can laugh you can deal with any situation even if it doesn't change. Of course, some people feel they have nothing to laugh about, aren't shown any tenderness at all and don't have anyone at all to call on for help. Everyone needs a helping hand sometimes. I know I do, but I'm fortunate to have a large family and friends to call upon. That is, if they're still speaking to me after reading this book.

P.S. I showed some of this book to Gina, my friend who does my ironing. She was very complimentary, saying, 'Coo that's t'rific Bren. But just imagine though if any o' that was true!'

APPENDIX – LIST OF WORK

Brenda Blethyn OBE was with the Bubble Theatre and the Belgrade Theatre Coventry, before joining the National Theatre in 1975.

FILM

ATONEMENT	Joe Wright
CLUBLAND	Cherie Nowlan
PRIDE AND PREJUDICE	Joe Wright

(2006 British Academy Nomination: Best Supporting Actress)
(2006 London Critics Circle Film Awards Nomination: Best Supporing Actress)

ON A CLEAR DAY	Gaby Dellal
PICCADILLY JIM	John McKay
BEYOND THE SEA	Kevin Spacey
A WAY OF LIFE	Amma Asante
BLIZZARD	LeVar Burton
PLOTS WITH A VIEW	Nick Hurran
LOVELY AND AMAZING	Nicole Holofcener
SONNY	Nicolas Cage
THE YELLOW BIRD	Faye Dunaway
PUMPKIN	Anthony Abrams/Adam Broder
SLEEPING DICTIONARY	Guy Jenkins
ON THE NOSE	David Caffrey

SAVING GRACE   Nigel Cole
(2001 Golden Globe Nomination: Best Actress)
(2000 British Independent Film Awards Nomination: Best Actress)
RKO 281   Ben Ross
DADDY AND THEM   Billy Bob Thornton
LITTLE VOICE   Mark Herman
(1999 Oscar Nomination: Best Supporting Actress)
(1999 Screen Actors Guild Nomination: Best Supporting Actress)
(1999 British Academy Nomination: Best Supporting Actress)
(1999 Best Supporting Actress, Dallas Forth Worth Critics Association)
(1999 Golden Globe Nomination: Best Supporting Actress)
GIRLS' NIGHT   Nick Hurran
NIGHT TRAIN   John Lynch
IN THE WINTER DARK   James Bogle
MUSIC FROM ANOTHER ROOM   Charlie Peters
REMEMBER ME   Nick Hurran
SECRETS AND LIES   Mike Leigh
(1997 Oscar Nomination: Best Actress)
(1996 Golden Globe Award: Best Actress)
(1997 Screen Actors Guild: Best Actress Nomination)
(1996 Best Actress: Cannes Film Festival)
(1996 British Actress of the Year London Film Critics Circle Award)
(1996 Boston Critics Circle Best Actress Award)
(1997 British Academy Award: Best Actress)
(1996 LA Critics Circle Best Actress Award)
(*Premier* Magazine Best Actress Award)
A RIVER RUNS THROUGH IT   Robert Redford
WITCHES   Nick Roeg

TELEVISION
MYSTERIOUS CREATURES   David Evans
WAR AND PEACE   Robert Dornhelm

BELONGING	Christopher Menaul
(Golden FIPA Award)	
(2005 British Academy Nomination: Best Actress)	
BETWEEN THE SHEETS	Robin Shepperd
ANNE FRANK	Robert Dornhelm
(Emmy Nomination: Outstanding Supporting Actress in a Miniseries or Movie)	
MONA	Herbert Wise
OUTSIDE EDGE	Nick Hurran
(1994 Best Comedy Actress)	
THE BULLION BOYS	Christopher Morohan
ALL GOOD THINGS	Sharon Miller
SLEEPING WITH MICKEY	Lowri Gwylim
(Bafta Cymru Nomination: Best Actress)	
BUDDHA OF SUBURBIA	Roger Mitchell
GROWN UPS	Mike Leigh
THE IMITATION GAME	Richard Eyre
THAT UNCERTAIN FEELING	Robert Chetwyn
FLOATING OFF	Tim Renton
CLAWS	Mike Vardy
YES MINISTER	Peter Whitmore
SHEPPEY	Anthony Page
ALAS SMITH AND JONES	Martin Shardlow
HENRY VI	Jane Howell
THE SHAWL	Bill Bryden
LABOURS OF ERICA	John Stroud
CHANCE IN A MILLION	Michael Mills
RUMPOLE	Rob Knights
MAIGRET	John Strickland
BEDROOM FARCE	Christopher Morahan
THE DOUBLE DEALER	Peter Wood
DEATH OF AN EXPERT WITNESS	Herbert Wise
TALES OF THE UNEXPECTED	Peter Hammond

THE STORYTELLER   Charles Sturridge
SINGLES WEEKEND
THE RICHEST WOMAN IN THE WORLD   Charles Jarrett

THEATRE

NIGHT, MOTHER	Michael Mayer	Royale Theatre
		Broadway
MRS WARREN'S PROFESSION	Peter Hall	Strand Theatre
HABEAS CORPUS	Sam Mendes	Donmar Warehouse
WILDEST DREAMS	Alan Ayckbourn	RSC
BEAUX STRATAGEM	Peter Wood	National Theatre
DALLIANCE	Peter Wood	National Theatre
A MIDSUMMER NIGHT'S DREAM	Bill Bryden	National Theatre
BEDROOM FARCE	Peter Hall	National Theatre
TROILUS AND CRESSIDA	Elijah Moshinsky	National Theatre
TALES FROM THE VIENNA WOODS	Maximillian Schnell	National Theatre
THE GUARDSMAN	Peter Wood	National Theatre
FRUITS OF ENLIGHTENMENT	Christopher Morahan	National Theatre
THE DOUBLE DEALER	Peter Wood	National Theatre
THE PASSION	Bill Bryden	National Theatre
MADRAS HOUSE	Bill Gaskill	National Theatre
THE PROVOK'D WIFE	Peter Wood	National Theatre
STRIFE	Christopher Morahan	National Theatre
FORCE OF HABIT	Elijah Moshinsky	National Theatre
TAMBURLAINE	Peter Hall	National Theatre
AN IDEAL HUSBAND	James Maxwell	Royal Exchange
A DOLL'S HOUSE	Gregroy Hersov	Royal Exchange
BORN YESTERDAY	Gregroy Hersov	Royal Exchange
ABSENT FRIENDS	Lynne Meadow	Manhattan Theatre

(1991 Theatre World Award for Outstanding New Talent)   Club N.Y.

Appendix – List of Work

BENEFACTORS	Michael Blakemore	Vaudeville, W.E.
(Nominated Best Actress, Olivier Awards)		
STEAMING	Roger Smith	Comedy Theatre
(Best Supporting Actress Award)		
CRIMES OF THE HEART	Simon Stokes	Bush Theatre
THE DRAMATIC ATTITUDES		Nuffield Theatre,
OF MISS FANNY KEMBLE	Patrick Sandford	Southampton

INDEX

BB = Brenda Blethyn

Index

Index

Index

The British Academy of
Film and Television Arts

The British Academy Awards

The Council hereby certifies that

Brenda Blethyn

won the

**BRITISH
ACADEMY AWARD**

during 1996 for

*Best Performance by an Actress
in a leading role*

· *Secrets & Lies* ·

President

Chairman

The British Academy Award is based on a design by Mitzi Cunliffe

Elyabeth R

Elizabeth the Second, *by the Grace of God of the
United Kingdom of Great Britain and Northern Ireland and of Her
other Realms and Territories Queen, Head of the Commonwealth,
Defender of the Faith and Sovereign of the Most Excellent Order of the
British Empire to Our trusty and well beloved Brenda Blethyn* Greeting

Whereas *We have thought fit to nominate and appoint you to be
an Ordinary Officer of the Civil Division of Our said Most Excellent Order
of the British Empire*

We do *by these presents grant unto you the Dignity of an Ordinary
Officer of Our said Order and hereby authorise you to have hold and enjoy
the said Dignity and Rank of an Ordinary Officer of Our aforesaid Order
together with all and singular the privileges thereunto belonging or
appertaining.*

Given *at Our Court at Saint James's under Our Sign Manual
and the Seal of Our said Order this Thirty-first day of December 2002 in
the Fifty-first year of Our Reign.*

By the Sovereign's Command.

Grand Master